MONTGOMERY COLLEGE LIBRARY
ROCKVILLE CAMPUS

THE PRIZE PLAYS

of TELEVISION *and* RADIO

1956

MONTGOMERY COLLEGE LIBRARY
ROCKVILLE CAMPUS

THE WRITERS GUILD OF AMERICA

presents

The Prize Plays

OF TELEVISION AND RADIO

1956

FOREWORD BY

Clifton Fadiman

RANDOM HOUSE · NEW YORK

FIRST PRINTING

© Copyright, 1957, by the
Writers Guild of America, East, Inc., and
Writers Guild of America, West, Inc.

All rights reserved under International
and Pan-American Copyright Conventions

Published in New York by Random House, Inc.,
and simultaneously in Toronto, Canada, by
Random House of Canada, Limited

Library of Congress Catalog
Card Number: 57-10042

The Golden Junkman, teleplay by Donald Sanford,
story by John Nesbitt, winner
in the Anthology Drama, Half Hour TV category,
could not be included because John Nesbitt
would not grant permission.

Manufactured in the
United States of America

Contents

PAGE VII   Foreword
CLIFTON FADIMAN

3   Requiem for a Heavyweight
ROD SERLING

51   Good-bye, Gray Flannel
J. HARVEY HOWELLS

83   A Night to Remember
GEORGE ROY HILL *and* JOHN WHEDON

121   Bring on the Angels
ALLAN SLOANE

141   The $99,000 Answer
LEONARD STERN *and* SYDNEY ZELINKA

155   She Walks in Beauty
KENNETH KOLB

175   Paper Foxhole
JAMES ELWARD

211   The Penny
STANLEY NISS

237   Decision for Freedom
ROBERT S. GREENE

251   The Edgar Bergen Show
SI ROSE

271   The Visitor
THELMA ROBINSON

301   The George Gobel Show
HAL KANTER, HOWARD LEEDS,
HARRY WINKLER, EVERETT GREENBAUM

Foreword

by CLIFTON FADIMAN

This collection is interesting
for at least two reasons

FIRST, both amateur and professional students of airwave drama will be curious to see what competent judges, reviewing a year's production in a dozen varied fields, will choose as their top awards. There is of course an interest attaching to any prize-winner, whether it be a giant pumpkin or an Oscar-crowned leading man. But, beyond this, these twelve shows (the only word that seems to cover adaptations, serial episodes, children's programs, straight comedies, comedy sketches, documentaries and serious dramas) supply a fairly clear bird's-eye view of an important area of radio-TV as it has developed to date. You may admire or you may scorn or you may work the field of judgment in between. In any case this book can provide you with your arguments. SECOND, it is interesting to determine what degree of readability remains in these shows. Less, of course, than in a comparable collection of material written for the legitimate theatre. More, much more, I think, than would inhere in an assemblage of prize-winning movie scripts. These shows were not composed with any reader in mind; there can never, in the very nature of the medium, ever be a closet drama of television. Not only is no reader assumed, but the authors are further impelled in the direction of impermanence by the lack of any continuing audience. Most of these shows were one-shots, written and built for their little hour, written to be forgotten. Some may be retrieved by revival (which is not the same as a re-run) but most will not be. Thus, keeping in mind that the radio-TV eats its own children, we must judge the lives of its products as we judge those of midges and may-flies, not carp and elephants.

That these shows are readable as they are—and in several cases rather more than that—is a kind of miracle. Consider what the TV and radio writer, whether in the field of comedy or drama or whatever, must contend with. First of all, he has only a vague notion of whom he is writing for. The author of the *Lassie* episode probably has a fairly clear notion of the composition of her audience; most of her colleagues are less lucky. Then, he is operating against the clock: the "hour" is fifty minutes, the half-hour is twenty-five or less, and even these curtailed segments may be broken up by commercials. He works also against other dramatic traditions: trying hard to discover just what form is proper for this still strange, still new medium, he cannot help being influenced by, often disturbed by, the powerful, successful techniques of the stage and the film. Among other restraints are two formidable ones: the fear of using language whose color or subtlety may puzzle a mass audience; the fear of making statements about human life that may baffle or upset them, or, worse still, baffle or upset the sponsor, the agency, or the network vice-president.

Finally, there are the demands of the machine itself, the marvelous miracle conceived in the brains of a few forgotten physicists (such as Henri Hertz) which at once makes so much possible and so much more difficult. For the paradox of radio, and more especially television, is that the very assemblage of wires and tubes and reflecting surfaces that makes feasible the instantaneous spread of the image and the idea also interposes hindrances to the perfecting of that image and that idea. It is a curious fact that the more machinery there is available to broadcast a given message the more troubling the limitation imposed upon the depth, the originality, and the penetrating power of the message. Jesus delivering the Sermon on the Mount and Billy (as I suppose I must call him, though we never have been introduced) Graham are not comparable with respect to the quantity and efficiency of the machinery at their disposal; nor comparable in other respects either. The problem of the television playwright is twofold: how to make use of the machine; how to outwit it. For it is a fact of nature that the mind of man was not constructed to serve the authority of the camera, but merely to think. That is what puzzles the Hollywood or network tycoon: he is unable to comprehend why such a simple, cheap, dull-looking thing as a book should somehow still wield more influence than all his glittering engines can; so much so that often, to feed these very engines, he must go back to a book and adapt it to his own purposes. If you were to tell him that the book penetrates because there is nothing between the writer and the audience except twenty-six black squiggles called letters and a half-dozen others called marks of punctuation, he would put you down for a fool.

That the TV writer can still make statements that are amusing or moving or merely interesting is a tribute to his ability to evade the pitiless eye of the camera and somehow establish communication with the audience. At times he is almost as successful in this endeavor as is the live actor or the platform orator. To use a medium beautifully adapted to the dispersion of news, weather reports and lectures on cosmetics and force it by ingenious pressures and evasions to transmit signals of the real lives of men and women is a remarkable achievement.

In theory it should be easy. Says Henry James, "If a woman stands and looks at a man in a certain way, that is drama." Is there any reason why a television performance should find it hard to convey this drama? Several. The most obvious—and therefore the least noticed—is that in the most literal sense the television drama does not exist. That is, it does not exist as a separate thing, to be judged on its own merits within an enclosing framework, like a book, a play, or even a film. It is part of a complex, continuous process called "television." The television day or evening is composed of many parts—the programs that precede and follow, commercials, spot announcements, station breaks, time signals, system signals. It is within this larger framework that even the most determinedly attentive viewer must watch any single unit of dramatic entertainment. It is small wonder then that few of us can recall anything we watched yesterday; fewer still anything that originated more than a week ago. The radio and TV dramatist is competing, not with other plays, but with a turbid miscellaneous flow of communication within which he must somehow contrive to make his own message stand out.

Some succeed. George Roy Hill and John Whedon succeed with their prize-winning documentary *A Night To Remember,* a work that does not have to fight the medium, that harmonizes well with it. I think Stanley Niss succeeds with his bitterly humorous radio play *The Penny on 21st Precinct*—which by the way would make far less appeal to the imagination were it transferred to television, with all its values literalized. Rod Serling, with his deservedly praised *A Requiem for a Heavyweight,* succeeds. It is interesting that these three prize-winners, all effective in the original medium, should also be pre-eminent when transferred to print. They are more than readable; they actually engage the reader's mind and heart.

Radio and television comedy, satisfactory enough on the air, generally has a hard time when printed. Thus the sketch from *The Honeymooners,* which doubtless deserves its award, is only mildly diverting to read. What it needs is what it originally had—Mr. Gleason, whose special qualities remain obdurate to translation to the page. On the other hand, the Gobel show writers, awarded a Certificate of Excellence in the field of comedy-variety, have managed to do two things at once: to shape the lines, as they should, to the special dimensions of George Gobel's talent, and at the same time to infuse into them genuine style. It is the style that comes through to the reader, an unlabored, slightly fey and (considering that there are four collaborators) oddly personal accent. Everything in this book is workmanlike. Everything does its job, which is to divert or interest for a half hour or an hour. Some of the entries do more than this.

There are nevertheless certain things that the two mediums have done in the past that, by chance perhaps, are not represented in this collection. One is the moving employment of elevated or poetic language. One misses that special note of high feeling that in years gone by was provided by such writers as Archibald MacLeish, Stephen Vincent Benét and Norman Corwin. The best dialogue in the book is that of the street, the slum and the dingy bar (see Mr. Niss and Mr. Serling). This is worthy of all praise; but one misses the utterance of people of less limited vocabulary and less limited mental perspectives.

This links with the fact that the statements about life, to be found in the more ambitious efforts, while clear and for the most part sincerely felt, are in no case original, unconventional, startling, or penetrating. They are standard statements (see *Decision for Freedom*) to which no exception can be taken but which we all feel, either uneasily or comfortably, we have met before. On the whole, however, this is, by the standards of the business, good work, technically deft, successful in achieving whatever the desired end may be, whether it be eight laughs per minute (Gleason) or the evocation of nostalgia (*Bring on the Angels*) or a light-hearted comment on American business (*Good-bye, Gray Flannel*) or the lump in the throat (*She Walks in Beauty*). The ends are not in all cases related to art; but they are the ends, the goals that radio and television at their present stage of evolution, believe proper and possible to the medium.

There follows the list of the final judges by category in this first Writers Guild Awards Contest: ANTHOLOGY DRAMA (*One Half Hour*) TV—John Frankenheimer, Walter Ames and Don Quinn; EPISODIC DRAMA (*One Half Hour*) TV—Edward Barry Roberts, Jay Nelson Tuck and Ross Donaldson; SITUATION COMEDY (*One Half Hour*) TV—Groucho Marx, Matt Weinstock, and Shavelson and Rose; COMEDY-VARIETY (*One Half Hour*) TV—Tom McKnight, Jerry Lewis and Jess Oppenheimer; DRAMA (*One Hour or More*) TV—A. B. Guthrie, Jr., Dorothy Hughes and Clifford Odets; COMEDY (*One Hour or More*) TV—Norman Frank, William Morwood and Newman H. Burnett; DOCUMENTARY (*Any Length*) TV—Gilbert Seldes, Martin Hoade and John Daly; CHILDREN'S PROGRAMS (*Any Length*) TV—Florence Britton, Ernest D. Ricca and Nina Foch; DRAMA (*Any Length*) RADIO—Norman Corwin, David Friedkin and Ronald Colman; COMEDY (*Any Length*) RADIO—Anthony Ellis, Jim Backus and Sid Saks; SERIES or SERIAL EPISODE (*Any Length*) RADIO—Paul Roberts, Ken MacGregor and Perry Lafferty; RADIO DOCUMENTARY (*Any Length*) RADIO—Robert Lewis Shayon, Edward King and Gerald Green.

Requiem for a Heavyweight

by ROD SERLING

CATEGORY:

Television Drama

(ONE HOUR OR MORE)

REQUIEM FOR A HEAVYWEIGHT

by ROD SERLING

Requiem for a Heavyweight
was first presented on "PLAYHOUSE 90" CBS,
under the direction of Ralph Nelson,
on October 11, 1956,
with the following cast:

HARLAN MOUNTAIN MC CLINTOCK · Jack Palance
MAISH · Keenan Wynn
GRACE CARRIE · Kim Hunter
ARMY · Ed Wynn
STEVE · Maxie Rosenblum
MIKE · Maxie Baer
DOC · Edgar Stehli
PARELLI · Stanley Adams
FOX · Harry Landers
JESSEY · Charles Herbert
BARTENDER · Ned Glass
FIGHTER IN BAR · Frank Richards
PHOTOGRAPHER · Lynn Osborn
FIGHT ANNOUNCER · Joe Abdullah
WRESTLERS · Ivan Rasputin
Ted Christie, Karl Davis
CHAMP · Young Jack Johnson

ACT ONE

We open on a long angle shot looking down a bare cement corridor dimly lit by intermittent green-shaded 25 watt bulbs. This is the underbelly of a fight arena and from off stage comes the occasional roar of the crowd.

On one far wall are visible a couple of fight posters announcing the cards for that night and the weeks to come. Two men stand close to one of the posters and talk in low voice. From the far end of the corridor appear "ARMY" and a fighter named HARLAN "MOUNTAIN" MC CLINTOCK, walking slowly toward the camera, the fighter leaning heavily on the arm of ARMY.

The two men pause under one of the lights and we get our first definitive view of the fighter's face. He has a bathrobe thrown loosely over his shoulders, and his body is a mass of red welts and skin abrasions. The bridge of his nose has a red crack down the middle of it. One eye is shut, the other is swollen almost to the same point, and on his cheek is a bleeding bruise and his chest is covered with sweat. ARMY is an ex-fighter, a small man, with long arms, in his late forties. He has thinning hair that reveals two thin scars that run down toward his cheeks on either side of his temple. Beyond that his face is open, kind of pleasant, rather intelligent.

ARMY: How about it, Mount, can yuh make it? Make it okay? (*The fighter nods, wets his lips as if to say something and then can't get it out. Over their shoulder we see MAISH, the manager, coming down the corridor. A man steps out from the wall and detains him.*)

MAISH (*Calls out to ARMY*): Army, stay here with him a minute, will you? I'll be right there. (*The camera moves over for a close shot of MAISH and the MAN.*)

MAN: Two words, Maish. Cough up.

MAISH (*furtive look toward ARMY and the fighter*): Will you relax? I'll get it. I'll get it. Tell him I'll get it. Tell him to phone me.

MAN: Mr. Henson's no collection agency.

MAISH: I know. I know. Tell him he'll get it.

(*With this the camera moves away leaving them talking in low unintelligible voices. ARMY and the fighter take a few more steps down the corridor until they stand very close to the two men who stand near one of the posters. They cast a few disinterested glances at the fighter and then continue their conversation.*)

3

MAN NUMBER ONE: So I told him. And he said I gotta.

MAN NUMBER TWO: So what did he say?

MAN NUMBER ONE: He says I gotta.

MAN NUMBER TWO: Cut ice?

MAN NUMBER TWO (*Shrugs*): Wid him? Illokadisguy. Itellimstraight djaeverseeanyguywalkinaringwidabustedhand?

MAN NUMBER TWO: Whaddehsay? Cut ice?

MAN NUMBER TWO: Neh!IgottaputiminnestT-ursday.

> (*At this point the camera pulls away from them so that we can no longer hear them, but see them in pantomime as they continue talking only an arm's length or so away from the fighter who stands bleeding in front of them, but totally oblivious to him.*)

WE CUT TO

> (*A shot of* MAISH *and* ARMY *appearing again at the far end of the corridor.* ARMY *now has his arms full with a bucket, some towels, and a pair of gloves. He starts to continue down the corridor when* MAISH *takes his arm and with a nod toward the fighter still standing there . . .*)

MAISH: How is he?

ARMY (*Shrugs*): This wasn't his night, that's for sure.

MAISH: You are so right.

> (*Then the two men continue down the corridor. They approach* MC CLINTOCK *from either side, each taking an arm, and help him move forward. They walk a few more feet and then stop by the door to the dressing room and usher him into it. A fighter and his* MANAGER *are just coming by.*)

MANAGER: What hit him?

MAISH: Don't get impatient, Jock. That's a fast track out there. (*Then he looks at the young fighter, obviously ill at ease*) You ought to see the other guy. (*The* MANAGER *hustles his fighter out. Then* MAISH *closes the door.*)

MAISH: Not a mark on him. (*Both he and* ARMY *help* MC CLINTOCK *on to a high rubbing table.* ARMY *pours some water into the bucket from a dirty sink, brings the bucket over to the table.* MAISH *takes a towel, dampens it and starts to wipe away the sweat and blood.*)

MAISH: Mountain, can you hear me okay? (*The* FIGHTER *nods.*)

MAISH: Give me some of that alum, will yuh, Army? (ARMY *digs into his pockets and brings out a little jar.* MAISH *dabs his finger in it and starts to apply it to the* FIGHTER's *face.*)

ARMY: I don't think alum'll do it, Maish. I think that's going to take stitches.

MAISH (*Peers into the* FIGHTER's *face more intently*): Yeah. They get wider and wider.

ARMY: The Doc's going to be coming in a minute anyway. He'll do it. (MC CLINTOCK *wets his lips and now he speaks for the first time. His voice is heavy, and belabored and still short of breath.*)

MC CLINTOCK: Maish? Hey, Maish . . .

MAISH: Go easy. Go easy, we've got a lot of time.

MC CLINTOCK: Maish—too fast. Much too fast.

MAISH (*Nods*): Bum night, Kid. Just a bum night all the way around. There'll be others.

MC CLINTOCK: Sure. Others. (MC CLINTOCK *moves a bandaged hand awkwardly down to his side and feels*) Check there will yuh, Maish? By the belt. (ARMY *hurriedly pulls the trousers down a quarter of an inch.*)

ARMY: You've got a little rope burn down there. It'll be okay. Rubbed a sore there. It'll be okay.

MC CLINTOCK: Hurts. (*Then he breathes deeply again and* MAISH *goes back to dabbing water on his face. The door opens and the* DOCTOR *enters. This is a thin, vinegar-faced old man in his sixties with a single-breasted, old-fashioned suit with a vest, all the buttons buttoned. He carries a beaten-up black bag, which he tosses on the foot of the rubbing table.*)

DOCTOR: Mountain, haven't you got enough yet?

MAISH: It's his eye, Doc.

DOC: I know. Just as well, Maish. If he hadn't folded I wouldn't have let him out for number eight. (MAISH *nods but doesn't say anything. He pulls out the butt of a cigar from pocket and lights it. The* DOCTOR *squints, pushes his arm away.*)

DOCTOR: Let me breathe, will you? (*He leans over the* FIGHTER *and examines the eye, then pushes the face to the other side a little roughly and examines the other bruises and cuts. Then he snaps his fingers at* ARMY *who picks up the bag and hands it to him.*)

DOCTOR: Where do you buy your cigars, Maish? I'll see that they condemn the store. (*Then he reaches in the bag and takes out some gauze, a stick with cotton on the end of it, and a bottle of medicine. He starts to administer to the* FIGHTER.*)

ARMY: How much longer you got, Doc? You're out this week, ain't you?

DOCTOR: Let's see. This is Wednesday—I leave Friday.

MAISH (*Staring down at the* FIGHTER *and obviously making small talk*): Vacation?

DOCTOR: Vacation? Retirement. I'm the one man in the fight business who walks away without a wobble. Thirty-eight years, Maish. Retirement.

ARMY (*Clucks*): Thirty-eight years.

DOCTOR (*Administering to the* FIGHTER *as he talks*): Thirty-eight years. Wife says I oughta write a book, but who'd buy it?

MAISH: You've seen some good ones.

DOCTOR: Good ones and bad ones. Live ones and a couple of dead ones. (*Then he straightens up, massages his back and points down with the stick toward* MC CLINTOCK) And almost dead ones. He's got no business in there, Maish. You hungry, is that it?

MAISH (*Picking up the* FIGHTER's *hand and massaging it absently*): What do you mean hungry? In 1948 he was number five. You can check that in *Ring Magazine*. I could show it to you, number five, and that was only in 1948.

DOCTOR (*Looks at him a little quizzically*): Only 1948. And this is 1956. And that means eight years ago. Too bad he isn't a machine, Maish. Too bad none of them are machines. (*Then he laughs softly*) I've seen a lot of them. Thirty-eight years. When I first come in they used to lay them out in front of me. They were human beings then. They were young men. Do you know what it's like now, Maish? Army? (*He leans back over* MC CLINTOCK *and starts to work again*) Now it's like a guy who grades meat in a packing plant. They roll the carcasses down the line in front of him and he stamps them. Beef. Understand? (*He motions toward* MC CLINTOCK) Just a hunk of something inanimate. That's what thirty-eight years has done. (*Then musingly*) Thirty-eight years. And suddenly I don't have a single patient with a first and last name. A set of scars. A blood type and a record—that's all *my* patients have. Look here, Maish, I want to show you something. (MAISH *leans over*) Look at his pupil. See? Known as sclerotic damage. Look at the tissue there. Couple of good solid rights to that eye—and you can buy him a tin cup and some pencils. (*He straightens up again, puts his things back in the bag as he says*) Or maybe that won't have to happen. Maybe some night he'll bang his head on a bathroom door and bleed to death. Either way, Maish. It could happen either way. (*Then a long pause and a deep breath*) No more. This was it. Mountain and I will both retire this week. (MAISH *looks from the* FIGHTER *to the* DOCTOR *and his voice is strained.*)

MAISH: What do you mean?

DOCTOR: No more.

MAISH: He could rest up. I've got nothing scheduled for him . . .

DOCTOR (*Interrupts*): He can rest up for the rest of his life.

MAISH: What're you talking about? He's fourteen years in this business. Suddenly he gets a cut and we've got to put him out to pasture?

DOCTOR (*Turns to him*): Suddenly. It doesn't go fourteen years and then suddenly. And it's never one cut. It's fourteen years of cuts. (*He stretches, hoists up the bag*) Yep, write me a book. All about my gladiator friends. You too can become pathological in thirty-eight years of relatively easy lessons.

MAISH (*Interrupts*): Joker. Big joker. (DOCTOR *walks over to the door, turns the knob, then looks back at* MAISH.)

DOCTOR: Joker? (*He shakes his head, nods toward* MC CLINTOCK) Who's laughing? (*He walks out of the room and shuts the door.* ARMY *and* MAISH *stare at each other, then both look toward* MC-CLINTOCK. ARMY *goes over and starts to cut away the bandages on his hands.* MAISH *stands back a few feet smoking the cigar thoughtfully. Finally* MC CLINTOCK *sits up, closes his eyes, moves his mouth and touches his jaw gingerly.*)

MC CLINTOCK: Doc here?

ARMY: He left.

MC CLINTOCK: It hurts, Maish.

MAISH (*Turns his back*): I don't doubt it. (*Then* MOUNTAIN *shakes his head, reacts with pain, touches the bandage on his eye.*)

MC CLINTOCK: Deep huh, Maish?

MAISH: Enough. You could hide your wallet in there. Go lie down. Rest up a minute, and *then* take your shower. (MC CLINTOCK *pushes his feet around heavily so that they hang over the side. Then he balances himself with his hands. His head goes up and down and he breathes deeply.*)

MC CLINTOCK: I'm coming around now. Oh Lordy, I caught it tonight, Maish. I really did. What did I do wrong?

MAISH: You aged. That was the big trouble. You aged. (MC CLINTOCK *looks at him, frowns. He tries to get some thread of meaning out of the words but none comes.*)

MC CLINTOCK: What do you mean, Maish? I aged. Don't everybody age?

MAISH (*Nods*): Yeah, everybody ages. Everybody grows old, kid. Go ahead. I think a shower'll do you good. Try not to get that bandage wet.

(MC CLINTOCK *gets on his feet, a little wobbly. He holds the table for support, then walks out of the room toward the shower.* ARMY *starts to pick up the dirty towels and put them in a big container alongside of the door.*)

ARMY (*Without looking up*): What're you going to do, Maish?

MAISH (*Shrugs*): I dunno. Maybe I'll cut my throat.

ARMY: Somethin's wrong, isn't there?

MAISH: Where were you when the lights went out? I just lost a boy! Get with it, Army.

ARMY: Besides that . . .

MAISH: Besides that nothing. Forget it. (*Then with a desperate attempt at a kind of composure*) I just gotta go huntin' and peckin' around, that's all. Find somebody else. Maybe try a lightweight this trip.

ARMY: I was just wondering—

MAISH: You wanna pull out, huh, Army? A million offers, huh?

ARMY: I didn't mean . . .

MAISH (*Interrupts*): Don't gimme a whole Megillah. I know you're good, Army. You're the best cut man in the city. I know that. You probably could take your pick. I don't know why you haven't before.

ARMY (*With his head down*): Never mind about me. What about the Mountain?

MAISH (*Reacts a little guiltily*): I dunno. He'll find something.

ARMY: It's been fourteen years.

MAISH: Fourteen years what?

ARMY: Fourteen years fight. Then one night you get out of the ring— it's all over. And what've you got . . .

MAISH: You made a living, didn't you? You did all right. (*Then he chuckles*) Remember how I used to tout you? "The Hero of the Argonne." I even gave you the name "Army." So don't complain, Army. You came out of it with a name at least.

ARMY (*In a kind of wistful voice*): Still—a guy ought to have something to show for it besides the name. (*At this moment the sound of the shower water is heard from offstage.* ARMY *looks up toward the shower.*)

ARMY: He was good, Maish.

MAISH (*Thoughtfully, turning toward the shower*): One of the best. He had everything that was needed. Hands, legs, brains. He could take a cannonball in his face and you could fix him up with an aspirin. He was good all right. Oh, brother—where am I ever gonna find one like him? (*The camera pans over to the door leading to the shower. We get a shot of* MC CLINTOCK *as he comes out from the waist up. He dries himself off with a towel, then looks up.*)

MC CLINTOCK: Hey, Army. Bathrobe, huh? (*The bathrobe is thrown to him and he puts it around him. Then we pull back for a cover shot as he walks back into the room toward the table. He stands there and does a little hop and jump routine on the floor, loosening up. Throwing his shoulders and head back, breathing deeply and moving his hands and feet.*)

MC CLINTOCK: Feel better, Maish. Lot better. Eye kind of feels funny but—I'll be okay now. Got a lot of spring yet, huh? (*He moves his feet around, shuffling ring-like. He shadow boxes a bit*) How about it, Army? Still there, huh? (ARMY *nods, not able to say anything. He exchanges a look with* MAISH.)

MAISH (*Finally*): Mountain—sit down, huh? (MC CLINTOCK *stops his dancing, looks from one to the other, goes over to the rubbing table and sits down.*)

MC CLINTOCK: Sure, Maish. Sure. (*Then he waits expectantly.* MAISH *starts to say something, then he looks at* ARMY, *who turns away. Then he wets his lips.*)

MAISH: The doctor looked you over.

MC CLINTOCK (*Grins*): Yeah. I thought he was in here. I wasn't sure, though. (*He taps his head*) A little groggy yet, you know.

MAISH (*Nods*): Yeah. Well anyway he looked you over good this time.

MC CLINTOCK: Yeah?

MAISH: He figures . . . he figures you've had it. (*Then he turns away, coughs, takes out a cigar and lights it.* MC CLINTOCK *stares at him for a long moment.*)

MC CLINTOCK: What did you say, Maish?

MAISH: The doctor says you've had it. No more. He says you've got to leave now.

MC CLINTOCK: Leave? Leave where?

MAISH (*Whirls around and shouts*): Army. Lay it out for him, will yuh? Mountain, no more fights. You get it? This is where you get off. You leave. (*There's another moment's pause.* MC CLINTOCK *gets off the table, walks over to* MAISH, *pokes at him with a forefinger.*)

MC CLINTOCK: Leave? Maish, that's . . . that's crazy.

MAISH (*Shrugs, turns away*): So it's crazy. Maybe I think it's crazy, but that's what the doctor says. Go fight the commission. (*Deliberately turning his back on* MC CLINTOCK) Have you got everything all cleared up here, Army? (ARMY *nods.*)

MC CLINTOCK: Maish . . .

MAISH (*Without turning to him*): What do you want, Mountain?

MC CLINTOCK: What'll I do?

MAISH: What'll you do? I dunno. You do whatever you want to do. Anything you like. It's as easy as that.

MC CLINTOCK: I mean . . . I mean a guy's got to do something.

MAISH: So? A guy's got to do something. So you do something. Do anything you like.

MC CLINTOCK (*The words come out hard*): Maish, I don't know anything but fighting. You know, fourteen years pro. You know, Maish. I've been with you fourteen years.

MAISH: And before that?

MC CLINTOCK (*Smiles and shrugs*): Before that what? Who remembers?

ARMY: Why don't you go back home, kid? You talk about it enough. The green hills of Tennessee. Is that what you call it? Go back home. Go back to Tennessee. The hills are probably still green.

MC CLINTOCK: What's back there? (*He takes a few steps toward the other two men and looks from one to the other as he talks*) What's back there? I haven't been back in all those years. I don't know anybody. Nobody'd know me. (*And then suddenly as if struck by an afterthought*) Maish, we could try another state, maybe?

MAISH (*Shakes his head*): Now *you're* talking crazy. If you don't pass muster in New York State, you don't pass muster any place else. You know that.

MC CLINTOCK: Maybe some club fights. You know, unofficial.

MAISH: Where've you been? Those kind of club fights went out with John L. Sullivan. (ARMY *nods, follows* MAISH *to the door, then turns back toward* MC CLINTOCK.)

ARMY: Want me to help you dress, Mountain?

MC CLINTOCK (*Shakes his head*): No. No, I can dress myself. (*Then he looks across at* MAISH) Maish?

MAISH: Yeah?

MC CLINTOCK: I'm . . . I'm sorry about tonight. I'm sorry I lost.

(*We cut to a very tight close-up of* MAISH *as his features work and then he has to turn his eyes away.*)

MAISH: That's okay, Mountain. Don't give it another thought. (*He goes out and closes the door.* ARMY *sort of hangs back by the door.*)

ARMY (*Finally*): We can go over to the hotel later on and—and talk this out, make some plans. (MC CLINTOCK *nods and doesn't say anything. Then* ARMY *goes out the door.* MC CLINTOCK *stands there numbly and motionless for a long moment. We cut to the corridor outside the dressing room.* MAISH *is walking very slowly down the corridor. He stops abruptly.*)

MAISH (*Waves and hollers*): Hey, Foxy. Hey, Fox! (*A figure ahead of him pauses, turns, walks back toward him. This is a little mousey guy in a jacket with a face like a weasel.*)

FOX: Whadda yuh say, Maish? I just seen Slaughter on Tenth Avenue. Was there enough left to sew together?

MAISH: Break your heart, does it?

FOX: I got my own troubles. (*And then very confident*) You want to see the kid now, Maish? I got him right out here. You said you might be interested . . .

MAISH: I said I *might* be.

FOX: Maish, he's a real sweetie. Middleweight. A good fast middle-weight, but he's built like a tank and I can't get him matched on accounta the business.

MAISH: How is the business? Did you get that fixed up?

FOX: I was one year revoked. But you know that was a bum rap, Maish. To pinch a guy like me for fixing fights. It's to laugh. I swear, it's to laugh. I couldn't fix a parking ticket. But . . . ah . . . meanwhile I got no contract with the kid because I got no license to manage, so if he could just hook up with someone—you know—a real solid guy to handle him for a bit . . .

MAISH: Foxy, don't dress it up, will ya, pal? If he's here, put him on the block. Let's take a look at him. But don't choke me with publicity.

FOX: Maish, you're a doll baby. You're an everloving doll baby. (*He turns and shouts*) Bobby! Bobby, Mr. Loomis would like to look at ya. (*At this moment a* FIGHTER *walks down the ramp from out of the shadows and approaches them. He walks with the stiff gait of an old rooster and his face looks like the Battle of the Marne*) Here he is, Maish. Bobby Menzey.

MAISH (*Looks him over with the practiced eye of a veteran*): So what's to tell, Foxy? I'd like to see him spar.

FOX: He'll spar—he'll spar. I'll get a boy lined up at the gym tomorrow.

MAISH: Tell me about him. (*The* FIGHTER *starts to say something.* MAISH *holds up his hand and points to* FOX) Let *him* talk.

FOX: Like I told you before, Maish, he's a sweetheart. He's fought mostly out West.

MAISH: What's his record?

FOX (*Wets his lips*): Like I say, he's fought mostly out West.

MAISH: Wins and losses. Lay them out. Is that hard?

FOX: Well . . . well, his record ain't so well known, Maish. He was fighting out West.

MAISH (*Suddenly reaches out and grabs* FOX *by the vest, pulling him toward him*): What are you trying to pull off, Fox?

FOX (*With a worried look toward his fighter*): Go easy on the kid, Maish . . .

MAISH: Kid? I'd hate to have my hands in boiling water since he was a kid. (*Turns to fighter*): What's your name?

FIGHTER: Menzey—Bobby Menzey. Maybe you heard of me.

MAISH: I heard about you yesterday. But the last time I saw you fight, your name wasn't Bobby Menzey. (*The* FIGHTER *gulps and starts to stammer.*)

FOX (*Hurriedly*): You've got him mixed up, Maish. Menzey. Bobby Menzey. M-E-N-Z-E-Y.

MAISH: Stop it! Correct me if I'm wrong. LaPlant, isn't it? In 1949 you were a lightweight—a real comer. Sixteen straight. Then you fought Red Johns in Syracuse. He knocked you out in the second round. Then you lost six or seven straight. After that I saw you in Detroit. That was three, four years ago. (*The* FIGHTER *looks at* FOX *helplessly.*)

FOX (*With a huge smile*): You got me, Maish. You really got me. I had him change his name—but that don't prove nothing about his fighting.

MAISH: It doesn't huh? It means you're trying to pass off a stumble-bum on me as a comer. (*He grabs* MENZEY's *face and turns it to the light*) Look at it. I know a bleeder when I see one. One punch and his face falls apart. And this is the sweetheart, huh? This guy will never live to see the day when he's anything else besides a poor, beat-up slob.

FIGHTER: What're you talkin' about? I'm as good as I ever was.

FOX: That's right. He's still got it, Maish. Would I try to put something over on you? (*He slaps him expansively on the arm*) Would I? A wise one like you? Think I'm crazy or something. It's to laugh, Maish. I swear it's to laugh. Go ahead, Bobby. Box around a little for him. Go ahead. (*The* FIGHTER *starts to shadow box in front of them.* MAISH *and* ARMY *exchange a look.*)

FOX: Who does he remind you of? Baer?

MAISH: Yeah, a big brown one with a ring in his nose.

FOX: Look, Maish . . .

MAISH: Knock it off. You'd better send him back to your factory. Right now.

FOX: Maish, give me a break, will ya?

MAISH: I've given you a break. I won't split your head. That's a break. I'll see you around, Fox. (*He turns and walks past him. The* FIGHTER, *suddenly seeing his shadow against a wall, begins to shadow box.*)

FOX (*Pushes him*): Mud for brains! So stop already. No deal. (*The camera picks up* MAISH *as he starts up the ramp. The man steps out from the wall once again and stops him.*)

MAN: Hey, Loomis . . .

MAISH: I'll get it! I'll get it! What does Henson need—bail money? I told you I'd get it for you. Now lay off, will ya?

MAN: Mr. Henson would like to know *where* you're going to get it.

MAISH: Mr. Henson'll have to guess.

MAN: Mr. Henson will take it out of your skin, Loomis. Just remember that. (*He walks up the ramp and disappears.* MAISH *watches him go and the tight, set look on his face disintegrates and suddenly he is very frightened. But he recomposes his face when he sees* ARMY *walking toward him.*)

MAISH (*With a forced smile*): Come on, I'll buy you a drink.

ARMY (*Looks toward the ramp*): Fox showing off his wares? You work fast, Maish.

MAISH: People have to eat—or are you different?

ARMY: I'm not the one drumming up trade five minutes after I get the word.

MAISH: I'm drumming it up for you, too, remember, boy scout! Fox has got a boy and he can't handle him. I've got no boy and I *can* handle him. That's simple stuff, Army. That's arithmetic. (*Then his shoulders sag*) What difference? He was a clinker. The worst.

ARMY: What now?

MAISH: I think I'll go shadow box off a cliff. Come on. I *need* a drink.

ARMY (*Nods toward the dressing room*): I'll wait for the kid.

MAISH: Sure. (*Then he looks up toward the ceiling and grins*) The kid. That's what I call him too. The kid. I think that's where we goofed. As long as they wear trunks and gloves we think they're kids. They're old men. They're the oldest. I'll see you later on, Army. (*He walks on up the ramp, pausing near the top to look at a poster which advertises the fight that night. On it is a picture of* MOUNTAIN *and his opponent and the words "Main Bout" are prominent. He takes a few steps further and looks at another poster. This one shows two big clowns in a plug for a wrestling match. He takes a few steps closer to the poster and stares at it, taps it thoughtfully with his finger.*)

(*We cut to a brief tight close-up of* ARMY *noticing this. Then we cut to a long shot as* MAISH *disappears up the ramp.*)

WE DISSOLVE TO

(*A shot of a little hotel and adjoining bar as seen through its front window.*)

WE DISSOLVE THROUGH THE INTERIOR

(*And get a cover shot of the entire place. This is about a twenty-foot-square dingy little bistro frequented by people in the fight business—mostly ex-fighters and ring hangers-on. On the wall are pictures of fighters going back to the 1800's. A championship belt is in a frame over the bar. Other than these the place has no pretensions. It is simply there to serve drink and make up for what is probably a loss in the hotel business alongside. At the far end of the room there's a handful of fighters, obviously in nightly clatch. One fighter is holding sway with an excited blow-by-blow from some monumental battle of years before. As we pan around the room we pick up part of his speech.*)

FIGHTER NUMBER ONE: So he comes in at me. (*He holds both his hands up.*)

FIGHTER NUMBER TWO: Yeah, yeah. Go ahead.

FIGHTER NUMBER ONE: He comes at me. I sized him up. He throws a left, I duck. He throws another left. I duck. Then he throws another left.

FIGHTER NUMBER TWO: You duck.

FIGHTER NUMBER ONE: No, I don't duck. I take it right smack dab on the jaw. I'm down. Oh, man, am I down.

(*We pan past them at this moment for a shot of* MC CLINTOCK *and* ARMY *as they enter. The bartender is a flat-nosed ex-pug who nods very briefly at them as they sit on the stools.*)

BARTENDER: How're you, Mountain? Army?

ARMY: Two beers, huh, Charlie?

BARTENDER: Two beers. (*He draws them and expertly shoots them down the bar one at a time.* ARMY *takes out some money. Three one-dollar bills, separates them, lays one on the counter.*)

BARTENDER: How'd you do, Mountain?

MC CLINTOCK: Not so good, Charlie. Almost went the route, though. Doc says I'm over the hill now.

BARTENDER (*Clucks*): That's too bad. (*Then philosophically*) So—now yuh can join the Wednesday-evening sewing circle! (*He jerks with his thumb in the direction of the rear of the room. Then with a long look at* MC CLINTOCK *he takes out a bottle and says*) Have one on the house. This is the only one in the house that ain't watered. (*He pours two healthy-sized glasses and shoves them in front of each of them, and walks back down the bar.*)

ARMY (*Turns to* MOUNTAIN, *holds up his glass*): To Mountain McClintock. A hundred and eleven fights.

MC CLINTOCK: He wasn't so good—but he never took a dive. (ARMY *returns the laugh, starts to drink. He takes only the barest of sips, looking over the top of his glass at* MOUNTAIN, *a sad and knowing look on his face. At this moment* ARMY *sees the reflection of* MAISH *in the mirror. He turns around.*)

ARMY: Hey, Maish. Here we are. (MAISH *walks over to them.*)

MAISH: Let's get a booth.

MC CLINTOCK: How're you doing, Maish?

MAISH: I'll tell yuh when we get to the booth. (*As they get away from the bar a drunk tipsily bangs into* MAISH, *and* MC CLINTOCK *rather firmly places him out of the way.*)

MC CLINTOCK: Watch it. That's my manager.

(*The three men go to the rear and sit in an empty booth.*)

MAISH (*Without any preliminaries. Obviously intent on getting this over*): What did you do with your dough, Mountain?

MC CLINTOCK: You mean . . .

MAISH (*Impatiently*): The dough for the fight. You got six hundred and thirty-three bucks, didn't you? Where is it?

MC CLINTOCK: It's mostly gone. I owed the hotel half of it, Maish.

MAISH (*Wets his lips*): What about the other half?

MC CLINTOCK (*Very slowly*): Well, I suppose I've got some of it . . .

MAISH (*Excited, blurts it out*): Look, don't get cute with me. This is Maish. I asked you a question now. Have you got any money at all? (MC CLINTOCK *reaches into his pants and pulls out a crumpled roll of bills. He lays them out one at a time on the table.*)

MC CLINTOCK: I've got some. Twenty, forty, fifty-five, fifty-six, fifty-seven, fifty-eight bucks, Maish. (*He collects and shoves it over in a bunch to Maish*) Here.

MAISH: Fifty-eight bucks. (*He picks it up and looks at it. He throws it back down on the table.*)

ARMY (*A little wisely*): What's the matter, Maish? You in hock?

MAISH (*Nods*): Heavy.

ARMY: How much?

MAISH: Three thousand dollars.

ARMY (*Whistles*): Three thousand dollars.

MC CLINTOCK (*Very worried*): Gee, Maish, that's a lot of money. How're we gonna get it?

MAISH: I don't know. But I haven't got much time.

ARMY: How did you get into that kind of a crack, Maish?

MAISH (*With side look at* MC CLINTOCK, *his tone changes*): You don't know, huh? Mountain when you were in the hospital last month with a bum hand—remember?

ARMY: That comes off the top. What're you givin' him?

MAISH: Sure. But I brought in a specialist, didn't I? And that came out of here. (*He pats his own pocket*) And the training camp. He wanted to go up to New Jersey, so he went up to New Jersey. How much do you think that cost me a month? A lot more than my cut, I'll tell ya.

MC CLINTOCK: Gee, Maish, I didn't know that . . .

MAISH: I'm not complaining. I'm not complaining. But the money goes, you know. And one half of your take hasn't been much lately. It doesn't cover expenses, so I've been filling up the rest of it for you. Well, now we've got to pay the fiddler, Kid. We're at the end of the line now.

MC CLINTOCK (*His face very concerned*): I've been thinkin', Maish, if I could get me a job—you know, something to tide us over . . .

MAISH (*Barely listening to him*): Sure. Sure. (*Then to* ARMY) Jack Green's got a lightweight he's touting. Maybe we could buy a piece. (*He looks up to the ceiling*) Yeah, we could buy a piece. With what? We could get his thumb. That I could afford.

MC CLINTOCK (*Very softly*): Get a new boy, Maish?

ARMY (*With a quick look at* MAISH): Not for a while yet, Mountain, just an idea.

MC CLINTOCK: Oh. Oh. I see. (*His eyes go around the room looking at the people, the tables and the pictures, very quietly*) I remember the first night I come in here, Maish. I remember the guy's name even. Shipsky. Morty Shipsky. I knocked him out in the first round. And you and Army stood up on the bar and you shouted . . . you shouted, "Everybody take a drink on Harlan McClintock the next champ." (*He looks from one to the other*) Remember? That was the night you give me the name "Mountain."

ARMY (*Quietly*): I remember.

MC CLINTOCK: Sure. You asked me where I was from and I told you. I told you I lived in Tennessee on a mountain. And that's when . . . that's when Maish here says, "That's what we'll call ya. We'll call ya Mountain." (*He looks around the room again*) How many nights we come in here, Maish? How many nights?

ARMY: A lot of 'em.

MC CLINTOCK: Couple of hundred, I guess? Couple of hundred nights. We could just sit and talk here by the hour about this fight or that fight, or some other fighter, or a fight we were gonna get. By the hour.

MAISH (*A little disjointedly*): It's the breaks that's all. It's the breaks.

MC CLINTOCK: All of a sudden I—I'm sittin' here and it becomes different. Like . . . like right now even . . . I'm on the outside lookin' in. Like . . . I didn't belong with you guys any more. (*Then suddenly his face becomes a mask as realization seems to flood into it and he slowly gets up on his feet.*)

ARMY: Look, Mountain . . .

MAISH: Why don't you sit down and have another drink? It's early . . .

MC CLINTOCK (*Shakes his head*): I think I'll just . . . I'll just take a walk. I'll see you later. (*He turns to go and is suddenly aware of the little knot of men in the back of the room still talking about fights. He looks at them for a moment, almost winces, and then to nobody in particular says:*) That's no way. That's no way at all.

ARMY: What did you say, Mountain?

MC CLINTOCK (*As if awakened suddenly*): Nothin'. Nothin', Army. I'll see you later. (*MC CLINTOCK turns and walks down the room to the door and goes out. The BARTENDER comes over with a tray and places it on the table in front of MAISH and ARMY.*)

BARTENDER: How about you, Army? You want something? (*ARMY doesn't answer him. He is staring toward the door. MAISH drops a coin on the tray and makes a motion with his head for the BARTENDER to get lost. The BARTENDER walks back toward the bar.*)

MAISH: Hey, Army.

ARMY (*Without looking at him*): What?

MAISH: Look at me when I'm talking to yuh, will yuh? I don't like talking to a guy's neck.

ARMY (*Reluctantly turns toward him*): How'd you lose the dough?

MAISH: How do you think?

ARMY: You bet against him, didn't you?

MAISH (*Not meeting his eyes*): Something like that.

ARMY: You don't sidestep very good.

MAISH: You want it clearer, huh?

ARMY: A little bit.

MAISH: I said he wouldn't go four.

ARMY (*Smiles a crooked little smile*): Big disappointment, huh?

MAISH: There was another way? The minute they tell me he was matched against Gibbons I figure we should throw in the towel while he's signing the contract. Save wear and tear. Gibbons! Thirty-one fights and thirty-one wins. He's got a lit fuse in each hand. And they match him against the Mountain.

ARMY: They match him?

MAISH: Did I? I just go through the motions. Good fast brawl, they said. Couple of nice crowd-pleasers in a pier six. Harlan Mountain McClintock, ex-leading heavyweight contender. Ex is right. Very ex. Eight years ex. He's past prime, Army. I take what I can find—you know that. They say fight Gibbons, I say OK. They say Marciano. I say bring on Marciano.

ARMY: You coulda tol' 'em . . .

MAISH: Tell 'em, tell 'em, tell 'em. Tell 'em what? Tell 'em I've got a dead-weight has-been on my back? That he shouldn't fight any more? And then what do I do? Put in for a pension? (*At this moment a* MAN *walks up to the table, nods briefly at* ARMY, *and then smiles broadly at* MAISH.)

MAN: What's the good word, Maish?

MAISH (*Staring straight ahead*): Blow. That's a good word. I don't want any.

MAN: How do you know what I'm selling?

MAISH: So pitch. I'm busy.

MAN: Mr. Henson sent me. (MAISH's *hand hits the ashtray nervously and knocks it off the table.* MAISH *bends down to pick it up and we:*)

CUT TO

> (*Tight close-up of the* MAN's *foot on* MAISH's *hand.* MAISH *looks up from the floor, his face dead white.*)

MAN: Now you pitch. Tell me when Mr. Henson can expect his dough.

MAISH: Soon.

MAN: How soon is soon?

MAISH: Three weeks.

MAN: You said two, didn't you? (MAISH *bites his lips. The* MAN's *foot remains on his hand.*)

MAISH (*His voice a croak*): Two weeks. (*The* MAN *lifts his foot, picks up the ashtray, sets it back on the table.*)

MAN: You dropped something, Mr. Loomis. I'll see you in two weeks. (*He turns and walks away.* ARMY *stares across the table at* MAISH. MAISH *takes out a handkerchief and wipes his face. Then reaches for a half-smoked cigar he pulls out of his pocket. Then he pats around for a match.*)

MAISH: Got a match?

ARMY: You and a mouse. That's a match.

MAISH: Who am I, Atlas? These guys play for real, Army, you know that. This is no bank transaction. If I welsh, you can take a spoon, scoop what's left of me off the wall and put it in a cup. That's how serious they look on bets. And if they don't go to that trouble—they'll get my license so quick they'll blur the ink. I won't be able to sell peanuts at a fight, so I'm licked either way.

ARMY: Who told you to bet?

MAISH: Who told me I hadda eat?

ARMY: You picked the sport.

MAISH: This isn't a sport. If there was head room, they'd hold them in sewers. So what do I do?

ARMY (*Very quietly*): What does the Mountain do?

MAISH: You tell me. That's this precious business of ours. He gives them a million dollars' worth of fighting for fourteen years. And then they're not interested in paying for the dump truck to cart 'em away. The sport. The sport and the precious crowd.

ARMY: *You* ever buy him a ticket back to Tennessee?

MAISH: Don't stick it on me. All I do is curry the horse. I'm one of the stable boys. I don't set up the rules. I get sucked in just like he does. (*He stares at the chair* MOUNTAIN *was sitting in*) He asks me . . . He sits there and he asks me "What'll I do, Maish?" He asks *me* what he's gonna do. Like I was the Book of Knowledge and I'm supposed to tell him. I don't know what to tell him. I'm so scared right now, Army, that . . .

ARMY: Stop it. You lost a bank roll and a meal ticket. But this poor beat-up kid—did you ever figure out what he lost tonight?

MAISH: You don't think I feel sorry for him. I don't want to hurt that kid, Army. I swear I don't want to hurt him. He thinks he's the only one that's got a memory. I got a memory too. I remember him like he was. Like the first day he comes into my office. All hands and feet and his mouth full of teeth and he talks like General Lee.

(*He shakes his head.* MAISH *pats in his pocket again for a match.* ARMY *lights his cigar.*)

ARMY: Take one on me. (*Long pause*) You talk about memories, Maish. Remember Christmas, 1945? Right at this table. We had six bucks between us. Four of it you spent on a beefsteak and a new tie for him. Remember that, Maish?

MAISH (*Nods*): Sure. That horrible-lookin' tie. He wore it until there wasn't anything left of it.

ARMY: I remember a lot of times like that. That time in Scranton when that big Swede knocked him out. Remember? We couldn't get him back on his feet. They took him to a hospital that night. I remember waiting outside in the corridor with you. (MAISH *nods*) You cried that night, Maish.

MAISH: All right, knock it off.

ARMY: Okay. But you hear me out now, Maish. I'm telling you this now. I'm telling you that I love this guy like he was of my flesh. And I figure if I don't watch for him and weep for him—now nobody else will, least of all you for some reason. So be careful, Maish. That's what I'm telling you now. Be careful. (ARMY *rises, leaves the table, goes across the room and out the door,* MAISH *watches him for a moment and then rises after him. He starts to walk slowly toward the door.*)

DISSOLVE TO

THE ALLEY OUTSIDE OF THE FIGHT AREA

(*We see* MC CLINTOCK *very slowly walking into the alley, aimlessly, without direction. Once in the center of the alley he leans against the wall, his back touching one of the torn fight posters. The crowd noise comes up momentarily loud and sharp.* MC CLINTOCK's *head goes up. He slowly turns so that he is face to face with the picture of a boxer on the poster with his hands up. And then for no rhyme nor reason* MC CLINTOCK *starts to spar with the picture. First lightly as if he knew it were a joke, then much more seriously until pretty soon his hands flick out in short jabs. They hit the wall and they hurt. He suddenly draws back with his right as if to smash at the poster when suddenly a hand comes down on his shoulder. He stops. His head comes down. We pull back to see* MAISH *standing near him.*)

MAISH: Mountain, take it easy.

MC CLINTOCK (*Nods slowly, numbly*): Yeah. Yeah, Maish. Take it easy.

MAISH: The world didn't end tonight. Remember that. The world didn't end because you left the ring. It didn't end for you either.

MC CLINTOCK: Sure. Sure, Maish. Just . . . just stick around for a little, will ya? I could always depend on you, Maish. I always . . . I always needed to depend on you. (MAISH *nods slowly, pats his arm, but as he does so his eyes travel down the wall to another poster showing a big, stupid Arabian prince in a wrestling costume. And there is a big sign "Wrestling" over the top of it.* MAISH's *eyes slowly move from the poster to* MC CLINTOCK, *who stares up at him hopefully like a pet dog desperately needing reassurance.*)

MAISH (*Wets his lips*): C'mon, let's get out of here. (*The two men slowly walk away and down the alley.*)

WE TAKE A SLOW FADE TO BLACK

ACT TWO

WE DISSOLVE TO

> *An anteroom of a small office with a sign on the door: New York State Employment Office. Sitting on a bench are* MC-CLINTOCK *and* ARMY, *the former appears nervous and fidgety. He is constantly running a finger through his collar that is much too tight, as is his suit, shirt and everything else that he wears. He looks helplessly at* ARMY *who pats his arm reassuringly.*

ARMY: You look fine. Don't worry. You look just great.

MC CLINTOCK (*In a whisper*): But what do I say, Army?

ARMY: What d'ya mean what d'ya say? Just tell her you want a job, that's all. It's simple.

MC CLINTOCK: But what kind of a job?

ARMY: You don't have to worry about that. You just tell her the sort of thing you can do and it's up to them to find you one.

MC CLINTOCK: Army, in the past two days I've been thirty-five places already. Most of these jokers won't even let me in the door.

ARMY: It's different here. This place is official. They're here just to get people jobs. People like you that can't find them easy on their own. (*At this moment a young woman appears at the door of the inner office.*)

GRACE: Mr. McClintock, please. (MC CLINTOCK *bolts to his feet, almost upsetting* ARMY.)

MC CLINTOCK: That's me! That's me!

GRACE (*Smiles*): In here please, Mr. McClintock. (MC CLINTOCK *turns to* ARMY *and grabs his arm.*)

ARMY (*Firmly removes his fingers*): I'm right here at ringside but I can't go in to fight for you. Go ahead. (MC CLINTOCK, *with another journey of his finger through his collar, walks hesitantly after the young woman. We pan with them into her office as the door closes. He turns around with a start at its closing.*)

GRACE: Sit down, Mr. McClintock. Right over here please near the desk.

MC CLINTOCK: Thanks. Thank you very much. (*He sits down with another eye toward the door. They both start to speak together.*)

MC CLINTOCK: I was . . .

GRACE: Now, Mr. McClintock . . .

MC CLINTOCK: I was just wondering if . . . Oh, I beg your pardon.

GRACE: You were going to say?

MC CLINTOCK: I was just wondering if my friend could come in.

GRACE: Is he looking for employment, too?

MC CLINTOCK: No. No, not exactly but—well, he's kind of my handler.

GRACE: I beg your pardon.

MC CLINTOCK (*Wets his lips*): It's okay, he'll stay out there. (*Then she looks at him and smiles, looks through a sheet of paper.*)

GRACE: Harlan McClintock. Your age is . . .

MC CLINTOCK: Thirty-three. (*She makes a little notation with a pencil.*)

GRACE: Place of birth?

MC CLINTOCK: Kenesaw, Tennessee.

GRACE: I see. Your education: (*She looks up at him*) Mr. McClintock, you left that blank here.

MC CLINTOCK: My education? You mean school?

GRACE: That's right.

MC CLINTOCK: Ninth grade.

GRACE: Then you left, is that it?

MC CLINTOCK (*Nods*): Then I left.

GRACE: Now, field of interest.

MC CLINTOCK: I beg your pardon?

GRACE: Your field of interest. What do you like to do?

MC CLINTOCK: Most anything. I don't much care.

GRACE (*Looks down at his sheet and frowns slightly*): Past employment record, Mr. McClintock. You have nothing written down there. (*Then she looks up at him*) Who've been your past employers?

MC CLINTOCK: Well ... you see ... I really haven't had past employers —I mean past employers like you mean down on that sheet. I've always been kind of on my own except you might say I've been working for Maish.

GRACE: Maish?

MC CLINTOCK: You see, all I've been doing the past fourteen years is fightin'.

GRACE: Fighting.

MC CLINTOCK: That's right. You know, in the ring.

GRACE: You mean a prize fighter.

MC CLINTOCK (*Smiles*): That's right. Prize fighter.

GRACE: A professional prize fighter.

MC CLINTOCK (*Delightedly*): Yeah, that's it. You catch on. A professional prize fighter. Heavyweight.

> (GRACE *stares at him for a moment and we cut to a tight closeup of* MC CLINTOCK's *face as he becomes conscious of her stare. He almost unconsciously puts one hand across his face to hide the scar tissue. He turns his face away ever so slightly.* GRACE *notices this and turns away herself, and then looks down again at the paper.*)

GRACE: That sounds like interesting work, Mr. McClintock.

MC CLINTOCK (*Looks up at her*): Well, it's ... it's a living. I don't want you to go to no trouble. Army says I should just tell you that ... well, anything you got's jake with me. Dishwashing, anything. (*She looks at him again for a long moment.*)

GRACE (*Kindly*): Let's see if we can't examine something else, Mr. McClintock—something you might like even more. How about factory work?

MC CLINTOCK (*Shakes his head*): I never worked in a factory. I wouldn't know anything about it.

GRACE: No sort of assembly-line work, blueprint reading, anything like that? (*He shakes his head. She wets her lips*) Anything in sales, Mr. McClintock. There's a lot of openings in that sort of thing now. Department-store work. Anything like that?

MC CLINTOCK (*Shakes his head*): I ... I couldn't do anything like that. I couldn't sell nothin'. (*Then with a kind of lopsided grin*) With my face I'd scare away the customers. (*He laughs lightly at this and when he looks up she is staring at him, not laughing with him at all. He becomes embarrassed now and half rises to his feet.*)

MC CLINTOCK: Look, Miss, I don't want to take up your time. (*And now in his hopelessness, the words come out; he forgets his embarrassment*) The only reason I come is because Army said I should come. I've been answering all these ads like I told ya and I've been getting no place at all. Maish needs the dough real bad and I can't do nothin' for him any more, and I got to. I got to get some kind of a job. Don't make any difference what I do. Anything at all.

GRACE: Mr. McClintock . . .

MC CLINTOCK (*Unaware of her now*): A guy goes along fourteen years. All he does is fight. Once a week, twice a week, prelims, semi-finals, finals. He don't know nothin' but that. All he can do is fight. Then they tell him no more. And what's he do? What's he supposed to do? What's he supposed to know how to do besides fight? They got poor Maish tied up by the ears and I got to do somethin' for him . . . (*He looks down at his hands. Then he pauses for a moment, then sits down hesitantly in a chair.*)

GRACE (*Quietly*): Mr. McClintock, we handle a lot of placements here. I'm sure we can find you something . . .

MC CLINTOCK: I know you're going to do the best you can—but (*He points to the paper on her desk*) I don't fit in any of the holes. I mean that question there. Why did you leave your last job? State reason.

GRACE: That's question nine. You see, Mr. McClintock . . .

MC CLINTOCK: I understand it but what do I write down? What do I write down that would make sense? I left my last job because I got hit so much that I was on my way to punchy land and I'd probably go blind. How would that read there?

GRACE (*Her eyes narrow*): Punchy land?

MC CLINTOCK: Sure. You fight so long and then you walk around on your heels listening to the bells. That's what happens to you. Doc looks at my eyes—says one or two more I might go blind.

GRACE (*Very softly*): I see.

MC CLINTOCK (*Getting excited again*): And that's not fair. It's a dirty break that's all. In 1948 they ranked me number five. I'm not kidding ya. Number five. And that wasn't any easy year neither. There was Charles and Wolcott and Louis still around. And they had me up there at number five. Maish was sure that . . .

GRACE: Maish? Who's Maish, Mr. McClintock?

MC CLINTOCK: Maish is my manager. And where does it leave him?

That's a nice thing to do to a guy who's kept you going for fourteen years. You stop cold on him. So it's a bum break. It ain't fair at all. (*Then he rises and he turns his back to her and he slowly subsides*) I'm . . . I'm real sorry, Miss. I didn't mean to blow up like that. You ought to kick me out of here. Honest I'm real sorry.

GRACE (*Again quietly*): That's perfectly all right, Mr. McClintock. As long as you've got your address down here we'll contact you if anything comes up, and we'll . . . (*She stops, staring across the room at him. At the big shoulders that are slumped in front of her and the big hands down by his sides that clench and unclench. A certain softness shows in her face. A pitying look. She wets her lips and then forces a smile*) Right after the war I did a lot of work with disabled veterans . . . (*As soon as she has said this she is sorry. His head jerks up and he turns slowly toward her.*)

MC CLINTOCK: Yeah? Go on.

GRACE: I meant . . . I meant you'd be surprised the . . . the different kinds of openings that come up for . . . (*She struggles for a word.*)

MC CLINTOCK: For cripples. For those kind of guys?

GRACE: I didn't mean just that. I meant for people who have special problems.

MC CLINTOCK: I've got no special problems. (*He takes a step toward her*) There wasn't no place on that question sheet of yours. But I was almost the heavyweight champion of the world. I'm a big ugly slob and I look like a freak—but I was almost the heavyweight champion of the world. I'd like to put that down some place on that paper. This isn't just a punk. This was a guy who was almost the *heavyweight champion of the world.* (*He slams his fists on the desk. And then as quickly as the anger came it leaves. Very slowly he takes his hat from off the desk. He looks at it briefly, closes his eyes and turns away again. He looks down at his hand and feels the bruise over his eye, and stands there looking away from her.* GRACE *is staring at him all the time.*)

GRACE: Did you hurt your hand, Mr. McClintock?

MC CLINTOCK (*Looks at his hand*): I guess I did. That's the . . . that's the thing of it. When you go for so long the hurt piles up and you don't even feel them. You get out of the ring and you go back to a dressing room and you look in the mirror. You look like somebody just ran over you with a tractor—but somehow it doesn't seem to hurt. There's always a reason for it. You know that . . . you know that you just took another step up. Then after the last one—when the wad's all shot, and you're over the hill and there aren't going to be any more—then suddenly you do start to hurt. The punches you got fourteen years ago—even them. And when Maish and the Doc and Army—they were all standing around me that night and I heard somebody say—he's wound up. Then it hurts. Then it hurts like you've got to scream. Like now. It hurts now. Before at least—before every little piece of skin they took off you—was part of the bill you had to pay. And then all of a sudden one night you have to throw all the fourteen years out into an alley and you know then that you've been paying that bill for nothing.

> (*We cut to a very tight closeup of* GRACE'S *face as she comes around from behind her desk. She touches his arm tentatively.*)

GRACE: Mr. McClintock—I think—I think we can get you something you'll like. Just give us time.

MC CLINTOCK (*Looks at her*): Something I'll like? Do that, Miss. I don't want much. Just . . . the heavyweight championship of the world. That's all. (*He stares at her and you can see in his face that he wants to say something—wants to apologize—wants to explain to her that this is a bitterness directed at no one, but it can't come out. It can't be articulated. He turns slowly and walks out of the room. She stands there watching him through the open door. We see* ARMY *rise. The two men exchange words and then they both leave.* GRACE *slowly closes the door, goes back to her desk pensively. We take a slow fade out on her face.*)

FADE ON

A SHOT OF MAISH'S HOTEL ROOM—NIGHT

> (*In the semi-dark room* MAISH *and* ARMY *play cards.* MAISH *slaps down a card with tremendous vigor.*)

MAISH: Jack of spades. (ARMY *goes through a series of facial and body movements, shrugging left and right, opening and closing his mouth, drumming on the bridge of his nose with his fingers.*)

ARMY: That's good to know. That's very good to know. (*He draws a card, throws it down.* MAISH *draws another. He throws it down.*)

ARMY: Queen of spades.

MAISH: That's what it looks like, doesn't it?

ARMY (*Nods*): That's good to know. That's very good to know. (*He goes through the series of motions again.*) That's very good to know.

MAISH (*Looks up at him*): Army, would you not say that any more, please?

ARMY: Say what?

MAISH: "It's good to know. It's good to know. It's good to know." Everything is good to know with you. (ARMY *grins, draws a card, throws it down face down, lays out his hand, throws a single card across the table.*)

ARMY: I'll knock for two.

MAISH: You've got me. I've got a Jack and eight free. You've got me . . .

ARMY: That's good to know. (*Then he ducks away jokingly.* MAISH *rises and flings the cards at him across the table.*)

ARMY: C'mon I'll play you another hand.

MAISH: Don't do me any favors. (*He rises and pats around his pockets.*)

ARMY (*Points to an ashtray*): It's over here. (MAISH *walks across the room, takes a half-smoked cigar out of an ashtray, lights it.*)

ARMY: One inch shorter you'd be smoking your nose.

MAISH: So does it hurt you?

ARMY: Wanna watch television? There's a fight on.

MAISH: You don't get enough of that, huh?

ARMY: It's somethin' to do.

MAISH: If it's somethin' to do, go to a bar, will ya. I get my gut full of it nine, ten hours a day. I don't like it in my hotel room.

ARMY: Cards?

MAISH: How about ice skating? You bored, Army? (*He chomps nervously on the cigar*) What am I going to do?

ARMY (*Shrugs*): Ask 'em for another week.

MAISH: Ask 'em, ask 'em, ask 'em! Do you think it'll cut ice with them. They want their money. (*The phone rings and* MAISH *nervously and quickly picks it up.*)

MAISH (*On the phone*): Hello. Yeah. (*A pause*) Well, when he gets in tell him I want to talk to him, will ya? No, I can't talk to you. I want to talk to Parelli himself. Thanks. (*He puts down the receiver and finds* ARMY *staring at him*) Well? You want to lodge a complaint? You look it.

ARMY: Parelli handles wrestling.

MAISH: Is that a secret?

ARMY: What do you want with a wrestling promoter?

MAISH: You got the longest nose in the business.

ARMY: You gonna answer, Maish?

MAISH (*With an enforced matter-of-factness*): For a kick, Army. We'll let the kid wrestle a few.

ARMY: Mountain?

MAISH: Why not? They pay good for that stuff, just like they pay actors or somethin'. I could work up a routine for him—ya know. We could make him something like . . . well, you know, like Gorgeous George and the Mad Baron—he'd be . . . he'd be Mountain McClintock the Mountaineer. We could dress him up in a coonskin hat and a . . . a . . . costume of some kind. And we could bill him as . . . (*He stops abruptly. He sees the other staring at him*) So what's wrong with it? It's money, ain't it?

ARMY: It's money, sure, but what kind of money is it, Maish?

MAISH: What difference does it make what kind of money it is?

ARMY: A guy like him don't take getting laughed at.

MAISH (*Whirls around at him*): What're you talking about—a guy like him? So what is he? A prima donna? All of a sudden he's sensitive! All of a sudden he's very fragile like precious china or something. Since when does a guy like him get sensitive all of a sudden!

ARMY: Since when? Since we knowed him! That's since when. You never see things like that, Maish.

MAISH: Maybe I got no time. Ever look at it that way? Maybe I'm too busy stitching him up so he can show the next week. Maybe I'm too busy on my hands and knees pleading with a promoter to use him so we can get groceries. Maybe I've got no time to hold these poor sensitive boys on my lap.

ARMY: Hey, Maish—you stink.

MAISH: Sure I stink. I'm a crummy selfish louse—because for fourteen years I nurse along a pug, and instead of three square meals for my old age, I got nothing but debts and a headache. You want to know who owes who? Okay. Just check the records. Look at the win and loss. The Mountain comes in at the short end. He owes me. I figure it's as simple as that. What do I ask of this guy? Stick on a costume and make a few people laugh a couple of minutes. Is that going to curdle his sensitive insides? (MAISH's *voice has a barely perceptible tremor in it.*)

ARMY: He's only got one thing left, Maish, that's his pride. You don't want to job that off . . . (MAISH *doesn't answer.* ARMY *walks over to him and grabs him*) Leave something, will you? You talk about him when he was number five contender in *Ring Magazine*. You want to remember him that way. Leave it so that's the way he'll remember himself. Not a . . . not a clown. Not like somebody who takes a pie in the face so he can eat that day. He was a somebody, Maish. Let it go at that. Don't turn him into a geek. (MAISH *looks intensely at* ARMY. *He can't vocalize his frustration any more than he can put into words the sense of the truth that he gets from what* ARMY *has told him, and it is a truth that* MAISH *cannot answer. Finally he kicks at a table, upsetting a lamp.*)

MAISH: So I'm selling his soul on the street! So light a candle! So weep for him! So rip your clothes a little. So I may take an inch off his pride, but, by God, he and I'll have a full gut to show for it. You can starve to death, wise guy. (*He turns almost aimlessly, not knowing what to do, and finally goes out the door and slams it.*)

DISSOLVE OUT

FADE ON

> (*With a shot of the Squared-Circle Bar as in Act One. It is mid-evening and the place is only partially filled. At the far end of the room the same group of old fighters stand in a semi-circle around one of the others.* MC CLINTOCK *stands on their fringe, listening, and as the men talk* MC CLINTOCK *studies their faces. All of them are scarred, ring-battered and there's a kind of sameness in each face.*)

FIGHTER NUMBER ONE: That was Keister. Willie Keister. Used to fight out of Philly. Lightweight.

FIGHTER NUMBER TWO: He wasn't never no lightweight. He always fought middle. I remember him good.

FIGHTER NUMBER ONE: Middleweight, your bleeding ears—He never weighed more than 135 pounds in his life.

> (*This talk continues underneath as the camera moves away to take in a shot of the bar and the archway that adjoins the lobby of the little hotel. From out of the lobby we see* GRACE *enter the bar. She looks around.*)

BARTENDER: Sorry, Miss, unescorted ladies ain't permitted.

GRACE: I was looking for Mr. McClintock. The man at the desk said he'd be in here.

BARTENDER: McClintock? The Mountain you mean. That's him. (*He points down toward the end of the room.*)

GRACE: Thank you. (*She walks very slowly toward the group of men in the rear and when she gets close we can then pick up what they are saying.*)

FIGHTER NUMBER ONE: So it's round four. He comes out real slow like he always does.

FIGHTER NUMBER TWO: Yeah. He always did come out slow.

FIGHTER NUMBER ONE: He jabs a couple of times. Remember how he used to do that? From way up high on the shoulder. You could hardly see it coming.

FIGHTER NUMBER TWO: You hardly ever could.

FIGHTER NUMBER ONE: He touches me a couple of times up on the forehead. I back off. He keeps coming after me. I want him to lead. Now this is a guy you got to let lead because he's the best counter puncher in the business.

FIGHTER NUMBER TWO: Yeah. He can always counter punch. Man, could that boy counter punch. I remember one time in Chicago . . .

FIGHTER NUMBER THREE: Go ahead, Steve. Go ahead.

FIGHTER NUMBER ONE: So, we keep sparring like that right on through the round. He don't hurt me, I don't hurt him. (*He continues to speak underneath as* MC CLINTOCK *turns and sees* GRACE. *He reacts, leaves the group and walks over to see her hurriedly.*)

MC CLINTOCK: Miss Carrie, what're you doing here?

GRACE: Well, I . . . (*She is suddenly conscious of the rest of the men looking at her and* MC CLINTOCK *sees this too. He takes her arm.*)

MC CLINTOCK: Let's go over here and sit down. (*He takes her across to a booth and they sit down. The men move away chuckling with an occasional glance at them.*)

GRACE: A friend of mine and I had dinner over at McCleary's. It isn't very far from here. She got a headache and went on home, and I . . .

MC CLINTOCK: Yeah?

GRACE: And I remembered your giving me your hotel and . . .

MC CLINTOCK: It was real nice of you to look me up. (*She looks around the room and smiles a little embarrassedly.*)

GRACE: You know—I've never been around here before.

MOUNTAIN (*Nods*): No change. If you're here once, you've seen it all.

GRACE (*Smiles*): Atmosphere.

MC CLINTOCK: Yeah, you might call it atmosphere. (*She looks over his shoulder at the men in the back of the room. One fighter is going through the motions of a battle.* GRACE *looks questioningly at him and then at* MC CLINTOCK.)

MC CLINTOCK: That? That goes on all the time around here. Maish says this part of the room is the graveyard. And these guys spend their time dying in here. Fighting their lives away inside their heads. That's what Maish says.

GRACE: That's . . . that's kind of sad.

MC CLINTOCK: I suppose it is.

GRACE (*With a smile leans toward him*): I've got a confession to make.

I didn't eat at McCleary's. I ate at home. I came on purpose. I asked for you at your hotel. I've been thinking about you a lot, Mr. McClintock. (*There is a long pause*) I was just wondering ...

MC CLINTOCK: Yeah? Go ahead.

GRACE: I was just wondering if you ever thought of working with children. (*There's a long pause.*)

MC CLINTOCK: What?

GRACE: Work with children. Like a summer camp. You know in athletics ...

MC CLINTOCK: I—I never give it much thought.

GRACE: Do you like children?

MC CLINTOCK: Children? Well, I haven't had much to do with kids but I've always liked them. (*Then thoughtfully, going over it in his mind*) Yeah, I like kids a lot. You were thinking of a summer camp or something ...

GRACE: That's right. That sort of thing. In a month or so there'll be a lot of openings. I was thinking, well, perhaps you ought to give that some thought.

MC CLINTOCK (*His hand goes to his face*): But they'd have to see me and listen to me talk and ...

GRACE: Why not? You've got to begin some place. You've got to give it a try.

MC CLINTOCK: Sure, I'm going to have to. (*Then he stares at her intently*) Why did you come here tonight?

GRACE (*Looks away*): I've been thinking about you. I want to help— if I can. (*Then as if to dispel the seriousness of the mood she cocks her head, grins very girl-like*) How about it, Mr. McClintock—could I have a beer?

MC CLINTOCK: A beer? You mean here?

GRACE: I kind of like it here.

MC CLINTOCK (*Grins at her*): Why, sure. (*He stands up and calls to the* BARTENDER *who is passing.*)

MC CLINTOCK: Hey, Charlie! Two beers, huh? (*The* BARTENDER *acknowledges with a wave, goes back toward the bar.* MC CLINTOCK *sits down again and looks across the table at her.*)

GRACE (*Points to the juke box*): How about music?

MC CLINTOCK: What?

GRACE: Don't you like to listen to music when you drink beer?

MC CLINTOCK: Music? Why ... I never even gave it much thought. Sure. Sure we can play music. (*He rises, fishes in his pocket, takes out a coin, puts it in the juke box.*)

WE CUT TO

> (*A tight close-up of* FIGHTER NUMBER TWO *across the room—a toothless, terribly ugly little man.*)

FIGHTER NUMBER TWO (*Smiles*): Hey, Mountain—play "My Heart Tells Me."

> (*There's laughter at this.* MC CLINTOCK *quickly turns his face away, shoves a coin in the slot, indiscriminately punches a few buttons, then returns to the booth.* BARTENDER *brings over two bottles of beer, slops them down in front of them.*)

MC CLINTOCK: How about a glass, Charlie, for the lady?

BARTENDER (*Over his shoulder as he heads back to the bar*): Fancy-shmancy. (*There's another moment's pause.*)

GRACE: Pretty.

MC CLINTOCK (*Listens for a moment*): Yeah. Yeah it is kind of pretty. Them are violins.

GRACE (*Smiles*): Beautiful.

MC CLINTOCK: I never paid much attention to music before. I never had much time.

GRACE: What's that?

MC CLINTOCK: Music. Just plain old music. (*He looks away thoughtfully for a moment*) The only music I know by heart really is the national anthem because they play it before every fight. The national anthem. (GRACE *smiles at this*) Oh, yeah—there was Smiley Collins, too.

GRACE: Who's Smiley Collins?

MC CLINTOCK: He was a fighter. He used to play a violin. (*A pause*) That's funny, ain't it? He was a fighter but he used to play a violin. (*As* MC CLINTOCK *talks we can see him losing himself in the conversation and in the sheer delight of having a girl across from him.*)

GRACE: He used to play the violin? Seriously?

MC CLINTOCK: Real serious. Oh, I don't know nothin' about his violin playing—but, oh, man, did that boy have a right hand. Like dynamite. He could knock down a wall with it.

GRACE: What about his violin . . .

MC CLINTOCK (*Interrupts her, not even hearing her*): I remember his last fight. He fought a guy by the name of Willie Floyd. Floyd had twenty pounds on him. (*At this moment the* BARTENDER *brings a glass, puts it down in front of* GRACE, *then walks away.* MC CLINTOCK *picks up her bottle and pours the beer for her.*)

GRACE (*Smiles*): Thanks.

MC CLINTOCK: They don't have many ladies here—that's the reason he forgets to put glasses out. (*He holds up his bottle to her glass*) Drink hearty. That's what Maish always says. Drink hearty.

GRACE (*Smiles*): Drink hearty. Drink hearty, Mr. McClintock. (*The two of them drink. His eyes never leave her face. She notices this, smiles again*) You think a lot of Maish, don't you?

MC CLINTOCK: He's number one. They don't come like him.

GRACE: He was your—manager.

MC CLINTOCK (*Nods*): Yeah, for fourteen years. He's been a real great friend, not just a manager. In the old days—in the old days when I was just getting started—Maish would stake me to everything from clothes to chow. He's a real great guy. (*Then he stops abruptly and stares at her*) Why ain't you married?

GRACE (*Laughs*): Should I be?

MC CLINTOCK (*Nods*): You're pretty. Not just pretty, you're beautiful.

GRACE: Thank you.

MC CLINTOCK: Pretty as a young colt. That's what my old man used to say.

GRACE: Your father?

MC CLINTOCK (*Nods*): Yeah. A girl's as pretty as a young colt, so he used to tell me.

GRACE (*Very interested*): Go ahead, Mountain . . .

MC CLINTOCK: About my father? Big guy. Nice old guy too. I remember once—I fought a guy named Jazzo. Elmer Jazzo. And he looked just like my old man. Spittin' image. And in the first round I didn't even want to hit him. Then in round two I shut my eyes and I . . .

GRACE (*Interrupts*): Mountain.

MC CLINTOCK (*Looks at her*): Yeah?

GRACE: There isn't much else is there—besides fighting?

MC CLINTOCK (*Very thoughtfully looks away*): No. No, there isn't I guess. I'm . . . I'm sorry . . .

GRACE: Don't be. It's just that there is so much more for you that you'll be able to find now. (*They look at each other and both smile. The music is playing and they are both aware of it suddenly*) Hey, Mountain . . .

MC CLINTOCK: Yeah?

GRACE: Them are violins.

> (*They both laugh. The camera pulls away from them as they start to talk, lost in an awareness of each other and in the*

*pleasantness of being together. We continue a slow dolly
away from them, and then a slow fade out to black. We fade
on with a shot of the alley outside the arena.* GRACE *and*
MC CLINTOCK *walk slowly away from the door toward the
street. They walk slowly, looking around.*)

MC CLINTOCK (*Kicks a can out of the way*): A garden, ain't it?

GRACE: Where are the flowers?

MC CLINTOCK (*Flicks his ear*) Right here. (GRACE *smiles a little
forcedly.*)

GRACE: It's late, Mountain. I've got to go home.

MC CLINTOCK: I'll get you a cab. (*She starts to walk off*) Grace . . .
(*She turns to him*) I . . . I've had a good time.

GRACE: I have too.

MC CLINTOCK: You know when we came out of the bar I heard Charlie
say that I had a pretty date.

GRACE (*Smiles*): Thank Charlie for me.

MC CLINTOCK: It wasn't just that he thought you were pretty. He said
that I had a date. It's like with the music, I don't even think I ever
had a real date in all this time. A real one. Not somebody I liked.
Somebody I wanted to be with.

GRACE: I think that's a compliment.

MC CLINTOCK: One time . . . one time Army had a girl friend living
in St. Louis. She had a friend. Army fixed me up. We were supposed to meet after the fight. These two girls were waitin' for us
outside. This girl that I was supposed to go with—she takes one
look at me and she . . . she . . .

GRACE: She what, Mountain?

MC CLINTOCK: She turned around and she ran away. She looked at my
face and she turned around and ran away. (GRACE *instinctively
touches his arm and holds it tightly*) That shouldn't have hurt. I
should have been used to it. I know what I look like. I know what
I sound like, too. But it . . . it did hurt. I didn't want it to happen
again so I never let it happen.

CUT TO

A TIGHT CLOSE-UP OF GRACE

(*As she stares at him and she wonderingly shakes her head,
feeling that acme of tenderness a woman can feel for a man.*)

GRACE (*Softly*): The cab, Mountain. It's late.

MC CLINTOCK: Sure. (*The two start walking again toward the opening
of the alley.*)

GRACE: Remember to think about what I told you. I think you'd like working with children.

MC CLINTOCK: I'll think about it. I'll think about it a lot. Don't build me up none, Miss Carrie. Don't say I'm anything special. (*A pause*) Tell 'em . . . tell 'em I fought a hundred and eleven fights. Tell 'em I never took a dive. I'm proud of that. (GRACE *looks at him intently for a moment and there's a continuing softness on her face.*)

GRACE (*Whispers*): Sure you are, Mountain. You must be very proud. (*She quickly kisses him on the side of his face, studies him for a moment and hurriedly walks away from him. He stands there touching his face, looking after her.*)

WE TAKE A SLOW DISSOLVE OUT TO

A SHOT OF MAISH'S HOTEL ROOM, THE SAME NIGHT

> (*The door opens,* MC CLINTOCK *enters. In the room are* MAISH, ARMY *and a* FAT MAN *who has been sitting in a corner of the room.* FAT MAN *rises.*)

MAISH: It's about time. Army was lookin' for ya. Somebody said you left the bar with a girl.

MC CLINTOCK (*Grins broadly*): I want to tell you all about it, Maish. No kiddin', she's a wonderful girl. Her name is . . .

MAISH: Tell me later. We've got business to attend to here.

MC CLINTOCK (*Filled to overflowing*): Army, it's the girl from the employment office. Miss Carrie.

ARMY: Pretty kid.

MC CLINTOCK: Beautiful. Beautiful girl.

PARELLI: How about it, Maish? I ain't got all night.

MAISH: Right away, Mountain, I'd like you to meet somebody. This is Mr. Parelli. Mr. Parelli promotes wrestling matches at Matthew's Arena.

MC CLINTOCK: I'm gladda know you.

PARELLI: Likewise. So get with it, Maish.

MAISH: We've got ourselves a nice deal here, kid. Want to tell him, Mr. Parelli?

PARELLI: There isn't much to tell. Maish here thinks you might be a good draw. Your name's pretty well known. I've seen you fight a couple of times myself. (MC CLINTOCK *smiles*) Yeah I think I can line you up with some matches. I think it might be worth both our while.

MC CLINTOCK (*His smile fades somewhat*): Maish didn't tell ya. I'm not supposed to fight any more. I don't think I can get my license back. (PARELLI *looks at* MAISH *questioningly and* MAISH *forces a smile.*)

MAISH: We're not talking about boxing now, Kid. This is for wrestling. I told ya Mr. Parelli promotes wrestling matches.

MC CLINTOCK: Wrestling matches? I don't know how to wrestle.

PARELLI (*Laughs*): You don't have to know how. Couple hours and you can learn the holds. There's really only two big things you've got to learn in my business, Kid. That's how to fake, make it look real, and that's how to land without hurting yourself. That's about it.

MC CLINTOCK: I don't get it.

MAISH: What do you mean you don't get it? He's laying it out for you. And listen to what else, Mountain. I've got a funny idea. We'll dress you up in a coonskin hat see, and you're going to be billed as the Mountaineer. How about that, huh? Just like old times. Even buy you some kind of a long squirrel gun or something. (*Then there's a long dead silence as* MC CLINTOCK *turns away.*)

MAISH: Well?

PARELLI: I don't think he goes for it, Maish.

MAISH: What're you talkin' about he don't go for it? Mountain, what've you got to say?

MC CLINTOCK: I'd lose you a fortune, Maish. I can't wrestle. I don't think I could win a match. (PARELLI *laughs.*)

MAISH: What do you mean win a match? These are all set up, Kid. One night you win, the next night the other guy wins.

PARELLI: It depends on who plays the heavy.

MC CLINTOCK: A tank job.

MAISH: Will you talk sense? This is an entirely different thing. Everybody knows there's a fix on in these things. It's a part of the game.

MC CLINTOCK: I never took a dive for anybody. A hundred and eleven fights. I never took one single dive.

PARELLI: It's like Maish says. These aren't exactly dives . . . (*Then there's a long pause*) Well, look I'll tell you what, you guys talk it over. Give me a call, Maish, by tomorrow. I've got to know by tomorrow.

MAISH: You get the contracts ready. We'll be ready to sign in the morning.

PARELLI: Sure. Nice meeting you, Mountain. (MC CLINTOCK *nods.* PARELLI *goes out. There is the off-stage sound of the door closing.* MC CLINTOCK *stares at* MAISH. MAISH *averts his glance.*)

MAISH (*With his back to him*): I figure you owe it to me. (*Then a pause*) What do you figure?

MC CLINTOCK (*Nods*): I guess so.

MAISH: So there's nothing more to it then. (MC CLINTOCK *turns, his face shows an anguish we haven't seen before.*)

MC CLINTOCK: But Maish—I was almost heavyweight champion of the world. (MAISH *turns, walks over to him and grabs him tightly. His voice is fierce and intent.*)

MAISH: Then you remember just that. When I stick you in a silly costume you just remember you were almost heavyweight champion of the world. And I'll remember I was the guy who managed you. We'll do this one with our eyes closed. (*Then he releases him. He breathes a little heavily*) Army, take him home. (*He turns his back to them.* ARMY *walks over to* MC CLINTOCK.)

MC CLINTOCK: Never mind, Army. I'll go home by myself. (MOUNTAIN *exits.*)

MAISH: He's upset—that's all. He just don't know.

ARMY: He knows. Believe me, he knows.

MAISH: But he'll come around.

ARMY: Sure he will. You'll fix it that way. You gotta knack, Maish. You violin him to death. And if that don't work—squeeze a little. Back him up. Twist it up a little for him. What a knack you got! (*He turns to go.* MAISH's *voice is soft, pleading.*)

MAISH: Army, stick, will ya?

ARMY: Stick?

MAISH: Help me with him. Just stay alongside.

ARMY (*Understanding now*): Partners again, huh? If he sees me, he'll move faster—that the idea?

MAISH: He'll want both of us. It'll help him, Army. A lousy one-night stand.

ARMY: Stop it! You break him into a dummy harness once—he'll stay with it. (*Pounds his fists silently*) It ain't enough I gotta watch him go down all these years. Now you want me in the pit. I gotta officiate at the burial.

MAISH: It don't have to be that way. (*And now desperately groping for the words and for the first time we're listening to the mind of this man.* ARMY *grabs him by the lapels and holds on to him very tightly.*)

ARMY: This is a slob to you, Maish. This is a hunk. This is a dead-weight—has-been. This is a cross you got to bear? I'll tell you what he is, Maish, this boy. This is a decent man. This is a man with a heart. This is somebody, flesh and blood, now, Maish. You can't sell this on the market by the pound, because if you do, if you do, you'll rot in hell for it. You understand me, Maish, you'll rot. (*He cries uncontrollably and then stops.*)

MAISH: Please, Army, for him at least. Don't leave him alone.

ARMY: Of course not. I can't leave him alone. He'll do it for you even if I'm not there. So I'll *be* there (*A pause*) Why is it, Maish . . . tell me . . . why is it . . . so many people have to feed off one guy's misery? Tell me, Maish . . . doesn't it . . . doesn't it make you want to die?

FADE OUT

ACT THREE

FADE ON

> (*With a tight close-up of a suit of buckskin, the coonskin hat, an old relic of a muzzle-loading Long-Tom rifle, a powder horn and a few other accoutrements. Then we pull back for a cover shot of the room. It is a small dressing room very similar to the one in Act One.* PARELLI *is looking over the costume and chuckling softly through his cigar. He picks up one of the legs of the trousers, examines it, laughs again, tosses it aside, then starts toward the door as it opens.* MAISH *enters.*)

PARELLI (*Nods*): Looks good. Where is he?

MAISH: He's coming.

PARELLI: The guy at the gym says he don't have those holds down at all. Didn't understand them.

MAISH: He will. Give him a little while.

PARELLI: He knows just what to do, doesn't he?

MAISH: Yeah. He's all zeroed in.

PARELLI: And this is important. When the other guy gets a lock on him or any kind of a hold—have him look in pain, you understand? That's important. He's got to look as if he's giving up the ghost. (*Then with a grimace*) Pain, you understand, Maish. Real pain. Torture. Agony.

MAISH (*Sardonically*): He'll die out there for ya. (*Then he looks out toward the open door*) How's the house?

PARELLI: The usual. Not good, not bad. They want action. It don't have to be good action, but it's got to be action. So tell your boy to move around.

MAISH: I told you he knows all about it.

PARELLI: Okay. (*He starts to walk by him and* MAISH *pinches his sleeve with two fingers.*)

MAISH: The dough, Parelli.

PARELLI: It'll be waiting for you after the fight. I don't know how you talked me into an advance. Most people can't.

MAISH (*With a grin*): With me, it's an art.

PARELLI: It must be. (*He looks at his watch*) He better get here soon. (*Then with a grin*) It's going to take him a long time to get into that outfit.

MAISH: He'll be right along. I just talked to him.

PARELLI: Okay. I'll see you later. (*He goes out of the room. He closes the door.* MAISH *walks over to the table that the costume is on. He picks up the pieces one by one and looks at them. He has a dull, emotionless look on his face. When he gets to the gun he picks it up, and the door opens.* ARMY *enters.*)

ARMY: What's the season—grouse? What you huntin', Maish?

MAISH: Right now I'm huntin' a wrestler named McClintock. Have you seen him?

ARMY (*Shakes his head*): Not since last night.

MAISH (*Slams a fist against his palm*): He's late.

ARMY: That's good to know. (*He kicks the door shut and walks over to* MAISH. *He looks down at the paraphernalia.*)

MAISH (*Stares at him*): Enough to make a fuss over? (*He points to the clothes*) Is it, Army?

ARMY (*Shrugs*): I don't have to wear it.

MAISH: If you did—it would break your heart, huh? (*At this moment there's the sound of the crowd from up above and both men look up and then look at each other.*)

MAISH: Army.

ARMY: Go.

MAISH: You know me, Army.

ARMY: You bet I do.

MAISH: I don't mean just that way. I mean you know me inside. You know how I hate this. You know how it keeps me from sleeping. You know how it eats away my stomach, Army ... (*At this moment,* MC CLINTOCK *enters. He smiles at* ARMY.)

MC CLINTOCK: I looked for ya. I was afraid you wasn't gonna come.

MAISH: He's here. You better get into this thing.

MC CLINTOCK: Sure, Maish. Sure.

> (*Then suddenly his eyes fall on the coonskin cap and cos-
> tume and the   gun leaning against the wall. His face goes
> numb. He walks over to them, lifts them up one piece at a
> time. He stares down at them.*)

MAISH (*Wets his lips, forces a smile*): Ain't that a lark, Kid? It's gonna
kill 'em. Gonna knock 'em dead. (MC CLINTOCK *nods dumbly.*
MAISH, *continuing, hurriedly*) You know you take it off when you
get in. You walk around the ring a couple of times and you take it
off. You don't have to wear it very long. (*His words tumble out in
a torrent*) And underneath you wear Long Johns and it isn't until
after the bout you've got to put the stuff back on . . . (*He stops
abruptly as* MC CLINTOCK *turns to him.*)

MC CLINTOCK: Clown.

MAISH (*Points to* ARMY): He called it that. You're taking it from him.
Can't you think a thought for yourself?

MC CLINTOCK (*Shakes his head*): He called it that but I call it that
too. (*He nods toward the hallway*) And everybody out there will
call it that, too. Clown. (*He puts the flat of both hands on the
table, and bends his head far down so that his face cannot be seen*)
Maish—*don't make me!*

CUT TO

A VERY TIGHT CLOSE-UP OF MAISH

> (*What we see on his features is a look of pain—a kind of
> sudden, personal agony, and then he composes his features
> almost one by one and his voice comes out loud again and
> shrill, along with a laugh.*)

MAISH: What do you mean don't make you? What am I, your father?
Don't make you. You don't do nothin' you don't want to do. If you
don't think you owe it to me. Okay. (*There's a knock on the door.*)

MAISH: Yeah?

> (*The door opens and* PARELLI *is standing there. Behind him
> a* PHOTOGRAPHER.)

PARELLI (*Grins into the room*): How about a couple of pictures,
Maish? We ain't had any with the costume yet.

MC CLINTOCK (*His head goes up*): Pictures?

PARELLI: Part of the build-up, Kid. One picture is worth a million
words. That's what the Greeks say. (*Then to* PHOTOGRAPHER) How
about it? You want 'em in here or out in the hall?

PHOTOGRAPHER: Out in the hall. I've got more room. (*There's a long pause.* PARELLI *waits expectantly.*)

PARELLI: So? What's he waiting for—a valet? Let's hurry it up. (*He goes out, closing the door.* MC CLINTOCK *rises, looks quickly at* ARMY *and then at* MAISH, *then turns back to the table and picks up the coonskin hat, puts it on his head. Then he puts his arms into the coat and slowly puts it on.* MAISH *turns away. We are looking from close up at him and at his face and features as they work, and a little of the agony returns. Over his shoulder we see* MC CLINTOCK *buttoning the jacket, then he takes the gun, looks at it.* MC CLINTOCK *goes to the door, stops with his hand on the knob, stands there motionless, his eyes closed.*)

VOICE: McClintock's on next. Let's go!

MC CLINTOCK (*Almost a whisper*): Tell 'em to go away, Maish.

MAISH: What're you talking about? (*There's a loud knock on the door and this time* PARELLI'S *voice.*)

PARELLI: What's going on in there? What're you trying to pull off here, Maish? Get your boy out there. Photographer's waitin' for him and his match is on.

MAISH (*Raises his voice but it still comes out weakly*): He'll . . . he'll be right out, Parelli. He'll be right there. (*Then he turns to* MC-CLINTOCK) Mountain, you cross me now—and I'm dead. Understand? I'm dead. (MC CLINTOCK *shakes his head back and forth, back and forth.*)

MC CLINTOCK: Can't. Can't, Maish. Can't.

MAISH (*Grabs him and holds him tightly by the shirt front*): You got a debt, Mister. You owe me.

MC CLINTOCK: Maish . . .

MAISH: I mean it, Mountain. I've got my whole life on the line now. I can't afford to let you cross me. (MC CLINTOCK *shakes his head.* MAISH'S *voice desperate*) I swear I'll beat you to a pulp myself! I wouldn't have been in this jam if it weren't for you.

MC CLINTOCK (*Looks up*): Maish, I'll do anything you want but . . .

MAISH: But it bothers you too much. Well, it didn't bother you last week to stand up in a ring with your hands down at your sides and let Gibbons beat you to a pulp. That didn't bother you a bit! *It didn't bother you that I had every nickel in the world tossed on a table to say that you wouldn't go three!* (*Then there's a long, long pause as* MC CLINTOCK'S *face shows a gradual understanding, and* MAISH *on the other hand looks like a man whose tongue has suddenly gotten red hot in his mouth.*)

MC CLINTOCK: Maish . . . Maish, you bet against me. (MAISH *doesn't answer him and there's another pause.* MC CLINTOCK *takes a step toward him.*)

MC CLINTOCK: Maish. Why'd you bet against me?

MAISH: Would it make any difference, Mountain, if I hocked my left foot to bet on you—would it have made any difference? You're not a winner any more, Mountain. And that means there's only one thing left—make a little off the losing. (MC CLINTOCK *takes another step toward him, and* MAISH, *whose back has been to him, turns to face him.* MC CLINTOCK *stares at him and his lips tremble.*)

MC CLINTOCK (*Finally*): You fink! You dirty fink, you, Maish! Dirty, lousy fink. (MAISH's *face goes white but he doesn't say anything.*)

MC CLINTOCK: And because I wouldn't go down—because I stood up and took it for ya—I've got to pay for it like this. (*He pulls at the costume*) Like this, Maish, huh? (*He turns and walks away from him, shaking his head, trying to articulate, desperate to let something that he feels now come out without quite knowing how to let it come out*) In all the dirty, crummy fourteen years I fought for you—I never felt ashamed. Not of a round—not of a minute. (*Then he turns to* MAISH, *looks down at himself, then across at* MAISH) But now all of a sudden you make me feel ashamed. You understand, Maish? You make me feel ashamed. I'd have gone into any ring barehanded against a guy with a cleaver—and that wouldn't have hurt me near as much as this.

ARMY: Mountain. Listen to me . . . (MC CLINTOCK, *suddenly unable to control himself any more, raises his hand and with the flat of it smashes* ARMY *against the face.* ARMY *goes backward, falling against a table and winding up on his hands and knees.* MAISH *starts toward him.*)

ARMY (*Picks up his head*): Get away, Maish. Get away. (*Then very slowly he rises to his feet, rubs his jaw briefly, looks at* MC CLINTOCK.)

MC CLINTOCK (*In a whisper*): Army . . . Army—for the love of God . . .

ARMY: That's all right, Kid. I rated it. I shouldn't have been here. I had no reason to be here. I had it coming. (*He turns accusingly toward* MAISH) Go on, Kid, go on and leave. Take what precious little you've got left and get out of here. (MC CLINTOCK *turns slowly and walks out of the room. After a few moments' pause,* ARMY *turns and goes to the door, looks down the corridor and says:*) Good night, Mountain. (*From down the hall at this moment comes a shouting, fuming, sweating* PARELLI. *He arrives at the door almost too excited to speak.*)

PARELLI: He's walkin' out! The boy's walkin' out! What's with this? What's with it? (*Then* PARELLI *walks over to* MAISH, *sticks his finger in his chest and prods him.*)

PARELLI: You know what I'm gonna do to you for this, don't you? (MAISH *keeps his head down. Shouts:*) I'm gonna see to it that you don't get a license to walk a dog from now on. You don't think I will? You don't think I will, Maish? Well, let me tell ya . . .

(*The camera moves back over to* ARMY, *still standing by the door.*)

ARMY (*Very quietly*): Good-bye, Mountain—

DISSOLVE TO

THE BAR

(*Dolly down through it until we reach the rear and a group of men talking fight talk. All of them living in a little round-by-round dream world.* MC CLINTOCK *stands a few feet away from the fringes, staring at them and listening. Finally one of them says loudly enough to be heard:*)

FIGHTER NUMBER ONE: That wasn't his name, Stevie. His name was Hacker. Charles Hacker. And he never fought Louis. (*Then he looks up over the crowd and sees* MC CLINTOCK) How about that, Mountain? You know him. Hacker. Charles Hacker. He never fought Louis, did he? (*The crowd turns and stares toward* MC CLINTOCK *who takes a step toward them.*)

MC CLINTOCK: No, he never fought Louis. He fought me, though.

FIGHTER NUMBER TWO: No kiddin', Mountain. No kiddin'? How'd you do? (MC CLINTOCK *takes another step and the men make way for him until he is standing almost in their midst.*)

MC CLINTOCK: It went three rounds. He was always strong in the beginning.

FIGHTER NUMBER TWO: Yeah, yeah. He was always strong.

MC CLINTOCK: He come in at me and he don't box none. He never did . . . (*Then he stops abruptly and he stares around the circle of faces. We pan with his eyes to take in a shot of each face, and then winding up on a tight close-up of his own as he suddenly slowly shakes his head.*)

MC CLINTOCK: I . . . I don't remember it. I'm sorry but I don't remember it. (*He turns, walks away from them and goes over to the bar*) Give me a beer, will you?

BARTENDER: Sure, Mountain. Comin' up.

(*The camera pulls away from the shot of* MOUNTAIN *sitting at the bar until he is framed in the window. It continues to pull away until we pick up a shot of* ARMY *across the street staring toward the window. Then we see* GRACE *approaching him.*)

ARMY (*Turns to her*): I'm over here, Miss.

GRACE (*Approaches him*): You're . . . you're Army?

ARMY: That's right. Thanks for coming.

GRACE: Tell me what happened . . .

ARMY: What happened is that he walked out of a match. But I want to make sure he *keeps* walking. I didn't want him to stop at that graveyard over there.

GRACE: How can I help?

ARMY: You can help him by not conning him. He's been conned by experts. He's riddled. He'll listen to you. When he gets out of there head him toward Grand Central Station and give him this. (*He takes out an envelope and hands it to* GRACE.)

GRACE: What's that?

ARMY: That's a train ticket to Kenesaw, Tennessee.

GRACE (*Studies the envelope for a moment*): Is that home?

ARMY (*Very quietly*): It was once. Maybe it'll be again. (*Then there is a long pause*) Do you love him, Miss?

GRACE: I don't know. I feel so sorry for him though, I want to cry.

ARMY (*Touches her arm gently*): You tell him that, Miss. Tell him you think he's a decent guy, and you like him. But tell him, for the time being, you don't come with a kiss. He's been chasing a ghost too long now—and the next thing he's got a hunger for—he oughta get. It's only fair. Thanks very much, Miss. (*Then there is a long pause*) You're a brick. (*He walks away. And as he does so* MOUNTAIN *comes out of the bar.* GRACE *walks over across the street to him. The camera stays with* ARMY *looking at the two of them over his shoulder. We can see them talking but can't hear them. Then we see* GRACE *hand* MOUNTAIN *the envelope. He takes it in his hands, they exchange a few more unintelligible words, and then* MOUNTAIN *starts to walk away.* GRACE *turns, starts across the street and then stops.*)

CUT TO

CLOSE SHOT OF GRACE AS SHE WHIRLS AROUND

CUT TO

> (*Very tight close-up of* MC CLINTOCK's *face in the lamplight of the street. The broken nose, the misshapen ears, scar tissues, bruises that never healed and never will any more. The battered ugliness that is a legacy of the profession.*)

GRACE: Mountain!

> (MOUNTAIN *stops, turns to her.* GRACE *runs over to him and very lightly kisses him.* MOUNTAIN *reaches up and touches his face wonderingly.*)

MOUNTAIN: Thanks for that. (*Then hesitantly, terribly unsure, he kisses her back*) Thanks for not running away.

GRACE: When you get home, when you get settled—write me and tell me what's happened.

MOUNTAIN: When I get home? (*He looks down at the ticket*) I'll go there—but . . . I don't know if it's home any more.

GRACE: Go find out. You look for it, Mountain. Because wherever home is—it's not over there. (*She points toward the bar. Then she hands him a slip of paper*) It's my home address, Mountain. Write me. (*He very tentatively takes the paper and then slowly shakes his head. He crumples it in his fist. She grabs his hand and guides it into his pocket.*)

GRACE: Good-bye, Mountain. (*He turns and walks slowly away.* GRACE *watches him for a moment and then starts to cross the street toward the camera. Halfway across the street her head goes down and her hands are down at her side. She blinks her eyes and very quietly begins to cry.*)

DISSOLVE OUT ON HER FACE TO

COVER SHOT OF THE DRESSING ROOM

IN SEMI-DARKNESS

> (MAISH *sits alone by the rubbing table. The only light comes from the bulbs out in the hall.* ARMY *appears at the door, peers inside, sees* MAISH *and enters.*)

ARMY: You gonna stay here all night?
MAISH: That's a thought.
ARMY: Fox is out there with some other guys.
MAISH: It comes, I figured.

ARMY: If it comes, it comes. Get it over with, Maish. (MAISH *studies* ARMY *intently.*)

MAISH: Hey, Army, what are you going to do?

ARMY (*Smiles*): Tomorrow I'll be for hire. You know, Maish—you said so yourself—I'm the best cut man in the business. And after I patch up my millionth cut, maybe somebody'll give me a gold watch.

MAISH: You're needed, aren't you?

ARMY (*Nods*): A little bit. C'mon, take your lickin' and let's get out of here. (*The two men walk out into the hall.* FOX *and the two other men are waiting.*)

FOX: Maish— (MAISH *stops dead in his tracks, staring straight ahead.* FOX *comes up behind him*) This ain't a payoff, Maish, relax.

MAISH: You here to give me a medal? (*Looks at the other two men*) It must be heavy.

FOX: We're here to give you a proposition. This is Mr. Arnold. (*A heavy-set man comes up alongside. He is the same man we saw in the bar.*)

MAISH: Mr. Arnold and I have met. You work for Henson?

MAN: Yeah.

FOX: Here's the proposition, Maish. It's a sweetie, a real sweetie. (*With this he propels the other man to the front and into the light. He is a young fighter in his late teens. At a first sudden glance there is a striking resemblance between this boy and* MOUNTAIN— *as* MOUNTAIN *must have appeared very early in the game.* MAISH *looks at him briefly.*)

MAISH: What's he want—a haircut?

FOX: Mr. Henson would like him managed. Managed good.

MAN: Groomed—that's the word.

MAISH: Why me? That's the question.

FOX: He wants a nice dependable guy with know-how, Maish, and you're it. Some guy who knows his business—and who'll go along.

MAISH: I know my business ...

MAN: And you'll go along.

MAISH: I've got a choice, huh?

MAN: Yeah, you've got a choice. You take this kid and make a fighter out of him—or the Commissioner gets a phone call that a certain manager's been making bets.

FOX: That's against the law, Maish.

MAISH: Is that a fact?

FOX (*Seriously*): You know it is. Pari-mutuels at race or harness tracks —that's the only place betting is permitted. They'd take away your license, Maish. It wouldn't be just a suspension, Maish—it'd be permanent. (MAISH *takes a step closer to the young fighter and studies his face in the light.*)

MAISH: Where're you from, Kid?

FOX (*Interjects*): It's an amazing coincidence. It really is, Maish. He's from Kentucky. You could call him Mountain . . .

FIGHTER: Who is Mountain?

MAISH (*His lip trembles perceptibly*): He was a good, fast kid. All hands and feet with his mouth full of teeth and he talked like General Lee. Like you do—like you look. You better go back there and work in a drugstore. (*He turns away.*)

FIGHTER: To hell with the drugstore. I want to be a fighter. (MAISH *studies him very intently for a moment, looking him up and down.*)

MAISH: You want to be a fighter? All right, check this. There's eight champions in this business. Everybody else is an also-ran. There's the good and the bad in it. The good's great—the bad stinks; so we'll give it a whirl. (*Then there's a long pause*) Army—you're needed. (ARMY *who has been standing by the door sighs resignedly, joins* MAISH, *and the two of them walk down the corridor with the young* FIGHTER *in the middle.*)

WE LAP DISSOLVE

(*To a film clip of a train and a section of a car.* MC CLINTOCK *sits across from a* WOMAN *and a little* BOY.)

BOY (*Suddenly leans over to him*): Hiya.

MC CLINTOCK (*Looks down in surprise*): Hiya.

(BOY *picks up one of* MC CLINTOCK's *big hands and examines it.*)

BOY: You're a fighter, aren't you?

MC CLINTOCK (*Looks down at him*): Yeah. I was a fighter.

BOY: I can tell by your ears. You got big ears. (*There is a long pause and very slowly* MOUNTAIN *grins.*)

MOUNTAIN: Yeah, cauliflower ears. (*The* BOY *returns his grin and we can see* MOUNTAIN *relaxing for the first time.*)

BOY: How do you get ears like that? I'd like ears like that.

WOMAN: Jeffey, don't be rude . . .

MC CLINTOCK: That's all right, Ma'am. (*The* BOY *goes over to sit next to* MC CLINTOCK.)

BOY (*Suddenly assuming a fight position*): Like this? This is the way you do it?

MC CLINTOCK (*Straightens the* BOY's *hands*): No, you hold your right down, keep that left up, hunch your shoulder like this. Okay. Now lead. No, no, no—with the left, and don't drop your right. Okay, now lead again. (*The* BOY *does all this, delighted.*)

WOMAN: I hope he's not bothering you . . .

MC CLINTOCK: Not a bit, Ma'am. I like it.

WOMAN: Where are you heading for? (*There is a long pause.* MC - CLINTOCK *reaches in his pocket and takes out the slip of paper that* GRACE *had given him. Unfolds it and smooths it out.*)

MC CLINTOCK: Home. I'm heading for home. I don't know for how long. Cause I . . . cause I'll probably be taking a job one of these days soon. Work with kids like Jeffey here.

BOY (*Impatiently*): C'mon, Champ. Let's you and me spar.

MC CLINTOCK: Okay, Champ. Now lead again. That's right. Right from the shoulder. Okay, now cross with the right. No, no, no—don't drop your left. That's right.

> (*The camera starts to pull away very slowly from them until their voices cannot be heard and all we can see is the pantomime of* MOUNTAIN MC CLINTOCK *and the little boy fighting the* MOUNTAIN's *greatest fight. We take a very slow dissolve to the film clip of the train as it disappears into the night.*)

A SLOW FADE TO BLACK

Good-bye, Gray Flannel

by J. HARVEY HOWELLS

CATEGORY:

Television Comedy

(ONE HOUR OR MORE)

GOOD-BYE, GRAY FLANNEL

by J. HARVEY HOWELLS

Good-bye, Gray Flannel
was first presented by Robert Montgomery
on the SCHICK TELEVISION THEATRE,
under the direction of John Newland,
on October 22, 1956,
with the following cast:

TERRY MAJOR · Lee Bowman
CARLA MAJOR · Diana Douglas
JIM FOWNES · John Shay
GEORGE · Ken Renard
VAN · Carl Redcoff
CLIFF · Ray Boyle
MR. GREEN · J. Robert Dietz
ICHABOD LEWIS · George Chandler
ABIGAIL LEWIS · Mary Grace Canfield

A private dining room in New York. Lunch is over. Male and female personnel of large New York ad agency sit at table, T-ed across the end is the head table at which sit the five principals of the agency. JIM FOWNES, *President, is in the middle, with* TERRY MAJOR *on his right hand. There is a cheerful babble of noise. This has been a two-martini lunch but nobody is drunk.* JIM FOWNES *rises to his feet. He does not need to rap for silence. There is instant quiet and all heads click around to face him. He is a man of great dignity, handmade suits and a sense of humor.*

JIM: At ease, everybody.—This isn't going to be a speech. As President of this agency for ten years—if I never make another speech—I've already made too many. (*There are appreciative smiles around the table*) I see you agree with me. Today I have mixed emotions—as the man said when he saw his mother-in-law drive his new Cadillac over a cliff. (*Laughter*) Terry Major is one of the truly great creative people in this advertising business of ours. I'm glad the success of our agency makes it possible for him to retire. I only wish I knew why the Sam Hill he feels it necessary. However—I'll swallow my chagrin and just say, Good luck, Terry. We'll miss you, boy! (*Applause and calls of "Good Luck, Terry." He is obviously well liked.*)

A MAN: Speech! Speech!

A WOMAN: Come on, Terry! (TERRY *rises slowly, a broad grin on his face. He wears a gray flannel suit and plain tie. He has had two martinis. He is relaxed but not drunk. He is comedic throughout this sequence.*)

TERRY (*To* JIM): Thanks for the kind words, Jim—Mr. Fownes. (*To the group*) I have mixed emotions, too. I've looked forward to this moment for longer than I can tell you. But, now it's here, I sort of hate to think you're seeing me as a fellow slave for the last time. Some day you may bump into a yokel with a straw in his mouth, staring up at the tall buildings. Don't pass him by. Look carefully. It might be me.

A VOICE: Not you, Terry. You'll always be one of us!

TERRY: No—not after today. Don't misunderstand me—I love the advertising business. It's fast, hard and exciting—and (*He grins*) you meet such interesting money! But twenty-five years of it—with a little time out for Hitler—is enough for me. I've never been a country boy—but I'm sure going to be one now—even if I am too old for the barefoot part. I'll be thinking of you lads and lasses—

struggling for ideas—creating like crazy—polishing your deathless prose till all hours of the night. Spare a thought for me now and then (*He grins*) rocking gently on my porch, watching my apples grow into money!

> (*Dissolve to a bar car on a commuter train bound for Connecticut, 5:15 of an evening. Sundry male commuters and a bartender. More commuters enter, all with serious mien, frazzled appearances and brief cases.* TERRY *makes an entrance, sober gray hat on the back of his head, his face one large grin. He pauses while his commuting friends study him and he them. He is blissfully happy but not drunk. Still comedic.*)

VAN (*Calling*): Terry! Over here. Sit down before you fall down.

TERRY: Fall down? No man falleth when the spirit soars! (TERRY *moves to the vacant chair between* VAN *and* CLIFF) Well, how was the rat race today? I see you're drinking your grain again.

CLIFF (*Admiringly*): I never dreamed you'd do it, Terry. I thought all this retiring talk was just—talk. (GEORGE, *the waiter, comes for the order.*)

TERRY: I'm a dangerous man, Cliff. I decide what I'm going to do— then I do it.

GEORGE: What'll it be, Mister Major?

TERRY: A gin and tonic, George—without the gin.

GEORGE: I didn't catch that, sir.

TERRY: Yes, you did, George. No gin.

VAN: Come on, Terry—let me buy you a drink.

TERRY: Not even for you, Van. One more's my limit—and I'm saving it for Carla.

MR. GREEN (*Glumly*): Tickets, please. (*The men pull out their commutation books.* TERRY *gives him a ticket.*)

TERRY: Mr. Green—I shall miss you. You have been my friend these many years. I know nothing of you—but your gay camaraderie has warmed my heart night and day. Have you a match?

MR. GREEN: Yes, sir. (*He strikes one from the holder on the large Pullman ash stand.* TERRY *holds his commutation book over it.*)

TERRY: Apply it to the badge of my servitude.

MR. GREEN: What you say?

TERRY: The book, man! Light the book! Burn the chain that binds me to New York.

MR. GREEN: You could get some money back on that.

TERRY: And do the New Haven out of its earnings! Why, Mr. Green, I'm ashamed of you. Light it and kindle the torch of my freedom. (*Shrugging,* GREEN *obliges and departs. The men watch the burning book.*)

CLIFF: Now, there's one fire I like to see. If I didn't have two kids to put through Vassar, I'd chuck my own book in with it.

VAN (*To* CLIFF): You should have in-laws living with you—like me.

TERRY (*Blissfully*): All I have is Carla—and my dog—and thousands and thousands of little apples.

GEORGE: Your drink, Mr. Major. I hope I got it right. (*He puts it down.*)

TERRY: No gin, George?

GEORGE (*Mournfully*): No gin.

TERRY (*Relaxing*): No more pencils, no more books—no more client's dirty looks.

VAN: Won't you miss all this ... The stimulation ...

TERRY: Stimulation. In New York, that's a euphemism for nervous tension. Yes, I'll miss it—with the greatest of pleasure!

VAN: How did you talk Carla into this? I always think of her as a real city girl.

CLIFF: Yeah. What's the formula? I'd like to try it on my wife some day.

TERRY: Carla loves New England madly.

VAN: Will she still love it with you under foot all the time?

TERRY: Your words depict a warped outlook, Van, my boy. Carla's looking forward to a future where her every wish will be fulfilled by her loving husband (*Dreamily*) who will have nothing else to do! No phone call from New York will ever again drag him back to put out a fire. Terry Major, boy fire-fighter, has turned in his axe!

MR. GREEN (*Calling*): We are coming into Westport. Don't forget your brief cases.

TERRY: Can the tooth forget its ache? Mr. Green, you are a sadist! (TERRY *rises first and walks dramatically through the car, staring at the occupants. As he reaches the exit, he turns and faces them. Dramatically*) You mean to tell me you poor souls will have to go through this again tomorrow—and tomorrow—and tomorrow? Ugh! What a life! (*One of the men throws a magazine at him. He ducks and exits, laughing.*)

> Dissolve to the MAJOR's New England bedroom. Birds are singing. CARLA, a seraphic smile on her face, is asleep in a

*double bed fourposter. A hideous metallic clanging breaks
out. She leaps out of bed and runs around the room. She
doesn't know where she is. She runs to the door and screams.*

CARLA: Terry! Terry! (*Her voice is unheard in the clamor. She grabs a
robe and hurriedly puts it on.*)

(*Cut to the empty kitchen-living room. The table is set for
breakfast. The bulldog lies beside it. Enter CARLA. The clanging ceases.*)

CARLA: Terry! Don't play games! Where are you? What's that noise?
What's happened? (*The noise stops.* TERRY *enters in impeccable
white coveralls. He has a six-foot poker in his hand.*)

TERRY (*Mildly*): I was just turning the heat on for you. Little chilly
this morning.

CARLA: What do we heat with—T.N.T.?

TERRY: I was only breaking up the clinkers. Sorry I woke you.

CARLA: Woke me! I thought the Russians had finally gone and done
it! (TERRY *unzips his coveralls. Underneath he has on slacks and a
plaid open neck shirt.*)

TERRY: Ready for breakfast?

CARLA (*Mock surprise*): You can cook, too? Am I going to be spoiled!
(*She sits at the table as* TERRY *puts down two plates with an enor-
mous stack of pancakes, six sausages and a mound of applesauce.*)

TERRY: I defend to the death man's inalienable right to spoil his wife.
(CARLA *eyes her plate.*)

CARLA: Who's coming?

TERRY: What d'you mean?

CARLA: Just what I say. Who's coming?

TERRY: Nobody.

CARLA: Then who's going to eat this?

TERRY: That black coffee and dry toast routine's all right around
New York. Up here, y'need a man-size breakfast.

CARLA: And you once told me my figure was a public trust! (*Manfully,
she takes a small bite of sausage.*)

TERRY (*Beaming*): Attagirl! Good sausages. Wait till we make our
own, though. Happy, darling?

CARLA: Thrilled! Who wouldn't be—with a full-time husband at last?
D'you realize I've hardly seen you in our fifteen years of married
life?

TERRY: Fifteen years. Is that all it's been?

CARLA: Coward! You wouldn't say that if you didn't love me. (*She looks at the dog*) Fownes been out yet?

TERRY: Out? Why, my dear girl, Fownes and I walked all around the orchard while you slept. I admit I had to carry him part way, but he'll learn to like the open spaces.

CARLA: How does the place look?

TERRY (*Ecstatic*): Wait'll you see it! You never saw so many apples.

> (*Dissolve to a corner of the orchard with split rail fence and part of one apple tree.* ICHABOD LEWIS *is on far side of fence, looking over at orchard. He is sitting on a small tractor. He is part of the countryside—drill pants, open-neck shirt with sleeves rolled up, old hat on head. Enter* TERRY.)

TERRY (*Ebullient*): Good morning, Ichabod.

ICHABOD (*Dry*): Mornin', Mistuh Majuh. Settlin' in?

TERRY: Sure thing. Got here about two o'clock this morning.

ICHABOD: Heard yuh. Ca' o' yours sure sounds loud—'specially in the da'k.

TERRY (*Jovially*): We won't be up that late any more. Us and the chickens bed together from now on.

ICHABOD: Be the only ones. Socials down to the Grange keep us all up, Mistuh Majuh.

TERRY: Now that we're going to be permanent neighbors, why don't you break over and call me Terry? (ICHABOD *ignores this. He stares up at the trees.*)

ICHABOD: Look good, don't they? Ought to run 'bout three thousand bushel.

TERRY (*Delightedly*): That many? Let's see—at fifty cents a bushel net profit . . .

ICHABOD: Countin' yer apples afore they're boxed ain't sma't.

TERRY: I guess not. You've done a swell job, Ichabod.

ICHABOD: Know m' business. Want me to keep on?

TERRY: Thanks—but no. These apples have to make money for me. Any profit has to go in my own pocket.

ICHABOD: That so? Well, now. When you figguh to pick?

TERRY: When they're ripe. They're not yet—not by a mile.

ICHABOD: Ripen in the box.

TERRY (*Hurt*): Oh, no. I'm going to ship tree-ripened fruit.

ICHABOD: Most folk can't tell a tree-ripened apple from a last-year turnip.

TERRY: My friends can.

ICHABOD: Well, 'tain't no conce'n o' mine, Mistuh Majuh. I sta't pickin' tomorrow. Might get weathuh any day now. (ICHABOD *goes to start tractor*.)

TERRY: Say, Ichabod. How about that power mower you wanted to sell me this summer? Still got it? (ICHABOD *gives him a long look*.)

ICHABOD: 'Tain't fer sale.

TERRY: You said it was—in July.

ICHABOD: Didn't know you wanted it then.

TERRY: How much?

ICHABOD: 'Tain't fer sale.

TERRY: Fifty dollars.

ICHABOD: 'Tain't enough.

TERRY: Sixty.

ICHABOD: Reckon I'll keep it. (ICHABOD *drives away on the tractor.* TERRY *stares after him.*)

(*Cut to kitchen-living room.* CARLA, *in trim-fitting blue jeans, is clearing the table. Dog lounges around her. Enter* TERRY.)

TERRY: That ruddy old pirate!

CARLA: Who?

TERRY: Ichabod—trying to country slicker me!

CARLA (*Laughing*): You're a neighbor, now—not just a summer visitor. (TERRY *is thoughtful.*)

TERRY: Anything you want from the village?

CARLA: Deserting me already?

TERRY: I'll be right back.

CARLA: Well, if that monster in the basement starts clanging again— I'm for the nearest tree!

(*Dissolve to the front of the local hardware store.* V*arious implements are in the doorway, including a new power mower with the price tag on it. We see the price*—$119.95. *A hand wrenches the price tag off. It is* TERRY, *as he stuffs it in his pocket. He's wearing an old fishing hat now. The owner of the store,* MARTIN LEWIS, *comes to the door.*)

MARTIN: Mornin', Mistuh Majuh. Thought I'd see yuh today. Heard yuh arrivin' last night.

TERRY: Yeah—I know. My car sounds loud in the dark.

MARTIN: Foreign, ain't it?

TERRY: Naturalized now. I've had it five years. Martin, I need your advice. Are these mowers in the mail order catalog any good? (*He pulls a page from a mail-order catalog from his pocket and shows it to a reluctant* MARTIN.)

MARTIN: Reg'luh machine. (*Pats handle*) Same as this 'un. Different name is all.

TERRY: Izzat so? What do you know! (*He compares the machine with the one in the catalog.*)

TERRY (*Doubtfully*): Looks just like it. What's the price?

MARTIN: On the tag. (MARTIN *and* TERRY *look for tag.*)

MARTIN (*Puzzled*): Where'd it go to?

TERRY (*Looking at catalog*): Catalog says ninety-nine ninety-five.

MARTIN (*Doubtfully*): More'n that—as I recollect. (TERRY *is examining the machine, as*)

TERRY: Must be a real problem—having stock left when the summer complaint leaves. Understand this company brings out a new model every year. What'll you do about this one then? (MARTIN *thinks about this.*)

MARTIN (*Suddenly*): Okay—y'got yerse'f a mowuh.

TERRY: Good! I'd much rather buy in the village—town. It's my town now, y'know. (TERRY *carries mower off camera.* MARTIN *quickly picks up a large gas can from inside door.* TERRY *returns.*)

MARTIN: Need a sealfast safety gas can to go with it? Ten dolluhs. Friendly price—to you. (TERRY *looks at Martin.*)

TERRY (*Grinning*): Okay. (*He takes the gas can*) So long, Martin.

MARTIN: C'n I he'p you?

TERRY: No, thanks. I'll just toss 'em in the car. (*He walks out of camera.* MARTIN *stares after him, an appreciative grin on his face.*)

MARTIN: Sma't—real sma't.

> (*Dissolve to the* MAJOR *parlor. Night.* CARLA, *in skirt and sweater, is sitting reading a magazine which we see is* The New England Pioneer. TERRY *enters, dressed as before, but with a lumber jacket over his shirt. He rubs his hands and goes to the fire to warm them.*)

TERRY: Turned cold all of a sudden. You sure notice the weather in the country.

CARLA: Why this sudden thought? We've always lived in the country.

TERRY: You call that country? That was still Madison Avenue—even if it was in Connecticut—Madison Avenue with pine trees.

CARLA: Fifth Avenue has trees.

TERRY: Poor spoonfed captives in cement.

CARLA (*Dreamily*): How lovely they were in the Spring! And the planting at Rockefeller Center.

TERRY: Reminds me of that crack of Alexander Woollcott's—What the Lord could have done if he'd only had the money!

CARLA: And the Christmas tree outside the RCA Building.

TERRY: And the statue outside the International Building—Atlas holding up an empty world.

CARLA: It wasn't empty for us. We were never like that.

TERRY: Never?

CARLA: Well—hardly ever.

TERRY: We were regular night owls. Plumage—gray with white and black markings. Natural habitat—any place where they served a cold, dry Martini.

CARLA: Not any more.

TERRY (*Lovingly*): No—not any more. These four weeks have been real living.

> (TERRY *comes and sits beside her. They kiss. A drumming noise starts to sneak in.*)

TERRY: Any regrets?

CARLA: None.

TERRY: D'you miss it?

CARLA: The bright lights? Not really. You're my only need—the only thing I've ever missed.

TERRY: Sleepy, darling? (CARLA *nods her head. They kiss. The drumming noise gets louder.* CARLA *hears it first.*)

CARLA: What's that noise?

TERRY (*Dreamily. He doesn't care*): Sounds like hail. (*He does a double take*) Hail!

CARLA: Dear Lord—the apples! (*They jump up, run to the window and try to peer out through a lashing hail storm.*)

CARLA (*Wails*): Oh, Terry! Our only cash crop! If we'd only listened to Ichabod!

> (*Dissolve to the corner of the orchard. A fifty-gallon barrel stands beside a cider press. Bushel baskets of apples lie around.* TERRY *staggers on, carrying a full basket, wearing very dirty white coveralls and a beekeeper's mask over his head. He puts some apples in the press, slapping furiously at himself to kill the fruit flies buzzing around. He is not very happy.*)

CARLA: Terry! Help! Come quick! (*He runs off camera.*)

> (*Cut to kitching-living room. Fownes under the table. The entire room is filled with bushel baskets of apples. Floors, chairs, tables, windowsills are covered. A large wash boiler is on the stove, bubbling loudly.* CARLA, *in blue jeans, is cowering away from it, hands over her face.* TERRY *dashes in, tearing off his mask. He has to pick his way through the baskets like a football player practicing broken-field running, as*)

TERRY (*Shouting*): What's wrong?

CARLA (*Wailing*): The apple butter! It'll boil over!

TERRY: Turn it off!

CARLA: I can't. It spits at me! (TERRY *grabs a towel, puts it over his head, drops to his knees, crawls to the stove and turns off burners. He hands* CARLA *the towel. She wipes her face.*)

CARLA (*Wailing*): I'm so sorry, darling. I tried to turn it off, but it kept popping and hitting me in the face!

TERRY: Poor kid! You're tired. Sit down and rest.

CARLA (*Looking around*): Where? The only place left is Fownes' bed. (TERRY *lifts two baskets off a window ledge. They perch on it.* TERRY *picks up a knee board with paper on it and pencil tied to it. He figures as they talk.*)

TERRY: Well, let's see how we're doing. I've pressed forty-seven bushels today. That makes two hundred and ten bushels into cider so far.

CARLA: I put up four dozen quarts of applesauce before I started on the butter.

TERRY: And you made two dozen yesterday—plus some pies.

CARLA: Some pies? Four dozen pies I've baked. There's no room left in the freezer.

TERRY: Maybe Martin'll sell me another one, cheap. How many did you dry?

CARLA: Six bushels.

TERRY: And you spiced . . .

CARLA: Two.

TERRY: Canned?

CARLA: Eight. And the butter'll use up two more—if I can find a way of boiling it without losing my face.

TERRY: Anything else you can do with apples? Can't you make flour or something? (CARLA *grimaces.*)

CARLA: How many bushel's that altogether?

TERRY: Processed—two hundred and thirty-three. Stored in the barn—one hundred.

CARLA: Oh, Terry—it's only a drop in the bucket!

TERRY: Some drop!

CARLA: But the bucket's so big.

TERRY: Must be over a thousand still on the trees. Means we've got less than three thousand bushels left to eat.

CARLA (*Shuddering*): Don't! Even steak tastes like apples to me now. (TERRY *jumps up and, as well as he can, paces the floor.*)

TERRY: It's so ridiculous! Why *can't* we sell 'em? (*He picks up an apple and bites into it.*)

TERRY: That's the best apple I ever tasted. Try it. (*He holds it out to her. She averts her head.*)

CARLA: I know, hon—They're divine!—What a rotten shame! Nobody'll buy them—with the skins all spotted from the hail.

TERRY: If they only knew! These hail spots are an outward and visible symbol of an inward and spiritual grace. (*He gets an idea*) Hey—wait a minute. That's it! Don't go away—I'll be right back! (*With knee board in hand, he executes his broken-field running again out the door.* CARLA *looks after him.*)

ACT TWO

(*The kitchen-living room. Same as before. Apples everywhere. Dog under table.* CARLA, *in blue jeans, is lighting burners on the stove.*)

CARLA (*To dog*): Fownes, old dog, you're such good scenery! Can't you do something to earn your keep? Wouldn't you like to eat up some apples—instead of that nasty, expensive beef? (TERRY *enters in same dirty white coveralls, although underneath he is now wearing rough plaid shirt, breeches and knee boots. He is staring at a paper in his hand*) Don't tell me you've found a way of making apple soup?

TERRY (*Modestly*): I've written a little something here. I'd like to run it up the flagpole and see if you salute it. (CARLA *grins. He reads from the paper, gesticulating as he does*) "Did you ever bite into an apple and wonder if you had picked up last year's turnip by mistake? The skin looked beautiful—but its promise was as insincere as a chorus girl's smile. Perhaps that apple was picked before it was ripe. Avoid that disappointment in future. Buy only Tree Ripened Apples! All my apples were left on the tree, soaking up the warm Fall sunshine, until they reached the very peak of juicy flavor! You don't have to take my word for it. You can prove it for yourself. All my apples have tiny brown spots on the skin. These spots tell you that the apple was left on the bough till the very last minute— till the first hail storm hit up here in October. I won't ship any apples without these tiny hail spots—unless it can pass the spot test! Of course, they cost a little more—but think of the joy of having an apple just like the one you plucked from the tree yourself, when you wore knickers and thought girls were for hair-pulling only!"

CARLA (*Laughing*): Terry—you're a devil! I *am* saluting!

TERRY (*Modestly*): Think it's all right? Of course, it needs polishing— but the basic direction's there.

CARLA: Who would you send it to?

TERRY: Every man in the *Advertising Register* making over ten thousand a year. They're all suckers for this kind of thing—especially the bit about kids in knickers.

CARLA (*Getting excited*): They'll buy 'em for their clients!

TERRY: Right! We'll make 'em a prestige item . . .

CARLA: Keep the price up, Terry . . .

TERRY: Wrap each one separately, in aluminum foil!

CARLA: School kids could help us on Saturday. We'll shine every one —the apples, I mean.

TERRY: Major and Major—Apple Growers Extraordinary!

CARLA: Apple *Sellers* Extraordinary. Anyone can *grow* apples. Takes brains to sell 'em! (*They kiss.* CARLA *looks around at the baskets of apples*) Oh—to have my own kitchen all to myself again!

> (*Dissolve to the corner of the orchard. An assembly line has been set up. Behind a long trestle table stand five teen age boys and girls. On the table are apple crates. A line of teen agers to right of table carries bushel baskets filled with apples. At the table, the first kid is polishing apples, the second wrapping in foil, the third packing in the crate, the fourth nailing the crate shut, the fifth stapling on labels. Another line at the left of table carries away crated apples.* TERRY *comes in, supervising them. He wears a rough plaid shirt, breeches, knee boots and a wide-awake hat, like an overseer on an East Indies plantation. He checks the addresses with a list in his hand.*)

TERRY: Mr. Jerry Stark, Five Shady Lane, Westport, Connecticut. Check. (*He jumps to the boy wrapping in foil*) Just a minute, son. That foil's split. Use another piece. Mr. Harry T. Jones, Old Orchard Road, Westport, Connecticut. (*He jumps to the boy placing them in the crate*) *Place* 'em in, lad. *Don't drop* 'em. One bruised apple spoils the crate. (*To all*) That's right, men. Keep 'em moving! Don't let the line slow down!

> (*Cut to the kitchen-living room still filled with apples.* CARLA *hasn't got it back—yet. With two fingers,* CARLA *is pounding a typewriter, perched on the window ledge. A line of teen agers, each holding a basket of apples, runs from the door up to* CARLA *and back to the door. She tears off an addressed label from machine and puts it in nearest basket. Teen ager moves away with it.*)

CARLA: Next! (*Another teen ager moves up.* CARLA *massages her fingers and starts to type the next label.*)

> (*Dissolve to* PRESIDENT JIM FOWNES *at his desk. An opened crate of apples stands on it. His* SECRETARY, *pad on knee, sits at his side. He is contentedly munching away.*)

JIM: Best darned apple I ever tasted! Help yourself, Miss Kelly. Take some home to your mother. Wonderful! Now—a letter to Mr. Major. Dear Terry. You are so right. Last time I tasted an apple like this, I shared it with a girl who now has six grandchildren. As a copywriter, you're an even better apple-grower. What's the secret? Was it really hail that put these little spots on them? (*His voice starts fading*) You could merchandise hair oil to Buddhist monks. I worried about you and Carla—but not any more.

> (*Dissolve to the* MAJOR *bedroom,* CARLA *in bed, reading. Clock says* 1 A.M. *She looks at it and makes a mild gesture of disgust.*)

CARLA (*Calling*): Terry! It's one o'clock! Come to bed.

TERRY (*Off stage*): Be right there, darling. (*He enters in dressing gown, yawning*) Boy, am I bushed!

CARLA: What was all this about early to bed? You haven't beaten midnight in a month! You're working yourself to a frazzle. (TERRY *grins sheepishly.*)

TERRY: It's all over now. I was just taking off the figures. The final net *net* is a dollar-eighty per box profit before taxes. That's counting everything. Cost of growing—paying the school kids—boxing—ship-ping—direct mail—upkeep of the house—my salary—your salary . . .

CARLA (*Surprised*): My salary?

TERRY: Sure—your salary. This has to be costed accurately or we'll never know where we are.

CARLA: When do I get paid?

TERRY: It's just bookkeeping. Doesn't make any difference if I pay you or not—tax-wise.

CARLA: Thank you, darling. You take care of me so well. Me and the Government!

TERRY (*Grinning*): You get paid, all right. (CARLA *ignores this.*)

CARLA: What's the total?

TERRY: Twenty-eight hundred boxes—at a dollar-eighty a box. That's five thousand and forty dollars. I'll give you the forty. (CARLA *burlesques figuring on her fingers.*)

CARLA: That's eight-tenths of one per cent.

TERRY: Then I'll take the forty and you can have the five thousand.

CARLA (*Smiling*): I've already got it. We used my checking account—remember? How many people did we have to refuse?

TERRY: Seven hundred boxes! (*Mad*) Wouldn't that frost you? Over a thousand dollars! (*He brightens*) Well—wait till next year. All the guys we couldn't supply will demand 'em next Fall. Make a thing hard to get and a New Yorker's got to have it!

CARLA: Where on earth will we get the apples? This year's crop was wonderful. Can't *order* more production from an apple tree.

TERRY: And it takes years for new trees to bear. (*He doodles*) Think I'll run over and see Ichabod in the morning.

(*Dissolve to* CARLA *in bed, alone. Ferocious clanging breaks out again. Lazily, eyes closed,* CARLA *reaches to night table, fumbles for and picks up cotton, sticks a piece in each ear. She opens her eyes, rises sleepily and puts on her robe. The clanging stops.*)

(*Cut to the kitchen-living room, empty. Only a bowl of apples on kitchen table.* FOWNES *underneath.* CARLA *enters, still yawning. She takes one piece of cotton out of her ear, listens, nods her head and takes the other one out. She picks up the coffee pot and pours herself a cup.*)

CARLA: Good morning, Fownes. I thought you were going to be the big outdoor dog. Looks like all you've done is change one kitchen for another!

(*Cut to the corner of the orchard. Bare tree, fence and no tractor.* ICHABOD *is leaning with his back on the fence.* TERRY, *in duffle coat with hood, leans in the same manner beside him.*)

ICHABOD: Yer powuh mowuh hold up?

TERRY: Yup. Nothing like a new machine.

ICHABOD: Cousin Ma'tin thinks so anyway, Mistuh Majuh.

TERRY: Terry (ICHABOD *ignores the invitation to the first name.*)

ICHABOD: Direct-mail business do good for yuh?

TERRY: Couldn't have done better. How'd you make out with *your* apples?

ICHABOD: Ain't complainin', am I?

TERRY: I netted a dollar-eighty a box.

ICHABOD: Did you now?

TERRY: I could sell double next year—if I had the fruit.

ICHABOD: Trees did good fer yuh this ye-uh. Can't expect mo-uh.

TERRY: Look, Ichabod—I don't know what you made on your apples —but I'll bet my whole profit you didn't net what I did.

ICHABOD: Could be so—could be not.

TERRY: Why don't you come in with me? I can sell your apples as easily as I can sell my own.

ICHABOD: You goin' to arrange with the Lord for anothuh hail storm like the last?

TERRY: If it's not hail—I'll—I'll think of something else. Wouldn't you like to make my kind of profit?

ICHABOD: Might. So might othuhs. Form an association, mebbe.

TERRY (*Doubtfully*): Well, I don't know. Associations are one heck of a lot of work. I just thought you and I . . .

ICHABOD: Cha'ge the growuhs by the bushel. How much you want to do the advertisin'?

TERRY (*Automatically*): Fifteen per cent.

ICHABOD: O' the net?

TERRY: Of the gross, you Yankee pirate!

ICHABOD: Ain't no easy ma'k yerse'f.

TERRY: Why don't we sleep on it?

ICHABOD: Done my sleepin'. When could you sta't?

TERRY (*Thinking*): I'd have to set up budgets. Plan a careful campaign that'd show a real profit for us all.

ICHABOD: Need 'n office? I got a piece o' prope'ty . . .

TERRY (*Quickly*): No! I'd turn the parlor into an office. Never use it anyway. I don't know what Carla'd say . . .

ICHABOD: Give yuh a nice tax deduction. Need a sekatary?
TERRY: Carla does all that.
ICHABOD: Association'd take more'n she could do. Abigail's a good
sec'etary.
TERRY: Your daughter? (*Pause*) How much?
ICHABOD: Fifty a week.
TERRY: Forty.
ICHABOD: Forty-five.
TERRY: Sold!
ICHABOD: She ain't Noo Yo'k—but she's sma't!

> (*Dissolve to a typewriter in action. We see female hands
> typing on office stationery headed "Tree-Ripened Apples,
> Inc." We should see enough of the typing to realize the
> typist is exceptionally fast.*)

January 10, 1956

Mr. J. Patrick Kidd
580 Bay Road
Pelham, New York

Dear Mr. Kidd:—

We cannot tell you how sorry we were to be unable to comply with
your request for apples. Frankly, the response to our letter was much
greater than we had expected. However, next year we will surely be
able to fill your order. We are putting your name on a special priority
list ...

> (*Cut to the* MAJOR *parlor. The old New England room has
> an office desk in it, a typist's desk and filing cabinets.* ABIGAIL
> LEWIS *is typing. She is a pretty girl in a simple, nice dress.
> Apart from her accent and restrained makeup, she might be
> a New York secretary. She is very efficient. Enter* TERRY,
> *plaid shirt, breeches, boots.*)

ABIGAIL (*Smiling*): Mornin', Mistuh Majuh.
TERRY: Good morning, Abigail. What d'you have for me this morning?
(*She gives him a folder.*)
ABIGAIL: These are the last lettuhs to the folks who didn't get apples.
I've also put togethuh pa't of the estimates of fuchuh production.
Then there's a lettuh from a Boston agency that wants to do your
advertisin'.
TERRY: Me hire an agency! Ernest Hemingway should hire a ghost
writer!

ABIGAIL (*Grinning*): Reg'luh leg slappuh, isn't it? Cousin Ma'tin down to the ha'dwa-uh sto-uh phoned. He has a new attachment for your powuh mowuh he thinks you'd like.

TERRY: The frenetic peddler! That power mower's like a camel. Once you let it get its nose in the tent . . . I'm sorry. He *is* your cousin and I *do* like him . . .

ABIGAIL: Sometimes he's mo-uh a go-gettuh than cousin. The secretary of the Merchants' Club wants to know if you'd speak on advertisin' at their next luncheon.

TERRY: Do I have to?

ABIGAIL: Be real nice. (*Warmly*) They want you to be a pa't of the community.

TERRY (*Pleased*): Okay. What else?

ABIGAIL: Fathuh said he'd like to come ovuh with Cousin Ma'tin at nine-thutty.

TERRY: What about? Never mind. Tell 'em to come.

ABIGAIL: They're pa'kin' the ca' right now.

> (TERRY *sits at his desk and opens his folder. Enter* ICHABOD *and* MARTIN *in business suits.* ABIGAIL *leaves.* TERRY *jumps up and greets them just as he would greet a client in New York.*)

TERRY: Good morning, Martin. Morning, Ichabod.

ICHABOD: Mornin', Mistuh Majuh.

TERRY (*Automatically*): Terry. What can I do for you gentlemen this morning? Sit ye down and have a cup of coffee. (ABIGAIL *enters with coffee which she smilingly gives each man, then exits.*)

ICHABOD: Know anything 'bout peaches?

TERRY: I've eaten a lot in my time but . . .

ICHABOD: Committee likes what yer doin' on apples.

TERRY: Well, we haven't really gotten going yet.

ICHABOD: We c'n tell sound plannin' when we see it. Want you to set up a Peach Association, too. Same idea.

TERRY: Now, just a minute! I don't even own any peaches . . .

ICHABOD: Ma'tin's got a two-acre pa'cel back of his apple stretch he'll sell yuh.

MARTIN: Cheap.

TERRY: Look—I'm supposed to be retired. There's a lot of work in setting up an association. I don't want to go back to working ten hours a day.

MARTIN: Need any he'p—my daughter Isabella's a good sec'etary. Forty-five a week.

ICHABOD: Forty.

TERRY: No! Now stop it, you two.

ICHABOD: Wouldn't be too ha'd. Same people grow apples, grow peaches.

TERRY (*Weakening*): That would make it easier. Maybe I could give you a hand in the beginning . . .

ICHABOD: That's settled, then. Now Ma'tin's got somethin' t'say.

TERRY: But . . .

MARTIN: You tell 'im, Ichabod.

ICHABOD: Nope. Every man cleans his own fish or he don't eat.

MARTIN: That's right. Well, sir, some of us ain't pleased with Congressman Pe'kins down to the Capital . . .

ICHABOD: Jackass!

MARTIN: Seems like he's had his nose in the trough too long.

ICHABOD: Feet, too. Get to the point, Ma'tin.

MARTIN (*A little nervous*): Pe'kins don't know anything 'bout fa'min' or apples. He's a foreignuh.

ICHABOD: City man—Boston. Point is, Mistuh Majuh, we'd rathuh have Ma'tin in Congress, 'stead o' Pe'kins.

TERRY (*Bewildered*): Congratulations, Martin. That's—that's great!

ICHABOD: No sense applaudin' when the cu'tain goes up. Be a big fight. Want you to handle it.

TERRY: Handle what?

ICHABOD: The campaign. Need good thinkin'.

TERRY: Well, I did this kind of thing in New York in fifty-two, but I don't know the ins and outs of local . . .

ICHABOD: Don't need to. We'll tell yuh. Need your ideas, though.

TERRY: But my ideas could be all wrong.

ICHABOD: Couldn't be wo'se 'n Pe'kins'.

TERRY: That's a matter of opinion. Have you any campaign funds?

ICHABOD: Don't need 'em. You're a fa'muh. Got a big stake in this.

TERRY: I know, Ichabod, but you can't run a political campaign without funds.

ICHABOD: Ma'tin's donatin' the printin'—postuhs and lettuhs.

TERRY: That's real white of you, Martin. How about mailing and handling?

ICHABOD: Figguhed on you for that.

MARTIN: Be a nice contribution.

TERRY: What're you two trying to do to me? I came up here to take it easy . . .

ICHABOD: Plenty o' time to take it easy when yer six foot unduh. Sho't campaign—three months.

TERRY: That isn't very long, is it?

ICHABOD: Fust meetin's tomorrow night—Ma'tin's sto-uh. Seven sha'p. Sobuh. Whiskey latuh. (*The men rise to go.*)

MARTIN: Mornin', Mistuh Majuh.

TERRY (*Bewildered*): Now just a minute, gentlemen. I haven't said I'll do it . . . (MARTIN *leaves as* CARLA *comes in.* ICHABOD *goes over close to* TERRY. CARLA *overhears.*)

ICHABOD (*Quietly*): 'Tain't no conce'n o' mine, Mistuh Majuh. City folk only ones dress like that up he-uh. (*He indicates* TERRY's *clothes.* TERRY *looks at them.*)

TERRY: But . . .

ICHABOD: Gray flannel be bettuh. Black tie. Conse'vative. Be a big man up he-uh some day. Mornin'. (*To* CARLA) Mornin', Missus Majuh. (*He exits.* CARLA *has a quick smile to herself.* TERRY *stares after him as if he had just been caught in a threshing machine.*)

> (*Dissolve to a booth in a deserted New England Main-Street restaurant, out of season.* TERRY, *in a rough tweed jacket, and* CARLA, *in a suit, are seated at it. The* WAITRESS *stands waiting for their order.*)

CARLA: Fifty miles is a long way to drive to meet your husband for lunch, but it's worth it. My, you're handsome.

TERRY (*Grins*): How about a drink to celebrate?

CARLA: M-m-m—that would be nice. Martini, please.

WAITRESS: Ma'tini.

TERRY (*Offhand. He's concentrating on* CARLA): And I'll have a Bloody Mary, please.

WAITRESS: What's 'at?

TERRY (*Still offhand*): Tomato juice, Worcestershire, vodka, salt and pepper.

WAITRESS (*Scornfully*): Fresh!

TERRY (*Realizing where he is*): Oh—guess that one hasn't reached here yet. Make mine a Martini, too—ice cold and powder dry. (WAITRESS *leaves.*)

CARLA: How are things (*She grins*) with the sma'test man in New England?

TERRY (*Mimics*): Nevuh bettuh! I've signed up almost one hundred per cent of the growers I've talked to.

CARLA: When are you coming home?

TERRY: Tomorrow night, I hope.

CARLA: That'll be almost a week. D'you realize I've seen less of you this month than I used to see you in New York?

TERRY: It's just for a little while—till I get things rolling.

CARLA: Terence Major, you've been singing that song to me since the day we were married!

TERRY: I promise . . . It won't last. I'm retired, remember?

CARLA: Funniest retirement in history! (*The* WAITRESS *delivers their drinks.*)

TERRY: Cheers! (*They drink.* TERRY *explodes. He eyes the drink.*) D'you suppose she heated it?

CARLA: It's out of season, darling. The good mixers have flown south to Florida. M-m-m, remember Leon's Martinis at the Brussels?

TERRY: And pretty girls having dinner with their—daddies?

CARLA: And handsome diplomats ordering in French?

TERRY: No taxis at theatre time . . .

CARLA: So you go in a lovely hired limousine . . .

TERRY: That costs you your left arm . . .

CARLA: From your nice, fat expense account . . .

TERRY: And a nice, simple lunch for two—ten dollars?

CARLA: Sunday brunch at the Plaza?

TERRY: And seven per cent state tax on top of federal?

CARLA: Afternoon tea at the Modern Museum?

TERRY: And a two-hour commute every day . . .

CARLA: The Christmas carols in Grand Central?

TERRY: And the drunks at the office party . . .

CARLA: Don't you miss it at *all?*

TERRY (*Thinking*): Sometimes I long to get into a blazing argument about Picasso or existentialism—or the latest opening night.

CARLA: That reminds me. Here's a letter from Jim Fownes. (*She hands him a letter.*)

TERRY (*Brightens*): Well, the old goat! Wonder what *he* wants. (*He opens and scans letter*) More apples for himself and fifty boxes for clients. Here's the list. The nerve of that guy! He'll be after our whole crop next. Wait a minute. Listen to this. (*Reads*) "Now that you have proved your independence and had your rustic fling, why don't you come back where you belong? The agency needs all the hands it can get. I won't say we can't get along without you, but life would be a lot easier for me if you were here." I'll bet it would!

CARLA: Why, Terry, how nice to know you're still needed.

TERRY: Of course he needs me! Life's rough in the agency business when there's no buffer between you and the clients.

CARLA: And you were such a good buffer.

TERRY: I should go back to that treadmill—back where you can't call

your soul your own? Not bloody likely! I've had it! "Quoth the
raven, never more." (CARLA *smiles*.)

CARLA: "Take thy beak from out my heart and take thy form from off
my door."

TERRY (*Grins*): That's telling 'em, fat lady!

ACT THREE

> *The parlor office. There are now more filing cabinets and an
> extra secretarial desk.* ABIGAIL *and additional secretary,* ISA-
> BELLA LEWIS, *are busily typing. The camera passes over bar
> charts on the wall, headed "Apple Production 1946-1956,"
> "Apple Sales Through Grocery Stores 1946-1956." A line map
> of the U.S. headed "Apple Prices 1955 by States." A poster
> headed "Look to* LEWIS" *above a large picture of* MARTIN.
> *Below the picture the poster reads "An Apple Grower Not
> an Apple Polisher."*
>
> *It is a very hot day in midsummer. The windows are open
> and blowing the papers.* TERRY *enters in a gray flannel suit,
> button-down collar, very Madison Avenue. He takes off his
> jacket, loosens his tie and mops his brow.*

TERRY: Whew, hot! Morning, Isabella. How's Martin this morning?

ISABELLA: Fathuh's just fine, Mistuh Majuh. (ABIGAIL *comes over with
a folder*.)

TERRY: Morning, Abigail. What's the news today?

ABIGAIL: Mornin', Mistuh Majuh. Aunt Hattie finally had her baby
last night.

TERRY: Well, now—that makes you both second cousins or something.
Should we send her some flowers?

ABIGAIL: Oh, Mistuh Majuh—Remembuh? Uncle Pa'kuh has the biggest greenhouse this side o' the White Mountains. Aunt Hattie
can't abide flowuhs. Candy'd be bettuh—especially from New Yo'k
(*Warmly*) if *you* sent it.

TERRY (*Pleased*): Anything you say. What else?

ABIGAIL: Congressman Cousin Ma'tin is takin' Cousin Ruth to New
York to celebrate his election. He wonders if you can get him tickets
for *My Fair Lady*. He wants two on the aisle—tenth row centuh.

TERRY: Sure he wouldn't like Rex Harrison to buy him dinner first?

ABIGAIL (*Smiling*): Also—he wonduhed if you'd fix it so he's a con-

testant on one of the quiz shows. No point in all that money goin'
to waste, he says.

TERRY: He'll probably end up winning the network. (*Phone rings.*
ABIGAIL *picks it up.*)

ABIGAIL: Mr. Fownes? From New York? (*She hands the phone to*
TERRY.)

TERRY (*Mopping his perspiring brow*): Hello, Jim. How's it with you?
Bet it's hot as the hinges down there.

> (*Cut to* JIM *on phone at desk. He is wearing his jacket, tie
> closed, sitting in immaculate air-conditioned room.*)

JIM: I suppose so. I haven't been out. Thank the Lord for air con-
ditioning!

> (*Cut to perspiring* TERRY.)

TERRY: You sure need it in New York.

JIM (*Offstage*): Say, Terry. I've got a box at the Polo Grounds for
Saturday. Be a big game. How about you and Carla coming down?
Spend the week-end with us on the boat afterwards. I've bought a
new ketch—forty-five footer.

TERRY: Business must be good—you fifteen per center!

JIM (*Offstage*): Can't keep up with it. How about it? You know how
Carla loves a ball game. Noisiest fan in the park.

TERRY: Love to, Jim—but I can't. I'm kind of busy right now.

JIM (*Offstage*): I thought you'd retired. What do you have to do to
apples? They just grow, don't they? (TERRY *is embarrassed. He
doesn't want* JIM *to know how hard he's working.*)

TERRY: Well, you have to kind of prod 'em along a bit, y'know.

JIM: If you won't come down, I suppose I'll have to come up. Sure you
can't make it?

TERRY: Sure, Jim. Sorry. Wish we could . . .

> (*Pause.* ABIGAIL *starts to type. Frantically* TERRY *signals her
> to stop, which she does.*)

JIM (*Laughs*): Isn't that silly? For a moment I thought I heard a
typewriter. Well, aren't you going to invite me up?

TERRY (*Wriggling*): Sure, sure. Just name the day.

JIM: I'll check at home and call you back.

TERRY: So long—so long, Jim. (*He hangs up.* ABIGAIL *and* ISABELLA
start typing like mad. CARLA *enters the room.*)

CARLA: Better get going, Terry, or your clients'll take a bite out of you,
instead of your apples. (ABIGAIL *and* ISABELLA *jump up.* TERRY *looks*

at his watch. He scurries around frantically. He picks up a giant layout carryall a yard square. He picks up three heavy blackbound books. He puts them all down, puts on his jacket and fixes his tie. ISABELLA *gives him a folder.*)

TERRY: Budget book. (ABIGAIL *gives it to him.*)

ABIGAIL: Budget book. (TERRY *puts it in carryall.*)

TERRY: Layouts.

ABIGAIL: Layouts. (*He puts them in carryall.*)

TERRY: Charts. (ISABELLA *gives them to him.*)

ISABELLA: Cha'ts. (*The whole sequence has the frenetic confusion of leaving for a client meeting, just like Madison Avenue. Laden,* TERRY *heads for the door.*)

CARLA (*Urgently*): Your hat!

TERRY: Blast my hat!

CARLA: You're conservative. Remember? Take your hat. (*She claps a gray homburg on his head. He pecks her a kiss and leaves.*)

> (*Dissolve to a meeting room in the Grange. One end of it is set up like a New York board room. Long table with pads, pencils, ash trays. An easel stands at the far end with charts and large blowups on it. Around this table are seated* ICHABOD, MARTIN *and six other members of the Apple Growers' Association, in business suits.* TERRY *is at the easel. He turns over the first chart. We see a picture of a parkway, jammed solid on one side, empty on the other.*)

TERRY: Gentlemen, first of all, I'd like to make a point. Have you ever been stuck on a parkway like this? If you could only get over on the other side, you'd have a clear road.

MARTIN: Be goin' the wrong way. (TERRY *looks at him, then goes on.*)

TERRY: That's just what we of Tree-Ripened Apples have. Our clear road is a better apple and a mailing list of *customers.* Not just people—customers.

MARTIN: How d'you know they're customuhs?

TERRY: Because they've been selected. I've put together a mailing list that's worth untold gold. Or—if you like—is worth fifty cents a box to you gentlemen.

MARTIN: Fifty cents. Lot o' money.

A MAN: Lot o' money.

TERRY: For every fifty cents you spend, I'll get you back a dollar-ninety. Ichabod, what did you net on your apples last year?

ICHABOD: Consid'able.

TERRY: Let me show you the figures as I've drawn them up. (*He turns over another chart. There are two lines on it crossing one another. Over the upper one is the word "Costs," and over the lower, the word "Profits") Now, as I see it, the big problem is to consolidate all our operations in order to cut costs. (His voice dies away in business gobbledgook)* By so doing, we can expedite the operation and concretize the net gains resulting from the shipping savings and the increased . . .

> *(Dissolve to same as before. The charts are all on the floor.* TERRY *has his jacket off and his tie loosened. He's a little frazzled. He has a sheaf of papers in his hands.)*

TERRY: That's it, gentlemen—except to read the actual copy. Martin, would you pass these around? (*Gives* MARTIN *the sheaf of papers.*)

TERRY: Before you read that, I'd like to explain it a little.

ICHABOD: You goin' along in the envelope to explain to the customuhs?

TERRY: Touché. Go ahead and read. (*The men start reading.*)

MARTIN (*He's using* TERRY's *own words*): Is this it, or are you jest runnin' it up the flagpole to see who salutes it?

TERRY: This is it.

MARTIN: I'm not an advertisin' man. I jest know ha'dware 'n' apples. Nevuh knew'n apple *explodin'* juice. Wouldn't dribble be bettuh?

A MAN: What it does—dribble.

TERRY: Poetic license. Better picture.

MARTIN: Mebbe we should throw a hose over it afore pourin' the concrete?

TERRY (*Desperately*): Look, gentlemen. I'm not writing to you. I *know* the people I'm writing to. And don't forget—I did it last year —and it worked. I could change every word in that letter to suit you, but then it wouldn't be the same letter.

MARTIN: Client's got to study every word. That's the way the cane breaks.

ICHABOD (*To Martin*): You been takin a correspondence course in how to talk like an advertisin' man? Mistuh Majuh's the writuh. You're not. I vote t'accept the campaign.

MARTIN: Money an' all?

ICHABOD: Yep. Money an' all.

MARTIN: I'm with yuh, skippuh—all the way. (*Everybody nods.* TERRY *heaves a big sigh.*)

TERRY: Thank you, gentlemen. I'll put it to bed right away. Now I'd like to talk to you about peaches. We can do for peaches what we've done for apples . . .

ICHABOD: Peaches kin come latuh. I got somethin' else to talk about fust. You're sma't, Mistuh Majuh. Associations don't take all yer time. We need yer brains down to the capital. Want you to be Publicity Directuh for the State. Big job. Pays eighty-five hundred a ye-uh. (TERRY *clutches his head.*)

TERRY (*Wails*): Oh, no! (*Slapping table*) Flatly and definitely NO!

> (*Dissolve to the parlor office.* ABIGAIL, ISABELLA *and two other girls are seated at typewriters, working madly. The walls are lined with filing cabinets. Camera pans over two charts and two posters: "Apple Production 1946-1956," "Look to* LEWIS," *"Peach Production 1946-1956." It holds on "Come to Glorious New England."*)

> (*Cut to the kitchen-living room.* TERRY *in gray flannel.* CARLA *in smart country cocktail skirt and sweater.* FOWNES *under table. We hear the typewriter.*)

CARLA: Can't you send the girls home now?

TERRY: The hotel owners want this mailing out tonight. Besides, I'd like to finish and have a quiet week-end to ourselves.

CARLA: What a heavenly thought! Just the two of us. I feel guilty, though—not asking Jim up. He could have come this week-end.

TERRY: And have him find that boiler factory in the parlor? I'd never hear the end of it. Retired? Huh!

> (*Cut to the outside of the parlor office.* JIM *stands in amazement, looking at the hive of industry. The girls don't see him. Quietly he tiptoes back off camera.*)

> (*Cut to the kitchen-living room.* CARLA *and* TERRY. *There is a loud knocking.*)

JIM (*Offstage*): Anybody home! (*There is a stunned silence, then*)

TERRY: Great balls of fire! Jim!

CARLA (*Urgent*): I'll bring him in here. You get rid of the girls.

TERRY (*Desperate*): I can't!

CARLA: Then keep the door closed and I'll stall him. (*Knocking is repeated.*)

JIM (*Offstage*): Terry! Carla! Everybody asleep in there?

CARLA: Scoot!

> (*They run off camera.* TERRY *runs back, takes off jacket, puts on smoking jacket and runs out again.* CARLA *returns with* JIM. *She helps him off with his coat, as*)

CARLA: This is a pleasant surprise, Jim. We were just saying how we wished we'd asked you up this week-end.

JIM: I knew I didn't really need an invitation from you two. What a charming place you've made of this kitchen! The center of the home, eh? I bet you never go in the parlor.

CARLA: Terry'll be with us in a minute. He'll be so glad to see you. He's just finishing up some typing. (JIM *listens to the four muffled typewriters.*)

JIM: Always had a heavy touch.

(*Cut to parlor office.* TERRY *is leaning over* ABIGAIL.)

TERRY (*Whispering*): How long'll you be?

ABIGAIL (*Still typing*): 'Bout ten minutes.

TERRY: Hurry it up! (*He goes to leave. Remembers something. Stage whisper*) Stop typing till I come back. (*The four girls look up at him and stop. He leaves.*)

(*Cut to kitchen-living room.* TERRY *enters, trying to be very relaxed.*)

TERRY: Well, Jim, you old goat! Welcome to Major Manor!

JIM: Let's have a look at you. Well, well, you haven't gained any weight! I thought this lazy life would have added pounds.

TERRY (*Uneasily*): Lots of physical exercise around an orchard. Carla, fix Jim a drink while I finish up. Be right back. (*He scoots out of room.*)

(*Cut to the parlor office. Girls with hands poised over typewriters.* TERRY *enters and closes door. He raises his hand like a conductor and signals "START." The girls pound away madly.*)

(*Cut to kitchen-living room.*)

CARLA: What would you like, Jim?

JIM: Some of that hard cider you put up last year. Any left?

CARLA (*Shuddering*): We had to move the car out of the barn to make room for it! (*As she pours a glass,* JIM *hands her a package.*)

JIM: A little gift for the house. (CARLA *opens it as*)

CARLA: Twenty-year-old Scotch! You darling! You shouldn't have.

(*Cut to parlor office.* ISABELLA *is wetting a row of envelope closures with a sponge. Others type.*)

ISABELLA: Sponge is dry, Mistuh Majuh. C'n I go wet it? (*She heads for the door.* TERRY *grabs her.*)

TERRY: No! No! (*He goes to the door, remembers, turns again signals "STOP." The typing stops.*)

(*Cut to kitchen-living room.* CARLA *and* JIM *each has a drink now.* TERRY *skids in, relaxes and goes to sink.*)

TERRY (*Nervously*): Ah! You've got a drink, Jim? Good! I just want a glass of water.

JIM: Water! How you've changed!

TERRY: Thirsty as a—a—sponge today. (*He exits. Typing starts again as* JIM *raises his glass.*)

JIM: Luck to the house—and to retirement à la Major! All the pleasures of life and none of the headaches. (*He drinks*) M-m-m, ambrosia—and all your own, Carla!

CARLA (*Sipping her Scotch*): M-m-m, divine Scotch, and I didn't have to make it. (*The typing stops suddenly.*)

(*Cut to parlor office.*)

TERRY (*To* ABIGAIL, *whispering*): You're an angel! (*To the group*) You're all angels! Lock the door and slip out the back way. Come late Monday. Our guest'll be gone by nine-thirty (*He blows them a kiss.*)

(*Cut to kitchen-living room.* TERRY *enters as*)

JIM: It's not just the new business, Carla. Our old clients have increased their budgets on an average of twenty per cent.

TERRY (*Pouring himself a drink*): How much have the headaches increased, Jim? Forty per cent?

JIM: You're right, Terry. You're well out of it. What's the good of beating your brains out? What's money? The Government takes it all anyway. You've got it made, son, sitting here in the quiet of the country... (*Phone rings.*)

TERRY (*Interrupting*): I'll get it. (*He goes to phone.*)

CARLA: How's Alice, Jim?

JIM: Splendid. She was so sorry not to be able to come with me.

TERRY (*On phone*): Hello, Ichabod. (*Hearing the name,* JIM *stares in disbelief.*)

JIM: Ichabod? I don't believe it.

TERRY: I don't see how I can. I have a guest—

ICHABOD (*Offstage*): Won't take long. Sta't early. Be back afore he's awake—if he's a Noo Yo'kuh.

TERRY: We'll be going hunting...

ICHABOD (*Offstage*): Do yer gunnin' latuh. This is business. No'the'n people come in—means a hunderd thousand boxes mo-uh next ye-uh. What's fifteen per cent o' that?

TERRY (*Wearily*): Okay. What time'll I pick you up?

ICHABOD: Six-thutty. Sha'p.

TERRY: Sha'p. (*Hangs up.* JIM *eyes* TERRY *quizzically, but says nothing.*)

TERRY: Mind if I leave you for a little in the morning?

JIM: Of course not, but who's this Ichabod who . . .

CARLA (*Interrupting*): Jim was telling me they've picked off three new accounts in the past two months.

TERRY (*Grins*): Anyone I know? (*Pause*) Are they big?

JIM (*Modestly*): Not bad—about two million total. Maybe we can make 'em grow, though.

TERRY: I saw a rumor in *Ad Age* that one of the automobile accounts was loose.

JIM: Could be.

TERRY: Why so non-committal?

JIM: Well . . .

TERRY: You don't have to keep secrets from me. I'm out of it. Remember?

JIM (*Smugly*): Ajax.

TERRY (*Amazed*): Ajax! Why, they must bill . . .

JIM: They're the biggest.

CARLA: Do you have a chance of getting it?

TERRY (*Thoughtfully*): Ajax. That would be a real coup.

JIM: Be tough to handle. I'd have to staff up.

CARLA: *You'd* have no trouble.

JIM: Good people are hard to find.

CARLA: And cost a lot.

JIM: I can afford it.

TERRY (*Deep in thought*): Ajax—the pioneer. They've led in engineering development for years, but they never tell anyone. All they talk about is color. Color and safety belts and trade-in values. Boy, would I like to get my hands on that!

JIM: I'll pay you sixty thousand a year.

TERRY: They could pre-empt the market. They've got more exclusives in their car . . . What did you say?

JIM: Plus bonus. Should run close to seventy, all told.

TERRY: Is this the reason you tore yourself away from New York, you huckster? Have you got that account in your pocket?

JIM (*Modestly*): Signed the letter of agreement this morning.

TERRY: You make Machiavelli look like little Eva!

JIM: Will you come back?

TERRY (*Distressed*): Don't, Jim. You know I can't resist a challenge. But how can I leave all this? I love it. Besides, I'd look like a fool!

JIM: The strayed lamb is always welcome. You'd have charge of all creative activity for the entire agency.

TERRY: I've worked toward retirement for years, Jim. A chance to relax. I've got everything I've ever wanted.

JIM: Including a parlor full of typists?

CARLA: Jim! You peeked! (JIM *nods his head, solemnly.*)

TERRY (*Suddenly*): I'm going out! (*He leaves.*)

CARLA (*Calling after him*): Terry! Dinner's ready! Jim must be starving.

> (*Cut to corner of the orchard.* TERRY *comes in, in duffle coat. He stares at the trees. He pats the trunk of one with affection. He bangs the split rail fence in frustration. This is a real problem.*)

> (*Dissolve to the kitchen-living room.* JIM *and* CARLA *have finished dinner.*)

JIM: Two pieces of apple turnover—and I never eat dessert!

CARLA: Terry's had nothing. Where *is* that fool husband of mine?

JIM (*Earnestly*): Have I a chance, Carla? From what you say, he's working as hard as he ever did. Will you help me get him back?

CARLA: No, Jim. This is Terry's life and I just go along. Oh, I miss the bright lights, but Terry is all I really need. It doesn't matter where we are. Maybe it's having no children—only Fownes. (*She pats the dog's head.*)

JIM: Fownes! You mean you gave that slavering monster my name? (CARLA *smiles shamefacedly.* JIM *is stunned, then he roars with laughter*) Wonderful! When I gave Terry a bad time, he could come home and kick Fownes.

CARLA (*Smiling*): He only scratches his back. (*Seriously*) Terry can no more retire than I can—can become President of the P.T.A.

JIM: I knew he couldn't quit. Once an advertising man, always an advertising man. It's a state of mind.

CARLA: The people up here have been so wonderful to him—to us both. They're clever and hard-working—and he's added an element they've needed. He's a big man up here.

JIM: He's a big man anywhere.

TERRY (*Offstage*): Come on in, Ichabod. (ICHABOD *and* TERRY *enter.*)

TERRY: Jim, this is my good neighbor and *client*, Ichabod Lewis.

JIM *(Smiling)*: How d'you do? I hear you're the only man in the Northern Hemisphere who can out-maneuver me.

ICHABOD *(Dry)*: Heard o' you, too. Wouldn't mind tryin' the best o' three falls with you any time. Hear you're danglin' fresh meat in front o' this young fella's nose.

JIM: If he wants to come back, I'd like to have him.

ICHABOD: Like him he-uh, too. Don't want to lose 'im.

TERRY: Now just a minute . . .

ICHABOD *(Ignoring TERRY)*: Come back, you resto-uh his pension seniority?

JIM: Maybe.

ICHABOD: You a woman?

JIM: Okay. Seniority back.

TERRY: Ichabod, how about letting me clean my own fish . . .

ICHABOD *(Still ignoring TERRY)*: Bo-ud membuh?

JIM: Perhaps not right away . . .

ICHABOD: Don't wriggle. Bo-ud membuh?

JIM: Well, as creative head . . . Yes, I suppose so. (CARLA *is fixing four drinks as she listens.*)

TERRY *(Shouting)*: Stop it! (ICHABOD *and* JIM *look at him in surprise. They had practically forgotten him.*)

TERRY *(Quietly)*: I know you two can't resist the chance to out-smart one another, but this is my problem. Mine and Carla's.

JIM: Don't forget my namesake.

TERRY: All right. It's Fownes' problem, too. I will only come back to New York—if . . .

JIM: If what?

TERRY *(Takes a deep breath)*: If I get three uninterrupted months up here every year.

JIM *(Uneasily)*: Of course, Terry, you can always come up here. You might have to pop back to New York to put out a fire or two . . .

ICHABOD: Nope. Heard tell o' yer fi-uhs befo-uh. Mistuh Majuh'll bring you two new accounts—wuth a million and half—'n' goin' up.

TERRY *(Grins)*: The State Publicity and the Fruit Association.

CARLA: *Fruit* Association!

ICHABOD: Yup. Pears, peaches, plums, grapes, cherries—*and* apples. Committee won't agree, though, 'less Mistuh Majuh spends three months he-uh each ye-uh, ha'd runnin'.

JIM *(Doubtfully)*: Well . . .

TERRY (*Softly*): A million and a half—and going up!

JIM (*Suddenly*): You win! I know when I've been mousetrapped. I'll have to cut the salary back, though. Fifty thousand.

ICHABOD (*To* TERRY): Fair enough?

TERRY: Fair enough. (*They shake on it.* CARLA, *who has heard it all, hands each a glass.*)

CARLA (*Raising hers, eyes shining*): Here's to Madison Avenue! Maligned, misunderstood, *moneyed* Madison Avenue—where there are more brains and drive per square foot than any place else in the whole wide world . . . (ICHABOD *coughs pointedly.* CARLA *looks at him and bows*) Except one! (ICHABOD *raises his glass to* TERRY.)

ICHABOD: Miss you when yer gone, boy, but good luck, Terry!

TERRY (*Stunned*): He called me Terry!

A Night to Remember

Adapted by
GEORGE ROY HILL *and* JOHN WHEDON
from the book by
WALTER LORD

CATEGORY:

Television Documentary
(ANY LENGTH)

A NIGHT TO REMEMBER

by GEORGE ROY HILL and JOHN WHEDON

A *Night to Remember*
was first presented on the KRAFT TELEVISION THEATRE
under the direction of George Roy Hill,
on March 28, 1956,
with the following cast:

NARRATOR · Claude Rains
MRS. ASTOR · Milette Alexander
MRS. RYERSON · Valerie Cossart
CAPT. LORD · Frederic Tozere
MAITRE D'HOTEL · Marcel Hillaire
COL. GRACIE · Larry Gates
MR. ANDREW · Patrick MacNee
WOOLNER · Peter Turgeon
HARPER · Anthony Kemble-Cooper
MR. STRAUS · Edgar Stehli

Television script based on A *Night
to Remember* by Walter Lord.
Copyright, 1955, by Walter Lord.
Used by courtesy of
Henry Holt and Company, Inc.

ACT ONE

FADE UP NARRATOR SEATED AT TABLE

NARRATOR: In 1898 a struggling author named Morgan Robertson wrote this book. (*He picks up the book*) It was fiction. It looked into the future and told the story of a fabulous Atlantic liner, far larger than any that had ever been built. Its displacement was 70,000 tons, its length 800 feet, its top speed 25 knots. On a day in April she departed on a voyage across the North Atlantic. Her capacity was 3,000 people, but since she was considered unsinkable, she carried lifeboats for only a fraction of that number. Four days later on a cold April night, she raced across the North Atlantic, heedless of iceberg warnings, struck an iceberg and went down, carrying the rich and complacent aboard her to the bottom. It symbolized the end of an age, of luxury, class inequality, of supreme self-confidence of man against fate. Robertson named his book, *Futility*. The name he gave his ship was the *Titan*. In 1912, fourteen years after this book was published, a British shipping company, the White Star Line, built a fabulous Atlantic liner, far larger than any that had ever been built.

CUT TO: FILM SHOT OF WHISTLE BLASTING

SOUND: *Whistle Deep Blast*

(*Dissolve to the bridge.* CAPTAIN SMITH *in command.* WILDE *and another officer.*)

CAPTAIN: Cast off spring lines.
WILDE: Cast off spring lines.
OFFICER (*Through megaphone*): Cast off bow lines!
NARRATOR: Her displacement was 66,000 tons, her length 882 feet, her top speed, 25 knots.
OFFICER: Lines cast off, sir.
CAPTAIN: Quarter speed astern.
WILDE: Quarter speed astern.

CUT TO: HAND MOVING TELEGRAPH

SOUND: *Telegraph*

CUT TO: FILM SHOT OF WHISTLE

SOUND: *Deep Whistle Blast*

CUT TO: DECK, LOWER LEVEL

SOUND: *Crowd Noises—Shouting Good-bye—Band Playing in Background—Tug Whistles*

(*People leaning over rail, waving. Dolly past them slowly. They are covered with confetti, cheering, shouting messages, etc.*)

NARRATOR: On April 10th, 1912, she departed Southampton on her maiden voyage to New York. (*The camera starts to boom to upper deck between lifeboats. People above also waving*) Her capacity was 3,000 people, but since she was considered unsinkable, she carried lifeboats for only a fraction of that number. (*The camera has brought in a front end of a lifeboat, seeing the people behind.*) The name the White Star gave to its ship was . . . (*Pan side of lifeboat and tighten on the painted side that reads Titanic.*) The Titanic.

CUT TO: WHISTLE AND STACK FILM

SOUND: *Whistle Blast*

DISSOLVE TO NIGHT SHOT OF THE TITANIC

AUDIO: *On dissolve to film bring in ship's orchestra softly in background. Bring up full on dissolve to grand staircase.*

Four days later, on a cold April night, she raced across the North Atlantic.

CROSSFADE TO THE GRAND STAIRCASE

(COLONEL *and* MRS. ASTOR *are on their way down. Also* HENRY SLEEPER HARPER *and others. A* MAITRE *stands at the bottom greeting them as they come in.*)

Carrying passengers worth collectively 250 million dollars. This is the story of her last night as remembered by those who survived. What you will see actually took place. It is as accurate as man can reconstruct that night. This is not fiction. It is fact. (*Super:* "A Night to Remember." *Lap to:* "By Walter Lord." *The* MAITRE *greets two guests.*

MAITRE: Good evening Mrs. Astor, Colonel. (*They go through*) Mr. Harper, Mrs. Harper, how are you this evening?

(*He goes through. There is a moment when the* MAITRE *is free. He looks off camera and snaps his fingers.* STEWARD JOHNSON *comes up.*)

MAITRE: Johnson?

NARRATOR: Although meals were included in the price of passage, here in the *Titanic* à la carte restaurant it was possible to be even more exclusive by paying handsome prices for them.

JOHNSON: Yes, sir?

MAITRE: The Wideners will be here any moment. Have arrangements been made?

JOHNSON: Yes, sir, at the corner table.

MAITRE: Good. The Captain will be dining with their party.

JOHNSON: I'll look after them myself, sir.

> (JOHNSON *leaves, and the* MAITRE *goes back to greeting the people.*)

MAITRE: Good evening, Mrs. Strauss—Mr. Strauss, Mrs. Ryerson, Mr. Ryerson—

> (*Dissolve to* THOMAS ANDREWS, *seated at table. He is dressed for dinner but does not have his coat on.*)

NARRATOR: Working in his stateroom at 6:45 that night was Thomas Andrews, builder of the *Titanic*. At 39 years old, the senior naval architect of Harland and Wolff Shipbuilders—a shipbuilding genius.

> (*Behind* ANDREWS, STEWARD *enters. Knock.*)

ANDREWS: Come!

STEWARD: It's nearly seven, Mr. Andrews. You'll be late for the Wideners' dinner.

ANDREWS (*Standing, but occupied with plans on the desk before him*): Alfred, I designed the first-class writing room as a place for ladies to retire after dinner, yet it hardly ever seems occupied.

STEWARD: If I may be allowed an observation, sir, the ladies of the twentieth century are not as retiring as formerly.

ANDREWS (*Being helped into his jacket, smiling*): I believe you're right. At any rate, I'm going to make it smaller and put in two more staterooms. (*He goes back over to the plans.*)

NARRATOR: Although this was a working trip for Thomas Andrews, his official capacity on board was that of a passenger. (*Dissolve to* ISMAY *in conversation with two men in the smoking room*) As was that of Mr. J. Bruce Ismay, president and managing director of the White Star Lines.

ISMAY: Of course we haven't begun yet to see what she can do. But I have asked for a speed run tomorrow, and we'll see what happens when we give her her head.

COL. GRACIE: Do you think we'll break the record to New York, Mr. Ismay?

ISMAY: Dear, no. I'm not out to set a speed record with the *Titanic*. But we should get her up to 25 knots with little trouble.

> (*The* CAPTAIN *comes over to him.*)

CAPTAIN: Mr. Ismay?

ISMAY: Excuse me, gentlemen. (*He goes to the* CAPTAIN *in front of the fireplace.*)

CAPTAIN: I wondered if you might have that message I gave you this afternoon.

ISMAY: Message?

CAPTAIN: The wireless message. The iceberg warning from the *Baltic*.

ISMAY: Oh, yes, of course. (*He reaches in his pocket, takes out his note wallet*) I was showing it to Mrs. Thayer and Mrs. Ryerson this afternoon. They were quite impressed.

CAPTAIN (*Taking it*): Thank you.

ISMAY: Are you going to dinner?

CAPTAIN: I'm being entertained by the Wideners this evening. I'm sorry.

ISMAY: I'll see you later then. (ISMAY *leaves*.)

(*The camera tightens on the* CAPTAIN.)

NARRATOR: Captain Edward J. Smith, fifty-nine years old, senior captain of the White Star Line. The man who had said:

CAPTAIN'S VOICE (*Recorded*): "I cannot conceive of any vital disaster happening to a vessel of today. Modern shipbuilding has gone beyond that."

NARRATOR: The wireless warning Captain Smith had asked Mr. Ismay to return at 7:10 in the smoking room was the third warning the Captain had received that day.

(*The* CAPTAIN *leaves with* MR. *and* MRS. THAYER. *Dolly past him to the picture and title* "Approach to a New World.")

CUT TO: ORCHESTRA AND DINING SALON

NARRATOR: The Titanic Salon Orchestra under the baton of Wallace Henry Hartley, the selection: "The Barcarolle" from *The Tales of Hoffmann*.

(*Beyond the orchestra on the balcony we see* OFFICER MOODY *enter. He comes down the grand staircase and looks around the room. He sees what he is looking for and walks out of frame.*)

CUT TO: THE WIDENERS' TABLE

(*The* RYERSONS *and* THAYERS *are there.*)

CAPTAIN: After all, it was Mr. Andrews who built this ship, yet he seems to spend most of his days prowling about trying to find fault with her.

MRS. THAYER: My dear, that's very alarming. What faults have you discovered in her, Mr. Andrews?

ANDREWS: If you are interested . . .

MRS. THAYER: But of course I am interested.

ANDREWS: Then, we are having trouble with the restaurant galley hot press, the color of the dashing on the private promenade decks is too dark, and there are too many screws in the stateroom hat hooks.

CLINCH SMITH (*Slams the table*): I want my money back.

> (*They all laugh as* OFFICER MOODY, *catching the* CAPTAIN'S *eye, bends over, whispers something to him and hands him a slip of paper.*)

NARRATOR (*As the camera tightens on* MOODY *and the* CAPTAIN, *and the* CAPTAIN *reads the message*): At 7:30 iceberg warning number four was received. It indicated an area directly in the path of the *Titanic*. (*The* CAPTAIN *nods to* MOODY *who retires.*)

CAPTAIN (*To the others, putting the message in his pocket*): You should have seen Tom here on the trials. There's not a detail of this ship he isn't familiar with. He's immensely conscientious.

CUT TO: MOODY GOING BACK UP THE STAIRCASE

> (*Pan him to door in the balcony over the orchestra, and then tighten on orchestra. Dissolve and segue music to tight shot of bagpipes.*)

NARRATOR: Four decks below, in the *Titanic's* steerage, were 712 souls: 179 women, 467 men and 78 children. At 9:00 that night, a young Irish couple were performing a jig. (*The camera pulls back to see a young couple watching and enjoying their performance,* KLAUS *and* HILDA CLASEN *and their daughter.* KLAUS *tries to persuade* HILDA *to join him in the dance, but she is shy. The dance comes to an end. The applause and laughter are suddenly interrupted by a scream and squeals from several women, who jump on their chairs.*)

GIRL (*Pointing*): A rat! (*Others take up the cry. They give chase. The women flee. One man grabs a chair and raises it over his head, running about after the rat. Another a fireaxe. The wife clings to her husband, who is laughing.*)

HILDA CLASEN: Klaus, it's a rat!

KLAUS CLASEN: So it's a rat.

HILDA: You don't mind?

KLAUS: Just so long as he stays on the ship. When he gets off I'll worry.

(The bagpipe player tunes up again and the folk dancing resumes.)

(Dissolve to the wireless room of the Titanic. *The operator is taking down a message. A steward picks up an empty coffee cup and thermos jug. As he does so, he glances over the operator's shoulder.)*

NARRATOR: The wireless room of the *Titanic*. First operator John George Phillips, on duty, was coming to the end of his fourteen-hour day, doing his job for which his pay was thirty dollars a month, or approximately seven cents an hour. The time, 9:30 P.M.

STEWARD: What are you getting?

PHILLIPS: Another ice warning. *(He tosses the message aside. The* STEWARD *picks it up and reads.)*

STEWARD: The *Mesaba* reports ice, Latitude 42°N to 41°25'N. *(Looks up)* Where is that?

PHILLIPS: I don't know. I'm no navigator.

STEWARD: Do you think . . .

PHILLIP: Look, leave me alone. I'm trying to get Cape Race.

STEWARD: What's Cape Race?

PHILLIPS: A relay station in Newfoundland. The passengers have got me loaded with messages to send to the States. They must think this is a toy. *(He picks up a message at random)* Listen. "Lovely trip. Found my beads. Guess who I ran into at the Vatican. Dying to see you. Love. Lily." *(He tosses it back on the pile)* Stacks of them. *(He gets a signal in his headset)* Wait a shake . . . that's Cape Race now. *(He throws the send-receive switch and starts to transmit. The* STEWARD *tosses the iceberg message on the desk. The camera pans with it.)*

NARRATOR: The fifth iceberg warning stayed in the wireless room. Had operator Phillips been a navigator, he would have known the *Titanic* was already well within the latitudes and longitudes described in the message.

CUT TO ENGINE FILM

(Dissolve to the bridge.)

LIGHTOLLER: What's the temperature, Moody?

MOODY *(Looks at thermometer)*: Thirty-three degrees.

LIGHTOLLER: Send word to the carpenter to see that the fresh-water supply doesn't freeze.

MOODY: Yes, sir.

LIGHTOLLER: And warn the engine room to keep an eye on the steam winches.

MOODY: Yes, sir. (*He relays the information through a speaking tube.*)

NARRATOR: The warning to protect the steam winches from freezing was sent by Second Officer Charles Herbert Lightoller at 10 P.M.

(CAPTAIN SMITH *arrives.*)

SMITH: Good evening, Mr. Lightoller.

LIGHTOLLER: Good evening, sir.

SMITH: Getting colder.

LIGHTOLLER: Yes, sir, one degree above freezing.

SMITH: There is not much wind.

LIGHTOLLER: No, sir, a flat calm. (*Pause*) Pity the breeze didn't keep up while we're going through this area. Ice is easier to see at night if there are waves dashing against it.

SMITH: Oh, we should have warning enough with a night as clear as this.

LIGHTOLLER: I should think so, sir.

SMITH: If anything becomes at all doubtful, I'll be in my cabin.

LIGHTOLLER: Right, sir. Good night, sir.

CAPTAIN SMITH: Good night. (*The* CAPTAIN *leaves the bridge.*)

BRIDGE OF THE *CALIFORNIAN*

(*Dissolve to:* GROVES *is peering out ahead, turns sharply.*)

NARRATOR: Thirty miles away, aboard the Leyland Liner *Californian*, bound from London to Boston. The time 10:30. Third officer Charles Victor Groves on duty.

CUT TO: HAND RINGING TELEGRAPH

(CAPTAIN LORD *appears on the bridge.*)

CAPTAIN LORD: What's the trouble, Mr. Groves?

GROVES: An ice field, Captain. We're blocked completely.

(CAPTAIN LORD *peers out ahead.*)

CAPTAIN LORD: You're right. Can't proceed through that—it's too dangerous.

GROVES: That's what I thought, sir.

CAPTAIN LORD: Very well. Shut down the engines. We'll stay where we are till morning. Warn all vessels in the area.

GROVES: Aye, aye, sir.

CAPTAIN LORD: I'll be in the chart room.

GROVES: Aye, aye, sir.

CAPTAIN LORD: And send that warning out immediately.

(*Dissolve to: The Wireless Room of the* Californian.)

NARRATOR: The wireless shack of the *Californian,* operator Cyril F. Evans on duty. Time, 11:00 P.M.

(GROVES *enters, hands* EVANS *slip of paper.*)

GROVES: Sparks, send this ice warning to all ships in range. We're stopped for the night, too dangerous to proceed.

EVANS: Right. (*He gets on the key and starts transmitting.*)

(*Cut to: Wireless room of the* Titanic. *Operator* PHILLIPS *suddenly gives a pained reaction and grabs his earphones.*)

PHILLIPS: Ouch! (*With the phones off his ears, he throws the send-receive switch and starts angrily tapping out a message.*)

NARRATOR: Aboard the *Titanic,* wireless operator Phillips got the *Californian's* signal, all right. They were so close, it almost blew his ears off. He didn't wait for the message, but snapped right back. His reply: "Shut up, shut up! I'm busy. I'm working Cape Race."

(*Dissolve to: Corridor in first class.* ISMAY, *going to his cabin, encounters Steward* ETCHES.)

ETCHES: Good night, Mr. Ismay, sir.

ISMAY: Good night, Steward. (ISMAY *goes into cabin. A* STEWARDESS *comes out of the next cabin.*)

STEWARDESS: Good night, Ma'am. (*She closes the door quietly. Steward* ETCHES *is disappearing down the long corridor. The* STEWARDESS *heads in the opposite direction.*)

NARRATOR: Aboard the *Titanic,* the passengers were settling down for the night—all but a few die-hards. (*Dissolve to: The first-class smoking room. In the background* WILLIAM CARTER *and* ARCHIE BUTT *are conversing over cigars. At a bridge table are seated* HUGH WOOLNER, *and three young men.* WOOLNER *is dealing*) Here in the first-class smoking room, the White Star Line's usual rule against Sunday card-playing had been relaxed, and a small group took advantage of the privilege. (*They pick up their cards and start sorting them*) Time all good people were in bed, really.

(*Dissolve to: The* RYERSONS' *cabin.*)

JACK RYERSON (*Calls*): Good night, Mother.

MRS. RYERSON (*Off*): Good night, dear.

(*Dissolve to:* LIGHTOLLER's *cabin, a close shot of his cap on hook and, below, his uniform on a hanger swaying slightly with the roll of the ship. Pan to* LIGHTOLLER *in bed, munching an apple and reading a magazine.*)

(*Dissolve to: An arm reaching out a door and depositing a pair of men's shoes outside—high laced shoes. Arm withdrawn, door closed. Pan up to long shot of the empty corridor.*)

NARRATOR: Everywhere quiet had settled down over the ship. . . .

(*Hold on empty corridor while we listen to the rhythmic sounds of the ship: The throb of the engines, the creak of the woodwork.*)

(*Dissolve to: The engine room. Two stokers are sitting on buckets turned upside down. A third reclines in a propped-up wheelbarrow, hands behind his head and a pipe in his teeth.*)

NARRATOR: Five decks below, even the stokers were taking their ease. It was 11:35—almost the end of their shift.

FIRST STOKER: Anybody want to bet we get up to 25 knots?

SECOND STOKER: I might take a little bet on that.

FIRST STOKER: You know what we're doing right now? Twenty-two knots! Which is not bad.

(*Dissolve to: The Lookouts in the crow's nest.*)

NARRATOR: Seamen Frederick Fleet and Reginald Lee were on watch in the *Titanic* crow's nest. Time, 11:40. Air temperature 32 degrees. Water temperature 31.

(LEE *slaps himself with his arms to stir the circulation.* FLEET *leans forward on the rail.*)

LEE: Like glass, isn't it? (*He turns aft and looks up at the sky*) If there was a moon now . . .

(FLEET *strains forward, as if trying to make out some object ahead.*)

FLEET: I say . . .

CUT TO: FILM OF ICEBERG IN DISTANCE
CUT BACK TO: CROW'S NEST

(*Hastily* FLEET *sounds the crow's-nest bell three times.* LEE *whirls about.*)

LEE: What? What? (*With his other hand,* FLEET *has grabbed the phone to the bridge.*)

CUT TO: THE BRIDGE

>(MURDOCH *on duty. At the sound of the buzzer,* MURDOCH *picks up the phone.*)

MURDOCH (*Calmly*): What did you see?

CUT TO: THE CROW'S NEST

>(LEE *is now peering ahead tensely.*)

FLEET: Iceberg right ahead!

CUT TO: THE BRIDGE

MURDOCH: Thank you. (*He peers forward and snaps a command over his shoulder*) Hard a-starboard!

CUT TO: QUARTERMASTER SPINS THE WHEEL
TO STARBOARD

>(MURDOCH *reaches for the handle of the engine room telegraph.*)

CUT TO: CLOSEUP OF THE TELEGRAPH INDICATOR

>(MURDOCH's *hand pulls the handle all the way to stop.*)

CUT TO: THE ENGINE ROOM

>(*A bell sounds and the engineer on duty looks up at the indicator.*)

ENGINEER: Stop engines!

>(*He leaps to action.*)

CUT TO: THE CROW'S NEST

>(LEE *and* FLEET *stare ahead, fascinated and appalled.*)

LEE: How long does it take to turn this thing?

CUT TO: THE BRIDGE

>(MURDOCH *reaches for the telegraph handle again.*)

CUT TO: CLOSEUP OF HIS HANDS

>(*It pulls the handle to "Full Speed Astern."*)

CUT TO: THE ENGINE ROOM

    (*Again the bell sounds.*)

ENGINEER: Full speed astern!

CUT TO: THE SMOKING ROOM

    (*The bridge players are proceeding with their game.*)

WOOLNER: Two no trumps.
PARTNER (*Looking at his cards*): Hmm . . . (*He glances at the opponent who is to bid next.*)

CUT TO: THE BRIDGE

    (MURDOCH *pushes a button labeled "Emergency Watertight Doors."*)

CUT TO: BOILER ROOM No. 6

    (*Two stokers are lounging near a doorway leading through a water-tight compartment. A warning bell sounds and a light flashes on above the door. The* ENGINEER *glances up quickly.*)

ENGINEER: The emergency! Watch it!

CUT TO: SMOKING ROOM

PARTNER: Two no trumps?
WOOLNER: Two no.

CUT TO CROW'S NEST

    (FLEET *and* LEE *riveted straight ahead.*)

LEE: She's swinging!

CUT TO THE BRIDGE

    (MURDOCH, *straining forward, watching.*)

CUT BACK TO CROW'S NEST

FLEET: She's swinging wide! We're going to miss her, we're going to miss her!

CUT TO FILM CLIP

    (*The entire bulkhead below decks in the* Titanic *giving way and the water pouring in.*)

CUT TO CAPTAIN SMITH IN HIS CABIN

> (*He has just entered and is about to put his hat on a hook when he stops, cocks an ear. Then he turns quickly and goes out.*)

CUT TO BRUCE ISMAY IN BED

> (*He sits bolt upright with a start.*)

CUT TO GIRL SITTING UP SLOWLY IN BED

GIRL (*Calling*): Father? Father, are we landing?

CUT TO MRS. ASTOR AND COLONEL ASTOR

MRS. ASTOR: It sounded to me as if something went wrong in the kitchen.

COLONEL ASTOR: I don't know. I'll go up and see. (*She sinks back into bed.*)

CUT TO CORRIDOR IN STEERAGE

> (CLASEN *comes up to his wife who is standing in her nightgown by the door to her cabin.*)

KLAUS CLASEN: We've hit something. Get dressed, quickly!

CUT TO: BLUE PRINT OF SHIP

NARRATOR: Depending upon their location in the ship, the initial jar was felt in varying degrees. (*Pan up to see* ANDREWS *working on plans*) Shipbuilder Andrews, concentrated on his work, did not feel it at all.

CUT TO FILM CLIP

> (*Water pouring through the hole into the boiler room.*)

CUT TO THE BRIDGE

> (*The* CAPTAIN *comes up quickly.*)

CAPTAIN: Mr. Murdoch, what was that?

MURDOCH: An iceberg, sir. I hard-a-starboarded and reversed the engines and I was going to hard-a-port around it, but she was too close. I couldn't do any more.

CAPTAIN: Close the emergency doors.

MURDOCH: They are already closed, sir.

CAPTAIN (*To officer*): Take a look below quickly and report back. Quickly!

CUT TO THE ENGINE ROOM

> *(Boiler room six. A small group of stokers arguing.)*

STOKER: We've run aground, that's what! We're aground on the Grand Banks.

CUT TO SMALL GROUP OF STEWARDS IN DINING LOUNGE

JOHNSON: I tell you, we've lost a propeller blade, that's what it was. I know the kind of shudder a ship gives.

SECOND STEWARD: You know what that means, lads. It's back to Belfast for repairs. A week at least in Belfast!

> *(Dissolve to first-class corridor. As STEWARD CUNNINGHAM starts down it, and is stopped by JACK THAYER, seventeen, who steps out of his cabin. They converse out of earshot as the NARRATOR continues.)*

NARRATOR: It went thus throughout the ship. Rumors, counter rumors, but above the depths of the ship, in first and second class, where the jar was barely felt, there was little excitement, little or no commotion. Young Jack Thayer of Philadelphia was reassured.

JACK: What was that noise, Steward?

STEWARD *(To THAYER)*: . . . I really don't know, sir, but I don't suppose it's much. *(He goes down the corridor to reassure another passenger.* THAYER *goes back into his cabin, as do the others.)*

NARRATOR: And at 11:45 life aboard the great liner returned to its usual pace. Nothing seemed amiss, everything seemed perfectly normal—yet not quite.

CUT TO JACK THAYER

> *(Standing by a porthole buttoning his pajama top. The sound of the ship's engines and the rhythmic creaking of the ship suddenly stops. He pauses, looks up, listening.)*

CUT TO OFFICER LIGHTOLLER IN HIS BUNK

> *(Sits up, listening.)*

CUT TO STEWARDS

JOHNSON: It's a propeller, I tell you. It happened once on the old Baltic . . . *(One of the others stop him. They listen.)*

CUT TO WOOLNER

> *(About to play a card, stops, listens.)*

CUT TO MRS. ASTOR IN BED

> (*She opens her eyes, listens.*)

CUT TO SERVICE BUZZER

> (*Lights all suddenly flashing on.*)

CUT TO FIRST-CLASS CORRIDOR

> (STEWARD ETCHES *starts toward a door.* MRS. RYERSON *steps out of her stateroom in a peignoir.*)

MRS. RYERSON: Steward?
ETCHES: Yes, Mrs. Ryerson?
MRS. RYERSON: Why have the engines stopped?
STEWARD: There's talk of an iceberg, ma'am. They have stopped not to run over it.

> (TWO GIRLS *have come out of their cabin and stand nearby.*)

FIRST GIRL: An iceberg?
STEWARD: So they say, Miss.
SECOND GIRL: I've never seen an iceberg!
FIRST GIRL: Neither have I!
SECOND GIRL: Let's run up and see it!

> (*They run off. The* STEWARD *smiles and moves down the corridor.* MRS. RYERSON *goes inside, stands for a moment, thinking. She goes to bed and looks at* JACK RYERSON.)

CUT TO COLONEL GRACIE COMING UP ON DECK

NARRATOR: A few of the more hardy among the passengers congregated on the deck. Among them Colonel Archibald Gracie and his old friend Clinch Smith.

> (GRACIE *has come up to* SMITH.)

GRACIE: What's up? Why have we stopped?
SMITH: Would you like a souvenir to take back to New York with you, Archie?
GRACIE: A souvenir of what?
SMITH: Ice.

CUT TO A SMALL PIECE OF ICE IN SMITH'S HAND.

> (*Pan up to* GRACIE's *face.*)

GRACIE: Where did you get that?

SMITH: Up forward. There are tons of it on the starboard well deck. Brushed off the iceberg when we went past it. Come ahead, I'll show you. Some of the steerage people are playing with it. It's quite a lark.

CUT TO FILM CLIP—WATER FILLING UP THE HOLD

CUT TO THE BRIDGE ON THE *TITANIC*

> (CAPTAIN SMITH. *Waiting. Sound of man running up steps. Officer reappears with* HUTCHINSON.)

CAPTAIN: Well? Well?

HUTCHINSON (*Arriving in a hurry*): She's making water fast, sir.

CAPTAIN: Where?

HUTCHINSON: Number six boiler room. Number five, too.

> (ISMAY *comes up the ladder, a suit over his pajamas, wearing carpet slippers.*)

ISMAY: What happened, Captain? What did we hit?

CAPTAIN: Were there any others damaged?

HUTCHINSON: I don't know, sir. That was as far as I got. The emergency doors blocked . . .

ISMAY (*Overriding*): Captain, what is going on?

CAPTAIN: I regret to say, Mr. Ismay, that we have struck an iceberg.

ISMAY: Do you think the ship is seriously damaged?

CAPTAIN (*Slowly, after a pause*): I'm afraid she is. I've sent for Mr. Andrews.

ISMAY: She can't sink with the watertight compartments, can she?

> (ANDREWS *arrives.*)

ISMAY: Mr. Andrews?

> (ANDREWS *looks at* CAPTAIN.)

ANDREWS: What's happened?

CAPTAIN: We've struck ice, Tom. She's taking water fast in number six and number five boiler rooms.

ANDREWS: We'd better have a look.

> (ANDREWS *and the* CAPTAIN *leave.*)

CUT TO ENGINE ROOM, FULL OF STEAM, WATER ON THE FLOOR

ENGINEER (*Shouting*): Shut the dampers! Shut the dampers!

STOKER: They're shut, you bloody fool!

ENGINEER: Hurry it up then, draw those fires! Get those boilers boxed up! If the water reaches them she'll blow! Let off the pressure! Let it off!

CUT TO HAND TURN LARGE VALVE

CUT TO FILM CLIP OF FUNNEL BLASTING. VERY LOUD

CUT TO JACK THAYER ON DECK

> (*He claps his hands over his ears.*)

CUT TO COLONEL GRACIE AND SMITH

> (*They both look up, try to converse, but can't.*)

CUT TO INSIDE LIGHTOLLER'S CABIN

> (*He comes back in, takes off his bathrobe and gets into bed pulling up the covers as the* NARRATOR *speaks:*)

NARRATOR: Second Officer Lightoller returned to his cabin from inspecting the deck. He knew something was wrong, but he was off duty and he should be where they would expect to find him in case of emergency. He waited, like the good officer he was.

CUT TO DECK AGAIN AND SOUND UP

> (ANDREWS *and* CAPTAIN *heading below. The* MAIL MAN *comes up to them, cupping his hands to shout.*)

MAIL MAN: There's water in the mail hold, sir! (CAPTAIN *holds his hand to his ear.*) There's water in the mail hold. It's filling rapidly!

> (ANDREWS *and the* CAPTAIN *look at each other and go below.*)

CUT TO THIRD-CLASS CORRIDOR "PARK LANE"

> (*It is full of people carrying trunks, talking in a mixture of tongues. Among them the* CLASENS *and* YOUNG IRISHMAN. CLASEN *is explaining to another man in a foreign tongue what happened.*)

IRISHMAN: I heard a crash, that's all I know. A horrible great crash. It sounded like the crack of doom.

> (*They are all ad libbing, and the* CAPTAIN *and* ANDREWS *push their way past.*)

HILDA CLASEN (*Pulling her husband out of the* CAPTAIN's *way*): Klaus, who are they?

CLASEN: The Captain. I do not know the other.

IRISHMAN: What are they doing down here?

CLASEN: I don't know.

IRISHMAN: I tell you there's something up!

FRIEND: I tell you what's up! It's up to my ankles in water! Go take a look back in my cabin!

CUT TO FEET SLOSHING AROUND IN SEVERAL INCHES OF WATER

(The room is also full of steam. Pan up to see stokers in boiler room trying to damp down the boiler.)

VOICE: That will do, lads! Out of there now! Let this one go, get back to boiler five! Get back to boiler five!

STOKER: Thank God for that. Come on, let's get out of here.

(They climb the ladder in the back out of the room.)

NARRATOR: With the fires nearly out in number six boiler room, the men started back to the next boiler room, where pumps were so far staying ahead of the water.

CUT TO THE CHART ROOM

(ANDREWS, CAPTAIN SMITH, ISMAY *in earnest conversation.*)

NARRATOR: At 11:55, back from their inspection, Shipbuilder Andrews outlined the situation to Captain Smith and President Ismay in the chart room.

ANDREWS (*Using his hands to explain*): . . . and there are sixteen separate compartments with water-tight bulkheads between each. She is taking on water in the first six compartments: the forepeak, number one hold, number two hold, the mail room, boiler room number six, and boiler room number five. That's six compartments gone. It means she's suffered a gash of nearly three hundred feet.

ISMAY: Never mind the mathematics. What are her chances?

ANDREW: It comes down to mathematics, Mr. Ismay. The *Titanic* can float with any two of her sixteen water-tight compartments flooded. She could even float with any three of her first five compartments flooded. She might even float with all of her first four gone. But, with the first six all gone . . . she cannot stay afloat.

ISMAY: But the compartments are water-tight. They're sealed.

ANDREWS: No, sir, they are not sealed on top. The bulkheads go only as high as E Deck. If the first five are flooded, the bow will sink so low that the water in the sixth compartment will overflow into the seventh, and when that is full it will overflow into the eighth and so on back.

ISMAY: Is there nothing we can do about it? Nothing?

ANDREWS *(After a moment)*: I'm afraid not, sir. The ship must go down.

CAPTAIN: How long do you give her, Tom?

ANDREWS: The water was about fourteen feet above the keel in the first ten minutes. *(He takes out his watch and looks at it as we tighten on him)* It is now nearly midnight . . . It's been twenty minutes since we hit the ice . . . *(He calculates to himself briefly, puts his watch back and looks up)* I'd say two hours. Certainly very little more than that.

FAST FADE TO BLACK

ACT TWO

FAST FADEUP TO: FILM—WHISTLE BLASTING

CUT TO OUTSIDE THE CHARTROOM ON THE
BRIDGE OF THE *TITANIC*

> *(Through the glass from the bridge we see* CAPTAIN SMITH *talking to* ANDREWS, ISMAY *standing beside them.)*

NARRATOR: The bridge of *RMS Titanic*, the time 12 midnight, April 14, 1912.

> *(*CAPTAIN SMITH *comes quickly out of the room.* ISMAY *follows closely behind him .The* CAPTAIN *goes to Officers* WILDE, MURDOCH, MOODY, *and* BOXHALL, *standing waiting.)*

CAPTAIN: Mr. Wilde, you will uncover the lifeboats immediately and have them swung out.

WILDE: Yes, sir.

CAPTAIN: Mr. Murdoch, have the passengers mustered on deck as quickly and quietly as possible. There must be no general alarm rung, nothing that might cause panic.

MURDOCH: Yes, sir.

CAPTAIN *(To officer)*: Break out the list of boat assignments for the crew. Wake up Mr. Lightoller and Mr. Pitman.

OFFICER: Yes, sir.

> *(They leave.* MOODY *passes on the word to a sailor, and the sailor leaves quickly. The camera tightens slowly on* ISMAY, *who is staring straight ahead of him.)*

NARRATOR: British shipping laws required all vessels over 10,000 tons gross to carry sixteen lifeboats. President Ismay's line, the White Star Line, met the requirements. The *Titanic*, 46,328 gross tons, carried sixteen lifeboats, which, along with four collapsibles was enough to accommodate a little over a thousand of its total capacity of 3,000 people. The law had been fulfilled.

> (ISMAY *turns and leaves the bridge hurriedly.* CAPTAIN SMITH *enters wireless shack.*)

CAPTAIN: Mr. Phillips!

PHILLIPS (*Having taken off his coat, his shirt half off, comes from behind the curtain*): Yes, sir.

CAPTAIN: We've struck an iceberg. Send the call for assistance.

PHILLIPS: The regulation distress call, sir?

CAPTAIN: Yes. At once. Here is our position.

PHILLIPS: Yes, sir. (*He takes the slip and sits back.* PHILLIPS *starts his set working, sending the call. Tighten on the spark.* CAPTAIN *leaves.*)

> (*Dissolve to wireless shack of the* Californian. *A headset lying on the desk. The chair is empty. Pan to show* OPERATOR EVANS *lounging on his bunk, reading.*)

NARRATOR: In the wireless room of the liner *Californian*, standing where she had stopped, ten miles away, Operator Evans, off duty since 11:30, was joined at 12:10 by Officer Groves. Groves was an amateur wireless addict.

> (GROVES *enters.*)

GROVES: Any news?

EVANS: Don't ask me. I'm closed for the night.

GROVES: Pretty soft life, if you ask me. (*He walks over to the set.*)

EVANS: You try working sixteen hours without relief.

GROVES: Mind if I fool around?

EVANS (*Without looking up*): Suit yourself.

GROVES: Any ships around?

EVANS: Only the *Titanic*.

GROVES: Oh, really? (*He fiddles*) Where's the receive switch?

EVANS: Bottom. On the left.

> (GROVES *throws the send-receive switch to receive position. He works the dials, listening intently. After a few moments of this he takes off the headphones.*)

GROVES: Nothing. (*He puts down the headphones and stands.* EVANS *glances up.*)

EVANS: No wonder. You didn't wind the detector.

GROVES: The what?

EVANS: The detector. It's magnetic—runs by clockwork. You have to wind it up if you want to hear anything.

GROVES: Oh, well . . . (*He dismisses the wireless set with a wave of the hand*) I'm tired anyway. I guess I'll turn in. (*He goes out the door.* EVANS *returns to his reading.*)

(*Pan up to clock saying 12:15.*)

CUT TO: FLOODED BOILER ROOM OF THE *TITANIC*

(*Gobo of furnace door. Stokers floundering about, up to their waists in water, shouting to one another, almost obscured by steam.*)

BELL (*From above, shouts*): Stick with it, lads! We've got to keep the generator going!

STOKER (*Shouts*): You just keep the pumps going, that's all! Keep the bloody pumps going!

CUT TO: DOOR OF LIGHTOLLER'S CABIN SUDDENLY THROWN OPEN

OFFICER: Lights! Captain wants you! You know we've struck an iceberg?

LIGHTOLLER: I know we've struck something.

OFFICER: The water is up to F Deck.

(LIGHTOLLER *springs out of bed.*)

NARRATOR: There was no general alarm—Captain's instructions. But quickly and quietly word passed among the passengers.

CUT TO: INTERIOR OF LUCIEN SMITH'S CABIN

(*He enters and turns on the light.* MRS. SMITH *is in bed. He sits down quietly beside her, gently smiling.*)

NARRATOR: Mr. and Mrs. Lucien Smith, of Philadelphia.

(*She opens her eyes.*)

MRS. SMITH: Darling, what's the matter?

MR. SMITH: It's all right, dear. We're in the north and we've struck an iceberg. (*She reacts.*) Now it doesn't amount to anything, but it will probably delay us a day getting into New York.

MRS. SMITH: Oh, you scared me.

MR. SMITH: However, as a matter of form, the Captain has ordered all ladies on deck.

CUT TO: GUGGENHEIM'S CABIN

> (STEWARD ETCHES *is trying to get him into his lifebelt, working like a solicitous tailor.*)

NARRATOR: Steward Etches and mining king Benjamin Guggenheim.

ETCHES: How's that?

GUGGENHEIM: It doesn't fit. It hurts.

ETCHES: We'll let it out a bit, sir. (*He adjusts the straps.*)

GUGGENHEIM: Where is that valet of mine? He's never around when I need him.

ETCHES: There. Is that better, sir?

GUGGENHEIM: No. I feel ridiculous.

ETCHES: (*Getting a heavy sweater*): You needn't, sir. They'll all be wearing them. (*He tries to put the sweater on and does so over the protest.*)

GUGGENHEIM: Look here, I don't need that.

ETCHES: It will be chilly, sir. You'd better wear it. (*He packs* GUGGENHEIM *off grumbling.*)

CUT TO: MILLING GROUP OF PEOPLE IN THIRD-CLASS LOUNGE

> (*They are asking questions of one another in various tongues.*)

NARRATOR: In the Third Class hallway on E Deck there was less formality—and even more difficulty. Steward John Edward Hart . . .

> (*Pull back to see* HART *at bottom of the stairs waving his hands for silence and attention.*)

HART (*Shouts*): There is no danger! But the Captain asks you all to put on lifebelts! (*There is a puzzled reaction*) Lifebelts! Life preservers! (*He picks up one and holds it up.*)

MAN: Ich weiss nicht was sie sagen.

WOMAN: Was sagt er?

HART: Never mind what they are! Just put them on! (*As the ad libs go back and forth, tighten on the* CLASENS, *worried, talking about what has happened in ad libs.*)

CUT TO: BRUCE ISMAY HURRYING DOWN STAIRWAY

> (CLINCH SMITH *watches him, then turns to* GRACIE, *at bottom of stairs.*)

NARRATOR: Others, like Colonel Gracie and his friend Clinch Smith, receiving no official word, put two and two together.

SMITH (*After watching* ISMAY): What do you think?

GRACIE (*Who has been staring at the floor and now at the ceiling*): Clinch.

SMITH: Yes?

GRACIE: Stand up straight.

SMITH: I am standing. . . . (*He stops, after a look at him, complies. Shifts his weight back and forth, looks at the floor and the ceiling.* GRACIE *watches him.* SMITH *looking back at him*) You're right. She's beginning to list.

GRACIE (*After a moment*): Clinch . . . if worst comes to worst, let's stick together. We might be of some help here and there . . . if it is serious.

SMITH: All right, Archie. (*They shake hands.*)

GRACIE: We'd better get into something warm. I'll meet you here in five minutes.

SMITH: Right, old boy. (*They separate.*)

CUT TO HANDS REMOVING THE TARP FROM THE LIFE-BOATS. STILL SOUND OF STEAM

NARRATOR: At 12:15 Chief Officer Wilde removed the covers from the lifeboats and Officer Lightoller started the loading.

CUT TO GROUP OF PEOPLE STANDING NEAR LIFEBOAT SIX

> (*Including the* ASTORS. *They are ad libbing and talking about what has happened and how ridiculous it is.* LIGHTOLLER *steps up and with one foot in Number Six and one on deck, he turns to them.*)

LIGHTOLLER: The Captain has asked for the women and children to board the boats, please. Come along, please! (*They hardly move*) Please come along. We haven't much time to get all the boats loaded.

> (*Finally a couple step up.*)

MAN (*To wife*): You go along, little girl. I'll stay awhile.

WOMAN: But it's silly.

> (LIGHTOLLER *takes her and puts her into the boat. Others follow slowly. He motions to* MRS. ASTOR.)

LIGHTOLLER: Step along please, Mrs. Astor.

> (ASTOR *stops her.*)

ASTOR: No. This is ridiculous. We're safer here than in that little boat. Come along inside, dear, where it's warm. You mustn't catch a chill.

NARRATOR: Colonel Astor expressed what they all felt. The loading at 12:15 was slow. (*Dissolve to wireless shack*) At 12:20 Wireless Operator Phillips received the first answers to his distress call. The North German Lloyd Steamer, *Frankfort*—150 miles away. The Canadian Pacific's *Mt. Temple* 50 miles away—but on the other side of the ice field. (*Dissolve to wireless shack on Bare Point. Dissolve to another one on top of building*) The news spread in ever-widening circles. Cape Race heard it and relayed it inland. On the roof of Wanamaker's Department Store in New York, a young wireless operator named David Sarnoff caught a faint signal and passed it on. (*Dissolve to desk. Sound of news room behind*) The time, 12:24. An Associated Press dispatch crossed the news desk of the New York *Times*. The *Titanic* was sinking.

MAN (*Who picks it up where it was tossed*): My God, I don't believe it!

NARRATOR: While the whole world was snapping to agonized attention, Henry Sleeper Harper, aboard the *Titanic*, remained unconvinced.

CUT TO GYM

> (A *group of people,* HENRY HARPER, MRS. HARPER, THE ASTORS.)

HARPER: Of course it's nonsense! Asking us to bob about out there in a rowboat in the dark, when we can stay in here. Besides it's freezing out there.

PULL BACK TO SEE COLONEL AND MRS. ASTOR

NARRATOR: And Mrs. Astor wasn't frightened—only curious.

> (COLONEL ASTOR *is cutting open a lifebelt.*)

ASTOR: Wait a moment . . . There you are. You see, it's cork inside.

MRS. ASTOR: How clever! (*He tosses the lifebelt in the corner.*)

CUT TO: THE BELT LANDING IN THE CORNER

> (*Dissolve to the back of a life preserver. On an old lady walking down the corridor. A* STEWARDESS *is shepherding them both.*)

STEWARDESS: There is nothing to be alarmed about, ladies. It's only a precaution. I'm sure you'll be back in your beds shortly. . . .

> (THOMAS ANDREWS *is coming up toward them. He stops the* STEWARDESS *and speaks quietly.*)

ANDREWS: The last time I saw you I told you to put on your lifebelt.
STEWARDESS: Yes, but I thought it rather. . . .
ANDREWS: Put it on; walk about; let the passengers see you in it!
STEWARDESS: It looks rather mean.
ANDREWS: If you value your life, put it on!

> (*He goes. She looks after him, startled, looks at the preserver in her hand.*)

CUT TO: MRS. LUCIEN SMITH BY HER DRESSING TABLE

MRS. SMITH: I thought this afternoon that we'd best not stay more than a day in New York.
MR. SMITH: I'll change the reservations. We can take the train to Florida on the 18th.
MRS. SMITH: Is this coat all right?
MR. SMITH: It's pretty cold on deck.
MRS. SMITH: I'll take them both. (*He starts with her to the door and she stops.*)
MR. SMITH: What is it?
MRS. SMITH: My jewelry.
MR. SMITH (*As she goes to table again*): My dear, it might be wiser not to bother with trifles.
MRS. SMITH: I'll just take these two.

> (*As she puts rings on, he comes up in back of her, kisses her fondly.*)

MR. SMITH: Come along now, dear. (*They leave.*)

CUT TO: PEOPLE GATHER AROUND A DOOR

PASSENGER: Unlock it!
MAN'S VOICE INSIDE: I can't!
PASSENGER: Turn it again, try the other way.

(The others ad lib suggestions. A man comes up with a fire axe.)

STEWARD: Here now, here now, what are you doing?

PASSENGER: Let him through. They're trapped inside.

STEWARD: That's company property!

(THE MAN sinks his axe in the door. THE STEWARD is frantic.)

STEWARD: What's your name there! Destroying company property. I'll report you and have the whole lot of you arrested when we reach New York.

(Dissolve to MURDOCH.)

MURDOCH: Come along, please!

NARRATOR: At 12:42 P.M., over one hour after striking the iceberg, it took more bravery, or more foresight to leave the *Titanic* than to stay aboard. And Officer Murdoch felt he could wait no longer.

MURDOCH *(Shouting)*: Lower away!

(Shot of seaman playing out the rope around a snub.)

NARRATOR: And the first boat, number seven, was lowered. Its capacity, 40. Its passengers, 20.

(Dissolve to ROWE pacing on stern of ship.)

NARRATOR: Time: 12:45. At the very stern end of the *Titanic*, Quartermaster George Thomas Rowe, pacing his watch, reported an unusual sight.

(He has done a take, and comes over to the rail, looking down. He rushes to his phone. He rings.)

ROWE: Sir? Sir, there's a boat afloat out here! I just saw it! Quartermaster Rowe, sir, stern watch. What sir? ...

(As camera tightens.)

NARRATOR: And one hour and ten minutes after the *Titanic* hit, Quartermaster Rowe became the last man to learn what was going on.

ROWE: Yes, sir! Right away, sir! *(He hangs up and runs.)*

(Dissolve to bridge. MOODY and the CAPTAIN. The CAPTAIN walks up to where MOODY is standing.)

MOODY: Captain? There's a ship off there, sir. Not more than ten miles away. We've been trying to reach her by Morse lamp.

CAPTAIN: Any reply?

MOODY: I thought there was for a while, but it seems to be their masthead flickering.

CAPTAIN: Rowe?

ROWE: Yes, sir.

CAPTAIN: Did you bring up the rockets?

ROWE: Yes, sir.

CAPTAIN: Fire one, and fire one every five or six minutes

ROWE: Yes, sir. (*He leaves.*)

CAPTAIN: She'll respond to those all right.

MOODY: Yes, sir.

CUT TO FILM CLIP OF A DAZZLING ROCKET DRIFTING DOWN SLOWLY. THEN ANOTHER

(*Dissolve to distant shot of it. Dissolve to* Californian.)

NARRATOR: On the bridge of the *Californian*, Second Officer Herbert Stone watched—and counted. By 12:55 he had counted five rockets.

GIBSON: I thought she was trying to signal us a while back, sir, but I think it was just her masthead flickering.

STONE (*After a moment*): Strange that she'd be firing rockets at night. (*He hands his glasses to* SEAMAN) Have a look at her now. She looks very queer out of the water—her lights look queer.

SEAMAN (*Studies the ship through the glasses*): She seems to be listing. Looks like she has a big side out of water.

(STONE *whistles down the speaking tube to the chart room.*)

CUT TO CAPTAIN LORD, ASLEEP, WAKING UP AND ANSWERING

LORD: Yes, what is it?

STONE (*Over speaker*): Sir, there's a ship off the port bow . . .

LORD: I know there is—what about it?

STONE: . . . she's been firing rockets. See five of them altogether.

LORD: Are they Company rockets?

STONE (*Over speaker*): I don't know, but they appear to me to be white rockets.

LORD: Uh . . . well, try the Morse lamp.

STONE: We did, sir.

LORD (*Sleepy*): Well ... try it again.

(*He hangs up, rolls over and goes back to sleep.*)

OVER CLOSE-UP OF HIS SLEEPING FACE SUPER FILM OF ANOTHER ROCKET GOING UP

NARRATOR: And at 1 A.M. Captain Stanley Lord of the *SS Californian* finally got to sleep.

SLOW FADE TO BLACK

ACT THREE

FADE UP FIRST-CLASS LOUNGE. THE BAND IN HAPHAZ-ARD UNIFORMS PLAYING A RAGTIME PIECE

NARRATOR: The time 1 A.M., April 15, 1912. The *Titanic* Salon Orchestra under the baton of Wallace Henry Hartley—the selection "Hello, My Baby."

(*Dissolve to: Film clip of rocket shot into the air. Dissolve to: The bridge of the* Titanic CAPTAIN *and* MOODY. MOODY *looking through binoculars.*)

CAPTAIN SMITH: Any response from that ship?

MOODY: I'm afraid not, sir. I thought for a moment she was signaling back, but it seems to be just her masthead flickering.

CAPTAIN (*Over his shoulder*): Fire another.

CUT TO: FILM CLIP OF ROCKET FIRED AT CLOSE RANGE

(*Dissolve to: Deck* 1—Titanic. *Passengers looking up, in alarm, at the bright glare of the falling rocket. Cut from passengers' faces to* ISMAY'S.)

NARRATOR: The sight of the *Titanic's* distress signals may have made little impression on the *S.S. Californian*, but aboard the *Titanic* they had their effect.

ISMAY (*Urging people along*): Hurry! Do hurry! There's no time to lose!

CUT TO DECK 4

LIGHTOLLER: Into the boat! Quickly! You, ma'am!

VOICES: Hold on there! Hold on there a bit!

(GRACIE *and* SMITH *arrive escorting a gorgeous woman,* MRS. APPLETON.)

NARRATOR: And the team of Gracie and Smith was already functioning smoothly.

GRACIE: Hold on there! (*He stops with her*) There you are, Mrs. Appleton.

MRS. APPLETON: Gentlemen, I don't know how to thank you, you've been so gallant...

> (*Two sailors lift her bodily into boat.* GRACIE *and* SMITH *smile at each other and nip off in search of other unattached ladies. Pull back to see* MR. AND MRS. LUCIEN SMITH.)

LIGHTOLLER: Step along, please, quickly, please.

MR. SMITH: Quickly, dear.

MRS. SMITH: No, no!

MR. SMITH: Dearest, I never expected to ask you to obey, but this is one time you must. It is only a matter of form to have the women and children first. The ship is thoroughly equipped. Everyone on her will be saved.

MRS. SMITH: Are you telling me the truth?

MR. SMITH: Yes!

> (*He kisses her and she steps obediently into the boat. She turns to* LIGHTOLLER.)

MRS. SMITH: Officer, won't you...

LIGHTOLLER (*Harshly*): Women and children only! Lower away!

NARRATOR: Women and children only was the rule of the night on the port side of the ship, where Officer Lightoller was in charge. But on the starboard side, Officer Murdoch was more lenient.

CUT TO: DECK 3 *TITANIC*

> (HENRY SLEEPER HARPER *entering Lifeboat Number Three.*)

MURDOCH: Come on, come on. Let's fill 'em up.

NARRATOR: Entering Lifeboat Number 3, Henry Sleeper Harper, his Egyptian dragoman Hamad Hassah, and ... (*Pan to Pekingese dog in* HARPER's *arms*) his prize Pekingese, Sun Yat Sen. (*Tighten on dog.*)

> (*Dissolve to: Bottom stairs 3rd Class Lounge. Face of child in mother's arms. Pull back to see her.*)

WOMAN (*With an accent*): Can we not go up yet, please?

STEWARD (*At barrier*): There will be someone here to escort the women and children up in a little while. Be patient, please!

(*They behave quietly, submissively.*)

NARRATOR: A small group of women and children had been sent up from steerage at 12:30. That had been a half an hour before. Now, at 1:05, steerage waited patiently for the most part . . .

(*The camera has been seeing past to the* IRISHMAN *and* FRIEND. *He turns and heads off in another direction. We see him take hold of a friend and motion.*)

CUT TO: CORRIDOR—3RD CLASS

(*They go around a corner and start down another corridor.*)

CUT TO: TOP OF SHORT STEPS TO ANOTHER BARRIER

(*They stop sharp at sign, "No Admittance, First Class." A* SEAMAN *steps in front of it.*)

SEAMAN: You can't go past here. I'm sorry.

FRIEND: And what's to stop us?

SEAMAN: It's against the rules.

FRIEND: Jam the bloody rules! Open up the gate! (*The* SEAMAN *throws him back. The* IRISHMAN *bounces up, howling.*)

IRISHMAN: Lay your hands on me, will you, I'll bust your bloody head!

(*He starts after the* SEAMAN *who retires past the gate in alarm. They break through and follow him up, several of them, including young* IRISHMAN.)

(*Dissolve to: The wireless shack of the* Titanic. PHILLIPS *at the set, receiving and writing down a message.* CAPTAIN *is over his shoulder expectantly.*)

NARRATOR: At 12:36 in the wireless room of the *Titanic*, operator Phillips received his first encouragement.

PHILLIPS: It's from the *Carpathia*, sir!

(CAPTAIN *waits anxiously.*)

PHILLIPS (*Taking it down*): She's fifty-eight miles away, sir. . . . She says she's coming hard!

(CAPTAIN *picks up the message.*)

CAPTAIN SMITH: Fifty-eight miles . . . (*Thinks a moment, shakes his head sadly*) They'll be too late.

CUT TO TIGHT SHOT OF ISMAY, DECK 3

ISMAY (*Yelling*): Hurry! There's no time to lose! We *must* get the women and children off! Hurry! (*Hanging onto davit with one arm, he swings the other in a circle, shouting*) Lower away! Hurry, man! Lower away! Lower away! Lower away!

LOWE (*Turning on him*): If you get the hell out of the way I'll be able to do something! You want me to lower away quickly! You'll have me drown the whole lot of them!

(ISMAY *walks away, abashed, to Number Three Lifeboat.*)

NARRATOR: There had been no need for a lifeboat drill aboard an unsinkable ship—no boat assignments, no procedure for abandoning ship. With no fixed policy to guide them, they behaved as the moment and their characters dictated.

(*Dissolve to:* STEWARD ETCHES, *on Deck 1.*)

ETCHES: Mr. Guggenheim! Where is your lifebelt?

CUT TO: GUGGENHEIM AND HIS VALET, RESPLENDENT IN EVENING CLOTHES

GUGGENHEIM: I gave it away. My valet and I have dressed in our best, and we are prepared to go down like gentlemen.

(*He looks to his* VALET, *who smiles proudly.*)

VALET: Yes, sir.

(*Dissolve to:* LORD AND LADY DUFF GORDON *approaching Lifeboat Number 3.*)

NARRATOR: As the moment dictated—Sir Cosmo and Lady Duff Gordon . . .

DUFF GORDON: May we get in?

MURDOCH: Yes, go ahead. Jump in.

(SIR COSMO *hands the ladies into the boat, then follows gingerly himself.*)

NARRATOR: The Duff Gordons' boat, number 1, was lowered at 1:10. Capacity 40, number of passengers 12.

(*Dissolve to: Elderly couple approaching lifeboat. Deck Number 4.*)

NARRATOR: As their characters dictated.

MAN: Please dear, go ahead.

LIGHTOLLER (*Trying to help her*): Take my hand, please.

WOMAN: I have always stayed with my husband. Why should I leave him now?

MAN: I beg you, my dear ...

WOMAN: Isidor, we have been living together many years. Where you go, I go.

HUGH WOOLNER: But all the other ladies are getting in.

WOMAN (*Shaking her head*): Where he goes, I go. (WOOLNER *turns to the* MAN.)

WOOLNER: I'm sure nobody would object to an old gentleman like you getting in, sir.

MAN: I will not go before the other men. (*They move away quietly.*)

NARRATOR: This was the decision of Mr. and Mrs. Isidor Strauss of New York City.

CUT TO MURDOCH AND MEN LOWERING BOATS

(*Montage back and forth.*)

MURDOCH: Lower away!

NARRATOR: Time 1:15, number ten lowered, carrying 53 passengers.

CUT TO

BOXHALL: Lower away!

NARRATOR: 1:20. Number nine lowered, carrying 55.

CUT TO

WILDE: Lower away!

NARRATOR: 1:25. Number 11 lowered, carrying 70. There was no longer difficulty filling the boats. The passengers knew.

CUT TO DECK NUMBER 6

(*Gun being fired three times rapidly.*)

CUT TO OFFICER LOWE

NARRATOR: At 1:30, Officer Lowe used his gun.

CUT TO BOY BEING FLUNG ON THE DECK, SOBBING

GIRL: Don't shoot him! Don't shoot him!

(LOWE *gives her a quick smile of reassurance and a pat on the head. Behind his back two men jump into the boat.*)

SEAMAN: Here! Get out of there! Clear out of there!

> (*The* SEAMAN *jumps into the boat and grapples with one of them.* ROWE *joins him. They grab the culprit by the arms and legs, haul him out of the boat. Two passengers—*WOOLNER *and partner—jump into the boat and drag the other man out.*)

NARRATOR: As their characters dictated.

LOWE (*Showing gun*): If anyone else tries that, this is what he'll get!

CUT TO

> (DANIEL BUCKLEY *cowering under a seat in the lifeboat, a woman's shawl pulled over his head. Deck Number 6.*)

> (*Dissolve to* ISMAY *at Lifeboat C, Deck Number 5.*)

NARRATOR: On the starboard side. At the moment there were no candidates at hand, and at 1:46 Presidence Bruce Ismay made his most important decision as president of the White Star Lines.

ISMAY (*He looks around*): Isn't there anyone else to go? There's room for one more! (*He looks into the boat*) No one else? (*He steps into the boat*) Lower away—lower away!

TIGHTEN ON ISMAY FAST

NARRATOR: At the time President Ismay left his ship, there remained on board 1643 passengers. Among them, 168 women and 57 children.

> (*Dissolve to the steerage. Third-class passengers who had been waiting patiently are beginning to become restive. A* STEWARD *stands at the foot of the stairs.*)

VOICES (*Ad lib*): When are they going to let us up? . . . What are we waiting for?

WOMAN: Can't we go up now? *Please?*

> (*The* STEWARD *looks back up the stairs, eager to get out of there himself.*)

WILDE (*Off*): Steward, send the passengers up!

STEWARD: Well, I . . . I suppose you can go now.

> (*The passengers surge forward, as he stumbles out of their way.*)

NARRATOR: At 1:55 the passengers from steerage lounge on E deck were allowed to find their way forward and up to the boat deck through the great ship by themselves. (*Dissolve to the deck. The*

ASTORS *approach Lifeboat Number 4. Deck Number 6*) At 1:56, at Lifeboat Number 4, the Astors had become aware of the situation.

LIGHTOLLER: Step along, please.

(MRS. ASTOR *gets in.*)

ASTOR (*To* LIGHTOLLER): May I accompany my wife? She's in a delicate condition.

LIGHTOLLER: No, sir. No men are allowed in these boats. It is women and children only, sir.

ASTOR (LIGHTOLLER *thought this was indignant, perhaps not*): What is the number of this lifeboat?

LIGHTOLLER: Number four, sir.

(ASTOR *nods, kisses his wife, who is put in the boat, crying.* MRS. RYERSON *arrives with her children.* LIGHTOLLER *takes a boy thirteen and pushes him aside.*)

LIGHTOLLER: Women and children only!

MRS. RYERSON: Jack!

(MR. RYERSON *comes up strongly with the boy again.*)

RYERSON (*Indignant*): Of course that boy goes with his mother! He is only thirteen.

(LIGHTOLLER *looks at him, pushes him into the boat.*)

LIGHTOLLER (*Grumbling*): No more boys!

CUT TO: CORRIDOR IN WATER

(*Steerage passengers up to their waists looking frantically where to go. Among them the* CLASENS.)

KLAUS (*Yelling, finding steps*): This way! This way! Up here! I've found the way up! Come on!

(*They plow through the water hurriedly, holding their children.*)

CUT TO BOAT "D" DECK NUMBER 6

NARRATOR: The time, 2:00 A.M. The last lifeboat on the *Titanic.* Officer Lightoller took a precaution.

LIGHTOLLER (*To members of the crew standing around*): Lock arms there! Let only the women and children through.

(*Two baby boys are handed over the barrier. Women are put in.*)

LIGHTOLLER: She's full up. Lower away!

VOICE (*Off*): Hold on there! Hold on! Hold on!

> (GRACIE *and* SMITH *rush up with* MRS. BROWN *and* MISS
> EVANS.)

NARRATOR: Mrs. John Murray Brown and Miss Edith Evans reached the boat, with the help of Gracie and Smith.

GRACIE (*Loudly*): Hold on. Two more women here! Two more here to go! (*He pushes them past the barrier*) Go along ladies and God bless you! Get along now! (*They go to the boat. It is full. They both stop.*)

LIGHTOLLER: Only room for one more!

MISS EVANS: Go ahead, Mrs. Brown, quickly! (MRS. BROWN *hesitates*) Quickly! You have children waiting at home!

> (MRS. BROWN *gets in as someone hollers "Lower Away," and
> the boat lowers. Tighten on* EDITH EVANS.)

NARRATOR: Last boat off the *Titanic*, 2:05. (EDITH EVANS *waves and smiles*) . . . and 1554 remained on board.

CUT TO THE STEERAGE PASSENGERS
ON DECK NUMBER 2

> (*Including the* CLASENS, *coming through a door, women, children, men. They stop and look around them quickly.*)

CUT TO THE ROPES HANGING EMPTY
FROM THE DAVITS

CUT BACK TO THEM

> (KLAUS *puts his arms around his wife and child. Deck Number 2.*)

CUT TO: THE WIRELESS SHACK OF THE *TITANIC*

> (PHILLIPS *is still on duty, sending out the distress call. His assistant,* BRIDE, *is standing beside him.*)

NARRATOR: Still on board, Operator Phillips, Operator Bride, Captain Smith.

PHILLIPS: The power's getting low. The spark is weak. (*The* CAPTAIN *enters.*)

CAPTAIN: Men, you have done your full duty. You can do no more. Abandon your cabin. Now it's every man for himself.

> (PHILLIPS *looks up for a second.*)

PHILLIPS: There's still a little power left. (*He goes on transmitting.*)
CAPTAIN: You look out for yourselves. I release you. (*He puts a hand on BRIDE's shoulder*) That's the way of it at this kind of time.

CUT TO BAND AT A PRECARIOUS ANGLE
ON DECK NUMBER 7

> (BANDMASTER HARTLEY *taps his stick. They steady themselves and begin "Autumn."*)

NARRATOR: Still on board, the *Titanic* Salon Orchestra. The time 2:15. The selection, the Episcopal Hymn, "Autumn." The orchestra's final performance under the baton of Wallace Henry Hartley.

CUT TO: GRACIE AND SMITH BY RAIL, DECK NUMBER 2

> (*The deck has lurched up again, throwing furniture down.*)

NARRATOR: Still on board, Colonel Gracie and his friend Clinch Smith.
GRACIE (*Smiling*): We didn't do too badly, Clinch?
SMITH: Not badly at all.
GRACIE (*Extending hand*): Good luck, Clinch.
SMITH: Good luck, Archie.

> (*The deck lurches again. They have to hold on.*)

NARRATOR: But of the two, Colonel Gracie proved the better swimmer.

CUT TO THE STERN OF THE SHIP, A RAIL AT A CRAZY
ANGLE. DECK NUMBER 5

NARRATOR: Still on board, young Jack Thayer and his friend, Milton Long.

> (*They are shaking hands.* THAYER *unbuttons overcoat.*)

BOTH: Good luck, Jack. Good luck, Milt.

> (MILT *climbs over the side.*)

MILTON LONG: You're coming, boy?
THAYER: Go ahead, I'll be right with you.

> (LONG *slides down, facing the ship.* THAYER *stands on rail and leaps out.*)

CUT TO THAYER HITTING THE WATER (ON FILM)

NARRATOR: Of these two techniques for abandoning ship, young Jack Thayer's was the one that worked.

(*Dissolve to crooked picture of the "Approach to a New World" in smoking room, set tilted.*)

NARRATOR: Still on board, Thomas Andrews—shipbuilder.

(ANDREWS *sits in chair, looking at it.* STEWARD *enters.*)

STEWARD: Mr. Andrews! (*No reply*) Mr. Andrews, aren't you going to have a try for it, sir?

CUT TO: ANDREWS CLOSE, TILTED

(*He looks up blankly, looks back down again.*)

CUT TO STEWARD ACROSS ANDREWS

STEWARD: But sir, there's still a chance if you . . .

(*A roar has started slowly—huge sound of the great ship's death cry. The* STEWARD *looks up sharply.*)

CUT TO CEILING OF SMOKING ROOM

(*A huge crystal chandelier. It has started to vibrate violently as the roar builds into a deafening crescendo.*)

CUT TO STEWARD

(*He takes a quick look at* ANDREWS *and runs for it. As he does, the roar reaches its peak—the set slowly tips up toward camera—the chandelier crashes onto* ANDREWS, *the picture crashes off the wall, and the floor of the set comes slowly straight up. The set sinks slowly into water.*)

NARRATOR: The time 2:20. The freezing waters of the North Atlantic closed over the grave of the *Titanic*. She carried with her 1502 souls. 1346 men, 102 women and 54 children, all but one of whom were steerage children. (*Dissolve to* NARRATOR) If the *Titanic* had heeded any of the six iceberg messages . . . if the night had been rough or moonlit . . . if she had hit the iceberg fifteen seconds sooner, or fifteen seconds later . . . if her water-tight bulkheads had been one deck higher . . . if she had carried enough boats . . . if the *Californian* had only heeded and come. Had any of these "ifs" turned out right, every life might have been saved. But they all went against her. And never again has man been quite so confident. An age had come to an end.

FADE OUT

Bring on the Angels

by ALLAN SLOANE

CATEGORY:

Radio Drama

(ANY LENGTH)

BRING ON THE ANGELS

by ALLAN SLOANE

Bring on the Angels
was first presented on CBS RADIO WORKSHOP
under the direction of Paul Roberts,
on June 8, 1956,
with the following cast:

LUIS VAN ROOTEN · MASON ADAMS
ED PRENTISS · ETHEL OWEN
DANIEL OCKO · JACKSON BECK
WALTER KINSELLA · JOHN GIBSON
JOE HELGESEN · IAN MARTIN

NOTE: The majority of the facts
dramatized in this play are from
Newspaper Days, copyright,
1940, 1941, by Alfred A. Knopf,
Inc. Other material is from *In
Defense of Women*, copyright,
1918, 1922, by Alfred Knopf,
Inc. Fragments are from *The
Vintage Mencken*, 1956,
edited by Alistair Cooke.
Vintage Books, New York.

MUSIC: KIND OF A SASSY FANFARE

OLD MENCKEN: It was the maddest, gladdest, damnedest existence ever enjoyed by mortal youth. A newspaper reporter in those days had a grand and gaudy time of it, and no call to envy any man. And yet I have marveled that the human race did not revolt against the imposture, dig up the carcass of Gutenberg and heave it to the buzzards and hyenas in some convenient zoo.

SOUND: A CLOCK'S RAPID SHARP TICKING. DOWN BEHIND

NARRATOR (*Close*): The man in the bed has had a stroke. A being full of gusto and sour joy, he is paralyzed. A master's master of words, he will never speak sense again. He is 68.

MUSIC: SNEAK NOSTALGICALLY

NARRATOR: His eyes are open, but there is no fire there. They see, instead, inward. What the sudden grab of thrombosis has left of his brain now gropes in the swirling mist of reversing time . . . seeks, finds . . . remembers.

MUSIC: UP AND AWAY

OLD MENCKEN: My father died on Friday, January 13, 1899, and was buried on the ensuing Sunday. On the Monday evening immediately following, I presented myself (*Sneak sound of two typewriters and someone calling out "Boy!"*) in the city room of the old Baltimore *Morning Herald*, and applied to Max Ways, the City Editor, for a job.

BRING UP SOUND, SEND IT DOWN FOR

YOUNG MENCKEN: Uh, Mr. Ways, sir . . .

NARRATOR (*Close*): I was eighteen years, four months, and four days old, wore my hair longish and parted in the middle, had on a high stiff collar and an ascot cravat, and weighed something on the minus side of 120 pounds.

YOUNG MENCKEN: Sir.

WAYS: What's your problem, Sonny?

YOUNG MENCKEN: I, uh, I'd like a job. (*Quickly*) A reporter's job.

WAYS: Got any experience?

YOUNG MENCKEN: Uh, no. No, sir.

WAYS: Been to school?

YOUNG MENCKEN: Baltimore Polytechnic Institute. But I've done some writing.

WAYS: Poetry?

YOUNG MENCKEN: Well, yes, yes, sir.

WAYS: What makes you think you want to be a newspaperman?

YOUNG MENCKEN: Well, I think it'd be inter— uh, exciting.

WAYS: Hah! (*Long pause*) You working?

YOUNG MENCKEN: Yes, sir. For my Uncle Henry at Mencken and Brother, the cigar factory.

WAYS: What's your name?

YOUNG MENCKEN: Mencken, sir. Henry Louis Mencken.

WAYS: Well, I tell you, Henry Louis, we don't have an opening right now. But you drop in now and then, evenings, say between seven-thirty and seven-forty-five. Something might turn up. (*Pause*) Boy!

MUSIC: UP BRIGHTLY AND AWAY

OLD MENCKEN: The next night, precisely at seventy-thirty-one, I was back. Max waved me away without parley. The third night he simply shook his head. The fourth, fifth, sixth—well, to make an end, this went on for four weeks, night in and night out, until Thursday, February 23, 1899. I found Max reading copy. For a few minutes he did not see me. Then his eyes lifted and he said casually . . .

WAYS: Go out to Govanstown and see if anything is happening there. We are supposed to have a Govanstown correspondent, but he hasn't been heard from for six days.

MUSIC: UP GLEEFULLY AND AWAY BEHIND

WAYS: What'd you get, Henry?

YOUNG MENCKEN: Well, there were only two lights burning in town, so I . . .

WAYS: The news, the news!

YOUNG MENCKEN: The Imperial Order of Red Men have postponed their oyster supper to March 6th.

WAYS: Stop the press. Anything else?

YOUNG MENCKEN: Yes, sir. A horse was stolen. . . .

WAYS: Gimme a stick.

YOUNG MENCKEN: Sir?

WAYS: A stick is one paragraph. Pen and paper over there.

MUSIC: UP AND AWAY

OLD MENCKEN: I was up with the milkman the next morning to search the paper . . .

SOUND: PAPER BEING RUSTLED EAGERLY

OLD MENCKEN: . . . and there it was.

YOUNG MENCKEN: A horse, a buggy and several sets of harness, (*Sneak music: A John Philip Sousa march, as of a parade approaching*) valued in all at about $250, were stolen last night from the stable of Howard Quinian, near Kingsville. The county police are at work on the case, but so far no trace of either thieves or booty has been found. He didn't change a single word!

MUSIC: UP BIG AND DOWN BEHIND

OLD MENCKEN: I was hooked. I was in print. I was a reporter. I was hired.

WAYS: Sonny, I'm going to give you a start. I'm going to put you on the payroll at seven dollars a week, and if you make good, you get a raise . . .

YOUNG MENCKEN: Aw, that's wonderful, Mr. Ways. . . .

WAYS: . . . to eight dollars. And the name is Max.

YOUNG MENCKEN: Yes, sir!

WAYS: You'll have pass privileges on the trolley cars, and in time, I might even get you a typewriter. Now—remember these things. First and foremost—never trust a cop. Always verify his report. Second, get your copy in early. Third, be careful about dates, names, ages, addresses, figures of every kind. And last—always be mindful of the dangers of libel.

YOUNG MENCKEN: I will, Max, I certainly will.

WAYS: And one more thing. Any *Herald* reporter who is worth a damn can write rings around a *Sun* reporter, and don't you forget it!

MUSIC: UP AND AWAY

OLD MENCKEN: It wasn't long before I had a typewriter, a spittoon of my own, and a beat. Max gave me Southern Baltimore, or, to speak technically, the Southern Police District. But my legwork carried me 'way out beyond the city line. I asked Max about that, how far I was supposed to go.

MAX: Henry, you stay on the road until you meet the Philadelphia reporters coming in.

MUSIC: UP AND AWAY, THE SOUSA MARCH AGAIN

OLD MENCKEN: Ah, the newspaper days, the happy days, when I laid in the worldly wisdom of the police lieutenant, the bartender, the shyster lawyer, the midwife. The days chased each other like kittens chasing their tails. And the very first week—I landed in court. On the witness stand.

SOUND: COURTROOM BABBLE, JUDGE'S GAVEL

OLD MENCKEN (*Quietly*): The reformers had blithered up a crusade against the bawdy dance halls, and I became an unwilling witness against two cops who had been aware of what was going on.

LAWYER: What were you doing there?

YOUNG MENCKEN: Covering the story.

LAWYER: And did you see the defendants?

YOUNG MENCKEN: Well, I was very busy taking notes . . .

LAWYER: Answer the question.

YOUNG MENCKEN: Well, I was there in my official capacity, and I presumed the police were.

LAWYER: Answer the question. Did you see the defendants there?

YOUNG MENCKEN: Well, I spoke to many officers of the law that night, I may have seen and spoken with the defendants. I remember asking . . .

OLD MENCKEN: The poor flatfeet were guilty, for I had talked with them there many times—but I managed to sophisticate my testimony with so many ifs and buts that it went for nothing, and they were acquitted.

MUSIC: A LIGHT STING

OLD MENCKEN: That was my first and last experience as an agent of moral endeavor. I made up my mind at once that my true and natural allegiance was to the Devil's party, and it has been my firm belief that ever since that all persons who devote themselves to forcing virtue on their fellow men deserve nothing better than kicks in the pants. Hence—Mencken's law: to wit:

YOUNG MENCKEN: Whenever A annoys or injures B on the pretense of saving or improving X—A is a scoundrel.

MUSIC: UP AND AWAY

OLD MENCKEN: I learned my trade from veterans who had seen Lincoln clear. Sometimes, for instance, it would be a matter of legging it to the iron wilds of Locust Point. But De Bekker was more experienced than I, and had a beard to prove it. So . . .

SOUND: FEET ON PAVEMENT. RATTLE OF BUGGIES, HORSES WHINNYING, KIDS YELLING, TROLLEYS BANGING

DE BEKKER: Two beers, dark.

SOUND: GURGLE, GURGLE

DE BEKKER: Aaaaah. Again. Henry, why should we walk our legs off tryin' to find out the name of a stevedore kicked overboard by a mule?

YOUNG MENCKEN: Well, the cops . . .

DE BEKKER: They're too busy dragging for the body. And when they do turn in the name, the spelling'll be so bad no union printer in Baltimore'll be able to set it up. And that reminds me. Charley, set 'em up again. (*Pause*) Aaaah.

YOUNG MENCKEN: But my City Desk . . .

DE BEKKER: The fact, my boy, that another poor man has given his life to engorge the interests is not news. It happens every ten minutes . . .

YOUNG MENCKEN: Well, kicked by a mule . . .

DE BEKKER: *That* is the story! Men are not kicked overboard by mules every day. That is the story, not the name. Therefore (A *slap on the bar*) I move you, my esteemed contemporary (A *gulp of beer*) that the name of the deceased be Ignaz Karpinski . . .

YOUNG MENCKEN: K-a-r-p-i-n-s-k-i.

DE BEKKER (*Goes on right over it*): That the name of his widow be Marie, that his age was thirty-six, that he lived at 1777 Fort Avenue, and that he leaves eleven minor children! Charley!!

MUSIC: UP AND AWAY

OLD MENCKEN: And so the sad facts were reported in all three Baltimore papers the next day, along with various lively details that occurred to De Bekker with successive beers. This labor-saving device was in use the whole time I covered South Baltimore, and I never heard any complaint against it. Every one of the three city editors, comparing his paper to the other two, was surprised and pleased to discover that his reporter always got names and addresses right. But we never stooped to faking . . . Well, hardly ever . . .

MAX: Henry.

YOUNG MENCKEN: Yes, Max.

MAX: This story about the wild man loose in the woods over the city line.

YOUNG MENCKEN: Wild man. Oh, the wild man, yes, Max?

MAX: He, uh . . . well, where'd you get it?

YOUNG MENCKEN: Lieutenant Dempsey.

MAX: Old Tom Dempsey, huh? Funny. He told me the same story fifteen years ago. (*Pause*) Or did I invent the wild man and sell it to him? Tcnk tcnk tcnk tcnk tcnk. Henry.

YOUNG MENCKEN: Well . . . it was Sunday. Quiet day. You know, Max.

MAX: Sure, Henry. (*Gently*) The trouble is, Judge Finnegan just sentenced some poor boob to six months as a result of the wild-man hunt.

YOUNG MENCKEN: That's all right, Max. I talked to him. He said he didn't mind. Winter's coming and he's out of work.

MAX: Well, watch yourself, Henry. (*Pause*) Nice writing though. From now on it's ten dollars a week.

MUSIC: UP AND AWAY

OLD MENCKEN: Thus I gradually took in the massive fact that journalism is not an exact science. I began to appreciate and understand my City Editor . . .

MAX: Henry, you've been here a year. From now on—fourteen bucks a week. But never forget, my boy, that the newspaper business builds its profits on the lifeblood and ambition of youth.

MUSIC: ACCENT

MAX: Henry, m'boy, that was a fine story on the judge and the wife-beater. Did he actually . . . Where's that copy?

SOUND: RUSTLE, RUSTLE

MAX: I quote: "The crime you are accused of committing," thundered Judge Grannan, "is a foul and desperate one, and the laws of all civilized nations prohibit it under heavy penalties. I could send you to prison for life, I could order you to the whipping post, or I could sentence you to be hanged. But inasmuch as this is your first offense, I will be lenient. You will be taken to the House of Correction, and there confined for twenty years. In addition, you are fined $10,000." Henry—did Gene Grannan actually say that—before he suspended sentence on the poor boob?

YOUNG MENCKEN: Well, not exactly. In the bar next door to court, he said he wished . . .

MAX: All right, Henry. (*He chuckles*) Nice story. Nice color. Writing, that's the thing, m'boy. From now on—sixteen dollars a week. But never forget, m'boy, that the newspaper business builds its profits on the lifeblood and ambition of youth.*

* This little saying, believe it or not, used to be the maxim with which the late Dr. Douglas Southall Freeman, Editor of the Richmond *News Leader*, used to close every session of his classes in the Columbia School of Journalism. I have given it to MAX because I like it and it is characteristic.

MUSIC: ACCENT

OLD MENCKEN: By this time, I had begun to reflect upon my trade. It worked me too hard—more than once I produced 5000 words of copy between noon and midnight, not in a single story.

SOUND: SNEAK TYPEWRITER BANGING. YOUNG MENCKEN YELLS "BOY"

But perhaps twelve or fifteen, every one of them requiring some legging. But there were compensations. Max put it best, I think, one night at the Stevedore's Club.

SOUND: BIG BRAWLING PARTY GOING ON

> (*German band in background. Lots of conversation, snatches of singing, and a voice is heard saying . . .*)

MAX: Henry, m'boy— you're a good writer. Too good for this trade. Some day you'll get out.

VOICE: Who touches a hair of your gray head, dies like a dog. March on, he said!

YOUNG MENCKEN: Well, I'd like to do a novel, or a play . . .

MAX: That's right, that's right. But where else, m'boy, where else can you see the show from a reserved seat in the first row? Eh?

YOUNG MENCKEN: You mean life . . .

MAX (*Roaring*): I mean humanity!

VOICE: Two beers?

MAX: Light for me, dark for m'nephew here. (*Pause*) Humanity, Henry! The rest of the boobs have to wait in line and shove for places—but we, we get in by the side door. (*Pause*) Here's to the Fourth Estate! Long may it slave!

MUSIC: SOUSA'S BAND UP AND DOWN BEHIND

SOUND: THE PARTY CONTINUES UPROARIOUSLY AND GOES BEHIND

OLD MENCKEN: The Stevedore's Club. Max proposed me for membership. I shall be grateful as long as my vital juices flow and tongue shall wag. Back in the city room, I learned to drink a potion called hand-set whiskey. The linotypers throve on it . . .

EDITOR (*Whisper*): Don't tell the other boys (*Irish accent*) the secret. You mix wood alcohol, snuff, tobacco sauce, and coffin varnish. It's the varnish gives it the body!

OLD MENCKEN: But in the Stevedore's Club, it was beer. Ah, the sixteen-ounce glass, the five-cent fee!

VOICE: Ten more!

OLD MENCKEN: But the Stevedore's Club. A professional society, it was. Met at Frank Junker's saloon opposite City Hall. Max explained the rules to me ...

MAX: Now the Stevedore's Club, m'boy ...

YOUNG MENCKEN: Why Stevedores, if it's for newspapermen?

MAX: Because the chief occupation is the unloading of schooners. Two, Frank! Light for me, dark for m'nephew! Now the rules are very few and very simple. One: all new members have to set up the drinks ...

YOUNG MENCKEN: Well, all right then ...

MAX: But be careful. They'll try to elect you *twice* in one night. Claim privilege.

YOUNG MENCKEN: Privilege. Right.

MAX: Other rule: guests are allowed to remain only if they treat the house. Guests are not to include musicians unless they bring actors, to whom guest privileges can be accorded by majority vote.

YOUNG MENCKEN: How about that fellow over there, what's he?

MAX: Him? Oh, he's a street cleaner. They're allowed if on Saturday nights proof of bath is furnished.

YOUNG MENCKEN: He seems to know you. He's coming over.

MAX: Never saw him before in m'life. Now another privilege here, reporters get special rates on deviled crabs—five cents apiece.

EDITOR: Say, Max ...

MAX: Now the twenty-five-cent businessmen's lunch is good here, but ...

EDITOR: Max.

MAX: All right, all right. Henry, meet my esteemed colleague, Mr. Walters, City Editor of the opposition paper whose dastard name shall never pass my lips in the company of callow youth. Chuck, my police man—Mencken.

EDITOR: Glad to shake the hand that shook the hand. Listen, Max. That story about the two Congressmen who got into a debate in Miss Nellie's music-room ...

MAX: Oh, yes. I've been wondering about that one.

HENRY: It's accurate, Max. One of them dented the other's skull with a spittoon.

EDITOR: That's the way we got it. Max, are we going to print that? Miss Nellie's got a nice reputation. Do we want to run her music hall down?

MAX: Oh, I wouldn't want to do that, Chuck. Miss Nellie is an awfully good news source.

EDITOR: Of course she is. Now if it's all right with you, I thought we might put the accident up in Mount Vernon Place—

MAX: The most respectable neighborhood in town, fine. All right, I go along with you.

EDITOR: Now about the spittoon . . .

MAX: Let's say one was opening an umbrella and the other turns suddenly.

EDITOR: We can do better than that. Say they got kicked by a runaway hack horse.

YOUNG MENCKEN: Excuse me.

MAX: What is it, m'boy?

YOUNG MENCKEN: Why not make it sound reasonable? Say they slipped on the icy pavement.

EDITOR: All right with me.

MAX: Fine by me, Chuck. Ice it is, Mount Vernon Place. (*Pause*) Set 'em up all around, Frank.

SOUND: THE PARTY GOES ON AND BEHIND

OLD MENCKEN: Thus, the co-operation of the press to protect a respected establishment, Miss Nellie's Music Hall. Scoops? Beats? There were plenty, but when the city editors agreed on the facts, that is how they appeared. Nor ever did one break his word. There is honor among thieves, editors, and sometimes even editorial writers.

MUSIC: UP AND AWAY

OLD MENCKEN: The Stevedore's Club. It was a time of giants, and the club was their stomping ground. Giants of the bended elbow and hollow leg . . .

VOICE (*From out of the babble: It sings*): "How dear to my heart are the scenes of my childhood, when fond recollection, presents them to view." (*A voice or two essays some harmony around the tune, then switches to various other barroom type songs.*)

OLD MENCKEN: Now fond recollection dredges up Printer Bill. Champion beer drinker of the Western Hemisphere. One night in 1902, I saw him get down 32 bottles in a row.

VOICE: Twenty-seven . . . Twenty-eight. . . Twenty-nine . . . Thirty . . . Come on, Bill! Thirty-two! (*A big loud cheer going behind.*)

OLD MENCKEN: What fetched him is still a subject of debate at John Hopkins Medical School.

MUSIC: NOW A PIANO BEGINS TO PLAY SOFTLY BACH'S PRELUDE NUMBER 1

OLD MENCKEN: Giants of the embellished fact, the expanded truth. Like Jones, our telegraph editor . . . claimed to have been a church organist once . . .

JONES: Well, there was the baby in the bank vault . . .

YOUNG MENCKEN: What was the baby doing there, Jonesy?

JONES: Why, Henry, the mother being wealthy had just forgotten about it in her eagerness to get the coupons over to the teller's window. So, they sent for me. I set up my organ in front of the vault . . .

YOUNG MENCKEN: Where'd you get an organ, Jonesy . . .

JONES: Borrowed it from a nearby Sailor's Bethel. Now I fooled around until I found a note that would vibrate steel—and shook the time-lock to pieces.

YOUNG MENCKEN: What ever happened to the baby?

JONES: Grew up to be a Congressman, I believe. Should have left him be. Frank!

MUSIC: UP AND AWAY UNDER

OLD MENCKEN: Jonesy had one failing. He took to handset whiskey on the job (*Sneak sound of telegraph keys*) and began scouring the world for ancestors. (*A little bell rings*) Whenever the AP would announce the death of some eminent man, he'd stagger into the city room with the flimsy, sobbing piteously.

MAX: What's the matter, Jonesy?

JONESY: Terrible thing, Max. Terrible.

MAX: What is it, Jonesy? Let's have it, man.

JONESY: Bismarck is dead.

MAX: Well, what of it? What do you care about him?

JONESY: You don't understand, boss. He was my father.

SOUND: TELEGRAPH KEY UP AND AWAY

OLD MENCKEN: When, in the course of one day's international wire, Jonesy had claimed for his parents a Confederate General, a Boston suffragette, a marshal Lt. Hung Chang—that was November 7, 1901—Max had to let him go. We were amazed when word drifted in that he was actually working as an organist in a Presbyterian church in a poor suburb, claiming to be a son of both John Calvin and John Knox.

MUSIC: THE PIANO UP AND BEHIND

OLD MENCKEN: Giants and sinners, all of us. What we did, we did with great gobs of gusto. It was a time of thoroughness, anyway.

SNEAK SOUND: WATERFRONT NOISES

(*Hooting of steamers, etc. Splashing of water.*)

OLD MENCKEN: I was sent down to the Patapsco to cover a suicide, one day. The unfortunate had been a bar owner. The cop couldn't even spell his last name.

COP: Kuno, old Kuno. The boob made the deal with the artists for free meals and beers if they'd do him a mural on his wall.

YOUNG MENCKEN: What happened?

COP: Well, it druv him to self-destroyal, Henry. At the end of a month, they'd guv him eight square feet of beautiful bims in peek-a-boo chemeesees—but it run him a hundred and twenty meals and five hundred some beers.

VOICE (*Way off*): We got him, we got him!

COP: Let's go, Henry. And take your hat off. The way we make it out, he clumb on the rail, tied a rope to it looped around his neck, swallowed a dose of arsenic, shot himself through the head, then fell or jumped into the river. You always want to say it like that, boy. Fell or jumped. Respect the family's feelin's.

MUSIC: UP AND AWAY

OLD MENCKEN: Sure, we worked sometimes. And hard. Rewrite men were unheard of. Every reporter came back to the office and wrote his story himself. But the *Herald* city room was the most modern in Baltimore. It had two telephones. Occasionally, somebody would get the right number.

SOUND: PHONE RINGS AND IS PICKED UP

YOUNG MENCKEN: *Herald*. Mencken.

MISS NELLIE (*Filter*): Henry? This is Miss Nellie.

YOUNG MENCKEN: Yes, Miss Nellie. How are all the girls?

MISS NELLIE (*Filter*): Fine, fine. But you'd better get down here. The most extraordinary thing has occurred.

YOUNG MENCKEN: Miss Nellie, I will take a hack immediately.

MUSIC: UP AND AWAY

OLD MENCKEN: Miss Nellie had appreciated my part in moving the cuspidorean Congressmen out of her precinct. So she'd called me on this one. *Her* story was succinct.

MISS NELLIE: Peebles the hack driver brung her. He says she gets out of the train and climbs into his cab and says—"Take me to an establishment for fallen women."

YOUNG MENCKEN: So he took her here. Did he say why?

MISS NELLIE: Because she was so young and innercent, and he din't know what to make of her. So with that, she tells me she comes from somewheres near a burg called Red Pion, P.A.

YOUNG MENCKEN: What's her name?

MISS NELLIE: Emmaline Berienblicker. A real redcheek Dutchman. Her father's one of them old rubes with whiskers.

YOUNG MENCKEN: Very strict people.

MISS NELLIE: Yes, sir. Now Emmaline had a beau in York, P.A., name of Elmer, and whenever he could get away from his work as train butcher on the Northern Central, he would come out to the farm and they would do a little hugging and kissing.

YOUNG MENCKEN: Same old story. No horsewhip?

MISS NELLIE: Now wait. Huggin' and kissin' was all they done. And one day, Old Whiskers caught them at it and hollered Emmaline out the house. Now Emmaline was a great one for readin' books. And while she packed her carpetbag, she remembered what girls in books done when they lost their honest name. They rush off to the nearest city, take up a life of shame, then go from booze to dope and die in the gutter. And their name is rubbed out of the Family Bible.

YOUNG MENCKEN: Well, why didn't she go to Philadelphia?

MISS NELLIE: Henry, nobody in their right mind goes to Philadelphia.

YOUNG MENCKEN: What do you want me to do, Miss Nellie? Print the story and ask Papa's forgiveness?

MISS NELLIE: Oh, no. This ain't for printing. I just want you to give the little girl some advising. I got her under lock and key upstairs. Wouldja, Henry? You're a writer. You can do it.

MUSIC: UP AND AWAY

OLD MENCKEN (*Dreamily*): Presently Miss Nellie fetched in Emmaline. She was no Lillian Russell, but she was far from unappetizing, in a country sassage schmierkase kind of way. Miss Nellie set her at her ease and soon she was retelling her story to a strange young man with a celluloid collar. Then, out of my worldly wisdom, I spoke.

YOUNG MENCKEN: My dear Miss Berienblicker—you have been grossly misinformed. I don't know what these works of fiction are that you have read, but they are wrong. The world no longer burns men for heresy, nor women for witchcraft, and it has ceased to condemn girls to lives of shame and death in the gutter for trivial derelictions such as those you acknowledge. The only thing that is frowned upon nowadays is getting caught.

NELLIE: What d'you think Emmy should do, Mr. Mencken?

YOUNG MENCKEN: I advise you to go home, make some plausible excuse to your pa for lighting out, and resume your faithful ministrations to his cows.

NELLIE: Now, you see, honey? Mr. Mencken says go home.

YOUNG MENCKEN: And at the proper opportunity, take your beau to the pastor and join him in indissoluble love. It is the one safe, respectable, and hygienic course. The primrose path, my dear, is not for you. It is beset with thorns, heartburn and corset stays.

MUSIC: UP AND AWAY

OLD MENCKEN: All the ladies of the resident faculty wept copious tears, took up a collection to which I added a dollar, the coachman another, and Miss Nellie ordered a box-lunch for the triumphantly repentant return to the parental pastures. Emma promised to send Miss Nellie a picture postcard of Red Lion showing the new hall of the Knights of Pythias, but it never arrived.

MUSIC: UP AND AWAY BEHIND

SOUND: HUGE NOISE OF DISHES, KNIVES AND FORKS, CHAMPAGNE CORKS POPPING, DINNER MUSIC, DOWN BEHIND

OLD MENCKEN: Yes, we were sinners in the days of the giants. But we felt the wind of the world in our faces, and we saw things with our own eyes. I believed then, and still believe today, that it was the maddest, gladdest, damnedest existence ever enjoyed by mortal youth. I was young, goatish and full of an innocent delight in the world. And tending to put on flesh.

SOUND: BANQUET PATTERN UP AND BEHIND

OLD MENCKEN: For a reporter could fill out the spaces in his belly left unfulfilled by his salary by covering banquets. Shall we ever see the like again?

SOUND: TYPEWRITER UP AND BEHIND

YOUNG HENRY: The dinner of the weekly meeting of the Merchants and Manufacturers' Association included . . . Chesapeake Bay Oysters . . .

SOUND: DISHES

YOUNG HENRY: Chesapeake Bay terrapin.

SOUND: CHAMPAGNE CORK

YOUNG HENRY: Chesapeake Bay wild ducks.

SOUND: WINE POURING

YOUNG MENCKEN: Various wines and champagnes, domestic and imported.

SOUND: MORE DISHES

YOUNG MENCKEN: Then the main course, consisting of Smithfield ham, potato salad, lettuce salad, fried softshell crabs . . .

SOUND: POURING OF LIQUOR

YOUNG MENCKEN: Beer.

SOUND: TYPEWRITER UP AND BEHIND

YOUNG MENCKEN: Harlequin ice cream, coffee, various liqueurs and brandy, and remarks by the Honorable Colonel Robert Cunningham, Confederate Army, retired.

MUSIC: DIXIE UP AND AWAY

OLD MENCKEN: Giants, giants, everywhere. Huge drinkers, vast eaters, cheerful sinners, honest geniuses . . .

SOUND: KNOCKING ON DOOR

HERBERT (*On*): Who is dere?
YOUNG HENRY: The press, Mr. Herbert. Baltimore *Herald*.
HERBERT (*On*): Come in.

SOUND: DOOR OPENS, CLOSES BEHIND

YOUNG HENRY: Sir, I'd just like a few quotations to go with my review of your new operetta. What do you think of our city?
HERBERT (*Bellowing*): Too hot! I wreck five size twenty collars every performance, conducting!
YOUNG HENRY: Ah, what do you think of our hospitality?
HERBERT (*Bellowing*): Rotten. I bring my own Rhine wine mit.
YOUNG HENRY: And to your music, Mr. Herbert. How did you get the idea for the lovely gipsy love-song in tonight's operetta, *The Fortune Teller*?
HERBERT: Damn if I know. They tell me Gene Cowles will sing tenor. I think how high he can holler, how low he can bleat—und I put

some schmier in between. You make you a name once, und anything
you do after, it's wunderschön. Chenius is a happy accident, nicht
wahr? Chohn Philip Sousa, him I envy. Everything goes oompa-
ooompa-ooompa-ooompa. I am a chenius in six-eight, he is a chenius
in two. In the middle is Shtrauss und dere is nobody else.

MUSIC: UP AND AWAY BEHIND, NOW COLORING
MORE TRAGICALLY

OLD MENCKEN: Victor Herbert, Reginald DeKoven, Printer Bill, William Jennings Bryan, Miss Nellie, Julia Marlowe, E. H. Sothern—
men, women, and fools, they were all bigger, those days. And the
stories, too. Bigger and better. I shall never forget my best.

MUSIC: UP AND AWAY INTO

SOUND: SNORING

OLD MENCKEN (*Fondly*): At midnight on Saturday, February 6, 1904
—by which time I was city editor—I put the *Herald* to bed, then
joined the exercises of the Stevedore's Club until 3:30. Catching a
nighthawk trolley, by four o'clock I was snoring on my celibate
couch in Hollins Street.

SOUND: PHONE RINGS. SNORING CHANGES TO A SNORT

OLD MENCKEN: But at eleven A.M. . . . .

SOUND: PHONE PICKED UP

YOUNG HENRY (*Sleepy*): How dare you disturb the peaceful Sabbath?
VOICE (*Filter*): Mr. Mencken, there's a fire down in Hopkins Place . . .
YOUNG HENRY: Let it burn.
VOICE (*Filter*): Sir, it looks like a dingwhistler.
YOUNG HENRY: Then let the dinged thing whistle! This is my day off!
VOICE (*Filter*): Mr. Mencken, sir, the fire department's talking of
sending to Washington for apparatus.
YOUNG HENRY: Well, why didn't you say so in the first place? Send a
hack up while I dress!

MUSIC: UP AND AWAY AND INTO

SOUND: IT SNEAKS, A LITTLE FARTHER ON:

> (*A confused pattern of fire engines, horses' hooves rattling,
> shouts, crackling, the works, the biggest you can put together
> and keep going.*)

OLD MENCKEN: I hoisted my still malty bones from my couch, and ten minutes later I was on my way to the office. That was at about 11:30 A.M. of Sunday, February 7. It was not until 4 A.M. of Wednesday, February 10, that my pants and shoes, or even my collar, came off again.

SOUND: PATTERN UP, DOWN BEHIND

OLD MENCKEN: For what I had walked into was the great Baltimore fire of 1904, which burned a square mile out of the heart of the town and went howling and spluttering on for ten days.

MUSIC: SNEAK GOTTERDAEMMERUNG ALONG
WITH SOUND

OLD MENCKEN: I can remember the eight-column streamer head I wrote, when three days later, burned out, we finally printed in Philadelphia.

SOUND: TYPEWRITERS, PHONES, ETC.,
HOLD CRACKLE BEHIND

YOUNG HENRY (*Exhausted*): Heart of Baltimore wrecked by greatest fire in city's history. (*Pause*) That's what I've always wanted to see. A double bank of stud-horse type.

MUSIC: UP AND AWAY

SOUND: THE FIRE

OLD MENCKEN: We had a story, I am here to tell you! Was there ever one that was fatter, juicier, more exhilarating to the journalists on the actual ground?

YOUNG HENRY (*Over the madhouse*): Apparatus from Washington, Philadelphia, Pittsburgh, New York, every block in midtown on fire—I need men! Cliff, get on the phone, check the bars and the poorhouses, find me printers and reporters!

MUSIC: UP TO COVER

OLD MENCKEN: It was grand beyond an adventure of the first chop, a razzle-dazzle superb and elegant, a circus in forty rings.

YOUNG MENCKEN: All right, close the first edition. If you need 20 pages take 'em. If you need 50, take 50!

VOICE: They're dynamiting in the next block!

SOUND: EXPLOSIONS

YOUNG MENCKEN: All right, everybody out! Everybody! Joe, grab the page proofs. Meek, get the galley proofs . . .

VOICE: Where we going, boss?

YOUNG MENCKEN: The hell out of here. We'll operate out of the Sloane Hotel! Everybody out!

SOUND: HUGE CRASH, THEN INTO

MUSIC: UP AND DOWN BEHIND

OLD MENCKEN: I went into it a boy. It was the hot gas of youth that kept me going.

YOUNG HENRY (*Bawling over racket*): Get me the AP, tell 'em to transfer our wire to Philadelphia . . .

VOICE: Philly? That's a hundred miles away . . .

YOUNG HENRY: I've tried Washington, the *Post* is loaded. We're going to Philly. Get hold of the President of the B. & O., tell him the *Herald* wants a special train to run staff up and papers back! Get on it!

MUSIC: UP AND AWAY, AND DOWN SOFTLY BEHIND

OLD MENCKEN: I went into it a boy. (*Pause*) When I came out of it at last, I was a settled and indeed almost a middle-aged man, spavined by responsibility. When it was all over, I returned to the ruins of the *Herald*.

MUSIC: THIN AND FAR OFF, ALMOST FILTERED, AS IS

OLD MENCKEN: It was easy to find the place where my desk had been.

SOUND: FEET SHUFFLING THROUGH DEBRIS

OLD MENCKEN: The desk itself was a heap of white dust. My clippings were gone, my poems, rejected short stories, spare collars and trolley passes. Even my collection of pieces of hangmen's ropes. I had always intended to present it, sooner or later, to the Smithsonian.

MUSIC: A LITTLE ACCENT

OLD MENCKEN: I did find my old copy-hook, twisted as if it had died in agony. I took it with me.

MUSIC: UP AND AWAY

OLD MENCKEN: I was a man. I was 24 years old. Two years later, in 1906, by then managing editor, I was to read to my staff a notice from the publisher.

YOUNG MENCKEN: Notice. Tomorrow the property of the Herald Publishing Company will pass into new hands, and there will be no further publication of the Sunday *Herald*, the Evening *Herald*, or the Weekly *Herald*.

MUSIC: UP AND AWAY

OLD MENCKEN: In my desk, I had a volume of stories by a new writer named Joseph Conrad. The man could write. His people were sailors, not newspapermen, but they spoke for me.

YOUNG MENCKEN (*Filter*): I remember my youth, and the feeling that will never come back any more—the feeling that I could last forever, outlast the sea, the earth, and all men. Youth. All youth! The silly, charming, beautiful youth!

OLD MENCKEN (*Filter*): *He crossfades in at* "I could last forever," *but we leave the* YOUNG HENRY *in at the same level, so that both, as it were, are speaking now and merged into one.*

SOUND: THE TICKING OF THE CLOCK UP AND DOWN INTO

MUSIC: FROM THE OPENING OF THE PIECE

NARRATOR: The man on the bed has had a stroke. But he shifts his eyes. They fall on a twisted, agonized, old-time copy-hook nearby, on his desk. The eyes find fire somewhere, perhaps purloined from the past. He, a writer who is to be paralyzed, who is never to speak sense again afterward, opens his mouth. And speaks.

OLD MENCKEN (*A sound*): . . . Ummmm. (*An attempt to shape words.*)

NARRATOR (*Quietly*): Yes, Mr. Mencken, what is it?

OLD MENCKEN (*He forces it out*): B—— Bring on the angels!

MUSIC: UP AND AWAY FOR

NARRATOR: The angels will treat him kindly. Why angels and not the more sulphurous visitants? Simply for this alone of all his writings.

OLD MENCKEN, YOUNG MENCKEN (*Together*): If, after I depart this vale, you ever remember me and have thought to please my ghost, forgive some sinner—and wink at a homely girl.

NARRATOR: Henry L. Mencken. 12 September, 1880, 29 January, 1956. Newspaperman.

MUSIC: UP AND AWAY FOR END

The $99,000 Answer

by LEONARD STERN
and SYDNEY ZELINKA

CATEGORY:

Television Situation Comedy

(ONE HALF HOUR)

THE $99,000 ANSWER

by LEONARD STERN and SYDNEY ZELINKA

The $99,000 Answer
was first presented on "THE HONEYMOONERS" program
by Jackie Gleason Enterprises, Inc., on CBS-TV,
under the direction of Frank Satenstein,
on January 28, 1956,
with the following cast:

RALPH KRAMDEN · Jackie Gleason
ALICE KRAMDEN · Audrey Meadows
ED NORTON · Art Carney
TRIXIE NORTON · Joyce Randolph

CBS Television is the owner and
distributor of "The Honeymooners"
series. "The $99,000 Answer," © 1957,
Columbia Broadcasting System, Inc.
All rights reserved.

As curtains part camera holds on establishing shot of stage setting for $99,000 Answer Show. Big Banner says "$99,000 Answer." Should be standard quiz show set of type used on audience participation shows. Center stage are MC and a male contestant. Contestant is bright-looking, conservatively dressed man in his middle forties. Music Playoff.

ANNOUNCER'S VOICE: Now back to Herb Norris and the $99,000 Answer . . . the show that gives away ninety-nine thousand dollars!

MC: Well, Mr. Parker, you have successfully gone over the $4,750 hurdle and now and it is time to make up your mind whether you are willing to go for the $9,500 answer.

PARKER: I am, Mr. Norris. (*Audience reaction.*)

MC: Good. I wish you luck, Mr. Parker. If you complete the $9,500 answer you will then be eligible to come back next week and try to clear the last hurdle for the $99,000 answer. Mr. Parker, are you ready?

PARKER: I'm ready, Mr. Norris.

MC: Fine, this question for your $9,500 answer was prepared by an expert in the field of banking and finance . . . Professor Walter Newman. Your question has to do with something you see and handle every day—a dollar bill. Now, disregarding the serial number, tell me how many times the figure "ONE" appears on a dollar bill, either in numeral form or spelled out. I'll repeat that. How many times does the figure one appear on a dollar bill, either in numeral form or spelled out! Give me the total and then tell me how many there are . . . you have fifteen seconds to give the $9,500 answer. . . . Your time is up! What is your answer?

MUSIC OUT

PARKER: The total number is twenty-five.

MC: That's correct!

PARKER: Sixteen times for the word "ONE" and nine times for the numeral "ONE."

MC: You're absolutely right!

LIGHTS UP—MUSIC—APPLAUSE—

MC: Mr. Parker, you've won yourself $9,500 of those one-dollar bills and you are now eligible to come back next week when you have the choice of taking the $9,500 or going for the last hurdle and $99,000! Good-bye—Good luck. (*Applause, music playoff as* PARKER *exits.*) And now, who is our next guest? (*A shot of a petrified* KRAMDEN *being led from wings by a lovely young girl. Over this shot,* AN-NOUNCER'S *voice speaks.*)

ANNOUNCER'S VOICE: Herb, here's our next guest ready to leap the first hurdle on his way to the $99,000 answer . . . from Brooklyn, New York . . . Mr. Ralph Kramden! (*Applause.* RALPH *is now standing downstage with* MC.)

MC: How do you do, Mr. Kramden. (*As* MC *extends hand,* RALPH *grabs for it as though it were a life preserver and continues to shake it in his nervousness.*)

RALPH: Buh—Buh— (MC *sizing up situation and anxious to get his hand back.*)

MC: Mr. Kramden, there's nothing for you to be nervous about. We're all your friends and everybody's rooting for you. (RALPH *nods with weak smile but keeps shaking* MC's *hand*) Just relax, Mr. Kramden. (RALPH *nods but keeps shaking hand*) It's certainly been nice shaking hands with you, Mr. Kramden. (RALPH *suddenly comes to his senses.*)

RALPH: Oh, buh, buh . . . buh . . . (RALPH *lets go of* MC's *hand and for a moment is at a loss as to what to do with his free hand.*)

MC: What kind of work do you do, Mr. Kramden?

RALPH: I'm a brus diver.

MC: A brus diver??

RALPH: Yeah. I brive a dus.

MC: Oh, you drive a bus!

RALPH: That's what I said, I'm a dus briver!

MC: Mr. Kramden, I can understand you being nervous, but it will be to your advantage to relax and calm yourself. Just remember we're all friends and I'm here to help you. (RALPH *smiles appreciatively*) Are you married, Mr. Kramden? (RALPH *nods "yes"*) What's your wife's name?

RALPH: Kramden.

MC (*Helpfully*): Her first name.

RALPH: Her—oh!—Alice!

MC: And you're from Brooklyn . . . have you lived in Brooklyn all your life?

RALPH: Er—not yet.

MC (*Amused*): I see . . . Mr. Kramden, I've always had great respect for the bus drivers of New York. It's been a constant source of wonderment to me how you men who have those huge buses to handle, and all the responsibilities that go with it, can remain as courteous and considerate as you do.

RALPH: Thank you, sir.

MC: Of course there always are exceptions to the rule—like what happened to me the other day. It was raining and I was waiting on Madison Avenue for a bus. Finally a bus came along and I signaled the driver. Not only did that driver ignore my signal, but he drove right by me through a puddle and splashed mud all over me!

RALPH: Was that you?

MC (*Good-naturedly*): Well. I hope you win some money . . . I've got a cleaning bill for you . . . Now, Mr. Kramden, it's time to choose your category from our list of subjects. (*Girl holds up cardboard for* RALPH *to look at; it has fifteen categories*) Take your time in picking your category because all your answers will be based on the category you decide upon.

RALPH: I think I'll take popular songs.

MC: Very well, popular songs.

ANNOUNCER'S VOICE: I'm sorry to interrupt, Herb, but our time is up.

MC: Mr. Kramden, I'm sorry but if you come back next week, you'll get your chance to reach the first hurdle and work your way up to the $99,000 answer . . . Can you be here?

RALPH: Yeah . . . Sure . . . Yes, sir!

MC: Thank you for being with us on the $99,000 answer. We look forward to seeing you next week. Good night. And good night, everyone.

MUSIC—PLAYOFF—DISSOLVE

> As curtains part camera holds on establishing shot of KRAMDEN kitchen. ALICE is in process of removing her coat. Door opens, a breathless TRIXIE enters.

TRIXIE: Alice! Oh, Alice! I couldn't wait until you got home. Ralph looked wonderful on television!

ALICE: Trix, it was so exciting.

TRIXIE: I'll bet. (TRIXIE *looks around*) Isn't Ralph here?

ALICE: He decided to stay downstairs. He's waiting for people to go by and recognize him.

TRIXIE: Who can recognize him at this hour? It's dark out. (ALICE *takes* TRIXIE *to window.*)

ALICE: He thought of that. (*Points out window*) There he is standing under the street light with his hat off!

TRIXIE: Well, on second thought, I don't know if I'd act any different, if I was on a big television program and I was seen by millions of people.

ALICE: Don't get me wrong, Trix. I'm real proud that Ralph's on the show. The only thing is that he gets over-enthused—runs away with himself. He can build himself way up to a let down and then he'll feel miserable.

TRIXIE: Yeah.

ALICE: Here he's acting like he's already given the 99,000-dollar answer and he hasn't even been asked the first question!

TRIXIE: Gee, wouldn't it be great if Ralph won 99,000 dollars?

ALICE: Take it easy, Trix. Let's be practical. Even Ralph knows he's no expert. The first two questions usually aren't so tough. If he can answer those and walk away with six hundred dollars, I'll be more than happy.

TRIXIE: You're right. Six hundred dollars can come in mighty handy . . . but just between us, Alice, you'd better hint to Ralph to always face the camera. When he stands in profile—brother! He's the biggest thing on television! (TRIXIE *goes to door as* ALICE *laughs good-naturedly.*)

ALICE: How about Ed, did he see the show?

TRIXIE: Yeah. He watched it with the boys over at the bowling alley. He'll probably stop in and see Ralph on his way upstairs. Night, Alice. See you tomorrow.

ALICE: Night,Trix. (TRIXIE *goes out.* TRIXIE *closes door behind her.* ALICE *picks up coat and carries it into bedroom.* RALPH *comes in. He's carrying large piece of cardboard. The blank side is visible.* ALICE *comes out of bedroom.*)

RALPH: Well, Alice, I've finally learned a lesson. This house is filled with nothing but jealous people.

ALICE: What are you talking about?

RALPH: There wasn't one person in this house, not one, waiting downstairs to congratulate me! They won't admit they saw me on the program.

ALICE: Ralph, don't talk that way. Norton watched it over at the bowling alley with all your friends and Trixie was just here to say she saw you.

RALPH (*Brightens*): Oh, she saw me. How'd she like me? How'd she think I was?

ALICE: She says you're the biggest thing on television!

RALPH: She said that? Nice girl, Trixie. And that Norton's a good guy too. They're real, true friends. Alice, they're gonna be with me when I celebrate my big night.

ALICE: What big night?

RALPH: When I win the 99,000 dollars! (ALICE *is struck speechless by* RALPH's *crazy confidence*) Yessiree, Alice. Soon we'll be livin' on Park Avenue. And just you wait and see how different this furniture'll look in a Park Avenue apartment! (ALICE *has to flag him down.*)

ALICE: Ralph, aren't you being a little too ambitious? You've heard some of the questions . . . they get awfully tough after the first two.

RALPH: Why do you think I picked popular songs as my category? I know all about them songs.

ALICE: But, Ralph, you're not an expert.

RALPH: Oh, no? I was interested in songs even when I was a little kid. And when I grew up I didn't waste my time like the other guys. While they were bumming around street corners and pool rooms . . . I spent every night of the week up at Roseland!

ALICE: Ralph, I'll be very proud of you if you just answer the first two questions and come home with six hundred dollars.

RALPH: Six hundred dollars! That's pennies!

ALICE: Ralph, I'm only talking common sense.

RALPH: Common sense? It's common sense to blow the opportunity of a lifetime? Look, I'll explain it to you real simple. (*He illustrates by putting imaginary piles of money on table*) Right over here is six hundred dollars. Over here is ninety-nine thousand dollars. I have a choice of taking either one of the two. Now my intelligence tells me that I gotta take the ninety-nine thousand. But if you're foolish enough to think I'm wrong, just tell me because I got an open mind!

ALICE: Well, you better close it before the rest of your brains fall out! . . . Stop dreaming, Ralph. They don't hand you that ninety-nine thousand. You've got to answer questions. And they're tough questions!

RALPH: Oh, so that's what you've been leading up to. Your husband's too dumb to answer questions. A twelve-year-old little girl can come on another program and win $16,000 but it comes out now you don't think I'm as smart as a twelve-year-old kid. Well, for your information, I can answer the toughest question they can think up because it stands to reason I gotta be smarter than any twelve-year-old kid!

ALICE: Spell Antidisestablishmentarianism. (RALPH *stares at* ALICE *for a split second.*)

RALPH: I can spell it. I can spell it, all right.

ALICE: Well, go ahead.

RALPH: Why should I? I'll spell it when you can give me sixteen thousand dollars for spelling it.

ALICE: Sixteen thousand for spelling it? I'll give you thirty-two thousand dollars if you can *say* it!

RALPH (*Reacts*): All right. All right, I will . . . some day.

ALICE: Ralph, I don't doubt you know a lot about popular songs. Let's even say you know *everything* about them. There's still one thing you're overlooking. That when you're on a television show, under pressure, with millions of people looking at you and with big money at stake, you're liable to get nervous and forget what you know. Any person could do that.

RALPH: Not this person. When I'm under pressure I'm at my best. I never get nervous.

ALICE: Oh, that's right, I forgot. You're always calm. You have to be in the work you do. You're a man who *brives a dus*. (RALPH *grunts*.)

RALPH: Alice, nothing you say is gonna make me change my mind. I'm gonna win that $99,000 and to make sure I do I ain't gonna leave a stone unturned. I'm staying home every night this week. I'm gonna study all the books on songs and songwriters. I'm gonna study every piece of sheet music. I'm gonna buy phonograph records. And that ain't all. I'm gonna rent a piano so that Norton can come down and play the tunes until I'm sure that I can recognize every one of them.

ALICE: Ralph, that's gonna cost a fortune. It'll take every cent we have saved. We'll have nothing in the bank.

RALPH: We'll have $99,000 in the bank . . . you ain't talking me out of it, Alice. I'm going for that pot of gold!

ALICE: Just go for the gold—you've already got the pot! (ALICE *turns and exits into bedroom, slamming door behind her.* RALPH *shouts at closed door.*)

> As curtains part, camera holds on establishing shot of KRAM-
> DEN *kitchen. Changes have been wrought. There's a piano
> upstage right, a portable hand-crank Victrola is strategically
> placed and piles of sheet music and records stacked all over
> the place. There's a knock on door.* ALICE *comes out of bed-
> room in robe and slippers. She goes to door and opens it.*

ALICE: Mother, what are you doing here at this hour?

MOTHER (*Hands* ALICE *a package*): Here's the dress material that you wanted.

ALICE: Oh, you didn't have to make a special trip for that, Mother.

MOTHER: I didn't. We went to a movie in the neighborhood, so it wasn't out of the way at all.

ALICE: Sit down. Have a cup of coffee.

MOTHER: I can't. Your father's waiting in the car. He's double parked. (MOTHER *looks around and takes the place in*) How's the brain doing?

ALICE: What a week! The piano and phonograph have been going every night until three in the morning. He's been fighting out the window with Mr. Garrity upstairs. Strangers have been stopping in to give him advice. He's gotten letters. Staying home from work without salary, paying for all this stuff? He'll have to win the $99,000 to cover expenses.

MOTHER: Where is he now?

ALICE: He's down at Mrs. Manicotti's. She's helping him brush up on all the popular songs that have been taken from Italian classics. This boy isn't missing a trick.

MOTHER: I've got to go. I'll keep my fingers crossed for Ralph tomorrow night.

ALICE: Thanks. Say hello to Pop. (*As* ALICE's *mother goes to door, it opens and* RALPH *comes in.*)

RALPH (*Sees* ALICE's *mother. His enthusiasm disappears immediately*): Alice, I was perfect. I . . . Oh, hello, Mother.

MOTHER: Hello, Ralph. Well, tomorrow's your big night. Alice and I were talking about it and there's just one thing I want to say . . .

RALPH: Save your breath! I know what you're gonna say and I ain't gonna do it! I ain't quittin' at six hundred bucks. I might've known you'd both get together to work on me. Well, Mrs. Buttinsky, you're wasting your time 'cause I'm goin' all the way.

MOTHER: But, Ralph, before you interrupted me, I was about to say I hoped you'd go for the $99,000 answer. (RALPH *is taken aback by* MOTHER's *statement.*)

RALPH: Oh . . . oh . . . you hear that, Alice? Why don't you listen to your mother once in a while? She's a smart woman. (*Pleased.*)

MOTHER: As a matter of fact, I can't wait for you to answer that question . . . want to see the expression on your face when you miss it. (MOTHER *hurries out and slams door.*)

RALPH: That does it! That does it! When we move to Park Avenue, I ain't givin' her our new address!

ALICE: Ralph, I must be crazy to even argue with you about this. You've got us living on Park Avenue, winning $99,000—Ralph, you haven't even answered the first question!

RALPH: There you go, tearing me down and upsetting me at a time like this. Mrs. Edward R. Murrow wouldn't act this way!

ALICE: What's Mrs. Edward R. Murrow got to do with this?

RALPH: Her husband's got a television show, too. (ALICE *looks at him as though this is the end. She's heard everything.*)

ALICE: I'm going to bed. (ALICE *goes into bedroom. Closes door.* RALPH *yells at closed door.*)

RALPH (*Shouts*): The truth hurts! (RALPH *crosses to piano and riffs through songs on top. Door opens and* NORTON *enters, singing happily. He is carrying an armful of sheet music.*)

NORTON (*Singing*): "Give me land, lots of land, deedle, deedle, deedle, dee—don't deedle dee . . ."

RALPH: "Don't fence me in" . . . written by Cole Porter . . . from the picture *Hollywood Canteen*, produced by Warner Brothers in 1944.

NORTON: When that master of ceremonies gets to you, Ralph, he's gonna run out of hurdles! How'd you do at Mrs. Manicotti's?

RALPH: I left her speechless. She kept trying to stick me, but I knew the English name for every song she sang in Italian.

NORTON: I picked up some more movie songs to try out on you.

RALPH: Well, come on, play them. I want to see if I know them.

NORTON: Okay, okay. (*He puts sheet music on rack; hand routine, loosening of fingers, etc.*)

RALPH: Will you come on! This is the last night I got. (NORTON *starts to play Swanee River and picks up.* RALPH *shoves him*) There you go again. You can't play a song without starting with that. (*Hums "Swanee River"*) Why do you have to do that?

NORTON: If I've explained it once, I've explained it a hundred times. It's the only way I can play the piano. A baseball pitcher's gotta warm up before he pitches—I gotta warm up before I play! . . . I hope I don't have to explain again! You ready?

RALPH: Yeah. (NORTON *plays "Swanee River" and pick up into "Shuffle Off to Buffalo"*) "Shuffle Off to Buffalo" by Warren and Dubin from *Forty-Second Street*. 1932.

NORTON: Perfect. Now hear this. (NORTON *plays "Swanee River" and pick up into "Too Marvelous for Words."*)

RALPH: "Too Marvelous for Words" by Johnny Mercer and Richard Whiting from *Ready, Willing and Able*, 1937.

NORTON: Right again. This is a tricky one, Ralph. Goes back a way. (RALPH *sings.* NORTON *plays Swanee and pick up into "Melancholy Serenade" fast tempo. It is interrupted by loud pounding at door.* RALPH *goes to door. It's* GARRITY.)

GARRITY: Shut up in here. You're driving everyone crazy!

RALPH: Oh, so it's you, Garrity. You're jealous, Garrity. You're jealous because tomorrow my picture's gonna be on the front page of every newspaper.

GARRITY: So will mine . . . for killing you! (GARRITY *leaves, slamming door behind him.* ALICE *appears in doorway.*)

ALICE: Ralph! (RALPH *opens door and shouts down hall after* GARRITY.)

RALPH: Ya satisfied, loud mouth! Now you woke up my wife! (*As* RALPH *comes back from door,* ALICE *addresses* NORTON.)

ALICE: Ed, I realize I can't talk to Ralph because he's stubborn and unreasonable. I've always had respect for your sense of fair play, so I appeal to you. It's late and people want to go to sleep. I think you ought to stop playing the piano. I'm sure you agree with me because you've always been fair and considerate—a reasonable man! (NORTON *caught between the devil and the deep blue sea looks from one to the other.*)

RALPH: Don't let her soft soap you. You're just as unreasonable as I am. Go ahead and play the piano!

ALICE: If you touch that piano again, I'll lose all my respect for you!

RALPH: Play that piano or our friendship is over! (*Poor* ED. *He looks from one to the other.*)

NORTON: If I play the piano I lose your respect. If I don't play the piano I lose your friendship. (*He looks heavenward, arms extended and speaks beseechingly*) Why, oh, why was I blessed with this musical talent? (*There's a knock on door.*)

ALICE: I wouldn't be surprised if that's the police. (ALICE *opens door.* MRS. MANICOTTI *enters*) Mrs. Manicotti! (MRS. MANICOTTI, *a woman with a purpose, looks right at* RALPH *and blasts out in opera style. Tune is "Come Back to Sorrento."*)

MRS. MANICOTTI: Guarda il mare come bello, spira tanto sentimento . . .

RALPH (*Proudly*): "Come Back to Sorrento" written by Ernesto Dicurtis in 1898.

MRS. MANICOTTI: I give up. (*Throws her hands up in the air and goes. Closes door.*)

ALICE: The whole house has gone crazy!

RALPH: Crazy? She's crazy because she helps me and roots for me? That's more than I can say for you!

ALICE: I've been trying to help you by being sensible. If you had listened to me you could have avoided all this pressure you're putting on yourself.

RALPH: For the last time, I'm going for $99,000!

ALICE: For the last time, I'd be very proud of you if you won six hundred.

RALPH: Six hundred bucks is peanuts! Peanuts! What am I gonna do with peanuts?

GARRITY'S VOICE: Eat them—like any other elephant! (RALPH *charges to window and opens it.*)

RALPH (*To* GARRITY): Garrity, when I move to Park Avenue, you'll be singing a different tune.

GARRITY'S VOICE: Yeah. "Happy Days Are Here Again" written by Yellen and Ager, 1929! (RALPH *slams down window, infuriated. He glares at* ALICE *and* NORTON.)

RALPH: Start playing, Norton. (NORTON *starts playing "Swanee River" intro.*)

RALPH: Oh ... No! (*... and sinks in despair.*)

DISSOLVE

As curtains part camera holds on establishing shot of 99,000 *set. Same as in scene one. As music dissolves,* MC *starts entrance.*

ANNOUNCER'S VOICE: . . . And now—the star of our show—Herb Norris! (*Audience applause.*)

MC: Thank you, and welcome to America's most exciting quiz show— the 99,000 answer. Tom, who is our first guest?

ANNOUNCER'S VOICE: Herb, our next guest ready to leap the first hurdle on his way to the 99,000 answer is our bus driver from Brooklyn, Mr. Ralph Kramden! (*Applause.* RALPH *is led down ramp by girl.*)

MC: Hello, Mr. Kramden. Nice to see you again.

RALPH: Thank you.

MC: Last week we just had time enough to get as far as picking your category—you picked popular songs.

RALPH: That's right, sir.

MC: Well, you had a whole week to prepare yourself. Did you do much studying?

RALPH: Oh, just a little.

MC: You mean just in your spare time.

RALPH: Yes, sir.

MC: Well, let's get on with our little competition. (*Girl brings questions to* HERB.) I have here your first question. Now, Mr. Kramden, you know how the 99,000 answer works. We start with the first question, which is our lowest hurdle. You get that right and get $100. Then you go over our second hurdle which is worth 600. After that our hurdles become higher and our questions naturally a little harder. Our third hurdle is worth $6,187.50, and if you answer that right, you will have a total of $12,375. Then we keep doubling until you finally get to the $99,000 hurdle. Any time you feel like stopping you can do so and keep whatever you have won. Of course if you miss, you go home empty-handed. Is that clear, Mr. Kramden?

RALPH: Yes, sir. But if it's all right with you I'd like to make a statement.

MC: Certainly. Go right ahead.

RALPH: I've made up my mind I'm going for the $99,000! (*Audience applause.*)

MC: Mr. Kramden, you don't have to make that decision now. You can decide as you go along.

RALPH: I know but I've already made up my mind.

MC: Have you discussed this at home? Have you talked it over with your wife?

RALPH: Yeah . . . but I'm goin' for it anyway! Making up my mind now's gonna save me a lot of headaches.

MC: That's quite a decision to come to. You certainly must know your popular songs.

RALPH: Yes, sir. And this way everything's settled. I know, you know and everybody lookin' in knows I ain't stoppin' until I've won the $99,000!

MC: I wish you the best of luck and here's your first question for $100. (*He reads from card*) Tell me, Mr. Kramden, who is the composer of "Swanee River"?

RALPH: "Swanee River"?

MC: (*Off to piano player*): José—a few bars of "Swanee River," please. (*Music off. Scene on piano only. "Swanee River." RALPH looks as if he's never heard of it. RALPH does eye bulge.*)

RALPH: That's Swanee River?

MC: Yes. Now who wrote it? (*RALPH is speechless*) Your time is almost up. Who wrote it? Make a stab at it. Take a guess!

RALPH: Ed Norton?

MC: Oh, I'm terribly sorry, Mr. Kramden, the right answer is Stephen Foster. But at least you have the satisfaction of knowing you have been a good contestant and a good sport. Good-bye, Mr. Kramden.

RALPH (*Looks lost at him*): Buh . . . buh . . . (*As jovial as possible, MC wants RALPH to leave.*)

MC: Well, Mr. Kramden . . . I'll be seeing you. (*RALPH half dazed automatically answers what he thinks of as a song title.*)

RALPH: "I'll Be Seeing You." A hit song written in 1938 by Irving Kale and Sammy Fain!

MC: But, Mr. Kramden . . . it's all over now.

RALPH: "It's All Over Now" words and music by Bazzy Simon. 1927.

MC: Good Night, Mr. Kramden, Good Night. (MC *motions off to* GIRL *assistant to come and help.*)

RALPH: There are two good nights. "Good Night, Irene" written by Lomax and Leadbetter and "Good Night, Sweetheart" by Rudy Vallee and Ray Noble and . . . (*The* GIRL *now has* RALPH *by arm.*)

GIRL: Please. This way, sir. Please.

RALPH (*As he is being led off*): "Please" sung by Bing Crosby in *Big Broadcast of* 1933. By Robins and Ranger. (*As they lead poor* RALPH *off camera.*)

BLACKOUT

She Walks in Beauty

by KENNETH KOLB

CATEGORY:

Television Episodic Drama

(ONE HALF HOUR)

SHE WALKS IN BEAUTY

by KENNETH KOLB

She Walks in Beauty
was first presented on the MEDIC program on NBC,
under the direction of John Brahm
with the following cast:

AINSLIE PRYOR · JAMES KARATH
ANNE STANTON · CARVLE WELLS
SAM FLINT · ANTHONY CARUSO
RICHARD BOONE

© Copyright, 1956
by Medic TV Productions, Inc.

FADE IN: DR. KONRAD STYNER—MEDIUM SHOT

(*The background is unrecognizable.*)

STYNER: Konrad Styner—Doctor of Medicine. Our story has the title: *She Walks in Beauty.*

FADE OUT

CLOSE UP—CENTER OF SHIELD

(*It contains a gnarled staff with a single serpent twined around it. The figure of the staff and serpent is in relief, finely wrought in metal. It is executed in scrupulous detail.*)

VOICE (*Off stage*): And the qualities of the worthy physician are three...

(*Camera pulls back slowly, revealing the entire shield. It is a detailed piece of metalwork hanging against a backdrop of rich drapery. The shield is marked off in thirds, all sections equal. The upper right portion contains the head of a lion. The upper left, the head of an eagle. The lower third contains the hand of a woman. All the figures are in relief, finely detailed. Lighting is low-key. Camera holds on shield.*)

VOICE (*Off stage*): ... the heart of a lion ... the eye of an eagle ... the hand of a woman.

(*The single word "MEDIC" is superimposed. The letters fill the entire screen.*)

FADE OUT

FADE IN: DR. KONRAD STYNER—MEDIUM CLOSE SHOT

STYNER: Our presentation tonight, the field of orthopedics. The object in point ... (*Displaying*) a book of poems. The case in point: Jenny Fallgren. She's twelve years old, in good general health, and happy as only a child on summer vacation can be. She has no idea that this will be the most important year of her life ...

DISSOLVE TO

INTERIOR FALLGREN LIVING ROOM—DAY—MEDIUM SHOT—GRACE FALLGREN

(*The living room is that of a low-middle income family in a small town. It is comfortably but inexpensively furnished. A stairway rises on one side of the room; the stairs are uncarpeted. A couple of windows are open, perhaps even the front door, which is covered by a screen door. MRS. GRACE FALLGREN is arranging flowers by a front window. She is a woman in her mid-thirties, growing a trifle plump; dark hair, pleasant face. She wears a summer cotton dress. After only a few seconds of this, she hears footsteps on the front porch.* GRACE *looks out, reacts in surprise, then goes out on the porch.*)

EXTERIOR FRONT PORCH—DAY

GRACE: You're early!

HENRY: The peeler broke down . . . Too late to fix it till tomorrow. (HENRY FALLGREN *moves in on this line. He is a year-round worker and summer foreman at the local canning plant. He is medium height, wide-shouldered and well-muscled, a man who has worked all his life at some sort of physical labor. He wears a pair of work pants and a work shirt open at the neck, sleeves rolled up. He carries two large, plump pears in his hands.*)

GRACE: Better now than later in the season . . . Is the fruit any good yet?

HENRY (*Extending a pear to her*): Fine! Some of the peaches are a little green still, but I've eaten a dozen of these things today . . . Thought you and Jenny'd like a taste.

GRACE (*Taking pear*): They look good. I just put dinner in the oven. It'll be an hour yet. (*She sits on the porch swing, dabbing at her face and neck. The kitchen has made her over-warm.*)

HENRY: I'm not too hungry yet. Anyway, it's cooler out here . . . (*He sits on the rail*) Where's Jenny?

GRACE: Up in her room, reading—as usual.

HENRY (*Smiling*): More poetry?

GRACE (*Nodding*): What else?

> (*Suddenly we hear the sound of* JENNY's *footsteps inside. Her steps form an irregular rhythm, halting—a quick step then a slow one.* HENRY *turns toward the sound, moves toward the screen door, half opens it.*)

HENRY (*Calling in*): Hi, punkin'!

JENNY (*Appearing on the line*): Hi, Dad! (HENRY *catches her in his arms, lifts her delightedly.*)

JENNY: What'cha doin' home early?

HENRY: Peeler broke down. Where's my kiss? (*She kisses him, and he makes elaborate groans at her tight hug. He puts her down.* JENNY *moves to the rail. She limps as she walks, but not badly, not enough to slow her down. She is a very pretty girl, rather thin, with delicate features and large, expressive eyes. She is twelve, a great reader, very*

SHE WALKS IN BEAUTY

sharp for her age, with quite a mature outlook. She wears a shirt and a pair of jeans.)

HENRY (*After embrace*): My little bookworm . . . You weren't reading lying down, were you?

JENNY: Huh-uh. At my desk.

HENRY: That's right. Bad for your eyes to read lying down. You hold the book too close.

JENNY (*Affectionately*): I know. You told me a dozen times.

HENRY: Brought ya something . . . (*He produces the pear, which he has kept hidden from her. JENNY shows pleased surprise, bounces off the rail.*)

JENNY: Oh boy! . . . Thanks. (*They both sit on the rail; GRACE watches them tenderly. JENNY brings the pear to her mouth and opens her jaws around it for a delicious bite.*)

GRACE: Ah, ah, ah, young lady. Not till after dinner. (*JENNY is just starting to bite as her mother's warning catches her. Her mouth remains opened longingly, but she is obviously going to obey.*)

GRACE: We're going to eat in an hour. You'll spoil your dinner. (*JENNY reluctantly lowers the pear from her mouth. She shines it on the leg of her jeans, then regards it briefly before handing it over to GRACE, who has moved in for it.*)

GRACE (*Going in*): I'll set the table.

JENNY (*Following GRACE into the house*): Can I go over to Dick's and play till dinner?

INTERIOR THE LIVING ROOM—DAY

(*GRACE deposits the pear in a bowl; HENRY has followed JENNY in.*)

GRACE: All right . . . but don't get any farther away. (*JENNY starts, gets almost to the door, then remembers something. She turns back to HENRY.*)

JENNY: Dick and I decided to get married. (*Her delivery is very matter-of-fact. A simple question settled. HENRY's eyebrows rise, but he quickly conceals his surprise and amusement.*)

HENRY (*Gravely*): Right away?

JENNY: Of course not! When we grow up.

HENRY: Do you think Dick can support you all right?

JENNY: Sure, he's gonna be a pilot and I'm gonna be a stewardess.

HENRY: Then I approve. Can I be best man?

JENNY: No, silly! You have to give me away. Haven't you ever seen a wedding?

HENRY: Only my own . . . and I was very nervous then.

JENNY: Oh! You're always fooling. (*Her tone is one of slight impatience mixed with tolerant amusement for this father who cannot comprehend a serious subject. She moves to the door, her hand upon it.*)

HENRY: What does your mother think of your engagement?

JENNY: I told her already. She said it's fine, if I can stand my mother-in-law.

GRACE (*Reprovingly*): Jenny! (*But* JENNY *is out the door and away.* GRACE *stares after her for a moment, then meets* HENRY's *eye. He is grinning broadly. In a second,* GRACE *gives a half-embarrassed smile.*)

INTERIOR LIVING ROOM—ANOTHER ANGLE—GRACE, HENRY

(*As* HENRY *moves to a small table, picks up the afternoon paper and settles himself in the armchair opposite the couch.*)

HENRY: Have to be careful what you say. She doesn't forget a thing. (*He unfolds the paper in front of him and starts to read.* GRACE *is looking at the front door, vaguely troubled. There is silence for a few seconds.*)

GRACE (*Bit troubled*): She's growing up so fast lately.

HENRY (*After pause, preoccupied*): Uh-huh.

GRACE: I found her trying out my lipstick the other day . . .

HENRY (*Still reading*): Oh? . . . What'd you do?

GRACE: Nothing, of course . . . There's no harm in it. But it gave me a shock when I looked at her.

HENRY: Must've looked like a clown.

CLOSE SHOT—GRACE

(*As she continues to work at her darning. Her face is deeply and genuinely troubled.*)

GRACE: No . . . she didn't. She looked like a young lady. (*Pause*) Now she's talking about getting married.

MEDIUM CLOSE SHOT—HENRY

(*As he reluctantly lowers his paper and looks at* GRACE. *He obviously does not want to be drawn into this discussion, but the seriousness of* GRACE's *tone compels him. He forces an amused laugh, then:*)

HENRY: When I was twelve I was gonna marry Flora Beesgartner and go be a fireman in Des Moines . . .

INTERIOR LIVING ROOM—MEDIUM SHOT—GRACE, HENRY

GRACE: I know it's only kid stuff . . . but . . . one day you watch them play at being grown-ups. You turn away—it seems for a moment only—and when you look again they've grown—suddenly.

HENRY: Don't worry. She's got years to think about marrying Dick— or anybody.

GRACE (*Quietly*): If she'll *ever* marry.

HENRY (*Startled*): What? (GRACE *puts down her darning. She hates what she knows she has to say.* HENRY *senses what is coming. They look at each other tensely for a moment.*)

GRACE: Who would there be? Who'll marry a girl with a club foot? (*The blow has fallen.* HENRY *folds his paper and thrusts it away with finality. His face is grave.*)

HENRY: Look, Grace, we've been all through this . . .

GRACE: We *haven't* been through it. We talked about it a hundred times. But it was always something off in the dim future . . . a problem we'd have to face someday . . . (*With despair*) Now it's here. She's not just a kid with a limp any more. She's a young lady with an ugly deformity. (*These words cost* GRACE *a terrible effort. But she has been worrying about the problem all day—since* JENNY'S *announcement—and she is determined to state it in the bluntest possible way. The words strike* HENRY *like blows. He breathes deeply, abruptly rises, walks to the open screen door and looks out till he can regain control of himself. There are tears in* GRACE'S *eyes*) We can't go on putting it off, Henry . . . (*He goes on fighting for control, becoming more and more subdued*) You can't pretend you haven't been worried about it—I've seen it . . . (*Pause.* HENRY *returns. There is no conviction in his protests.*)

HENRY: She still seems like such a baby to me.

GRACE: Only because you want her to be. So do I. But we can't fool ourselves much longer. We've got to do something.

HENRY: What?

GRACE: Someth·ing we should've done long before this. (*She looks over at the phone, and he follows her eyes, looking too.*)

INTERIOR LIVING ROOM—ANOTHER ANGLE—GRACE, HENRY

(*Camera shooting from point near telephone table as* HENRY *crosses to it. He moves slowly, reluctantly. He picks up the*

> *telephone receiver, dials one number, then breaks the con-*
> *nection with his finger. Still holding the receiver, he turns to*
> GRACE.)

HENRY: She's so happy now . . . Can't we wait? . . . Just a little longer?

GRACE (*Looking up*): Until she really wants to get married? There'll be dates—*real* dates, sooner than you think . . . and then the *real* humiliation begins . . . one hurt after another . . . How long will she take *that* before she starts to hate us?

MEDIUM CLOSE SHOT—HENRY, PHONE

> (*As his face reflects his decision. Abruptly, he begins to dial the phone, his fingers moving swiftly.*)

DISSOLVE TO

INTERIOR FALLGREN LIVING ROOM—MEDIUM SHOT— GRACE, HENRY, DR. BAIRD

> (*They are seated in conversation as scene opens.* GRACE *and* HENRY *have changed clothes. They are better dressed than we saw them yesterday, but still informal.* DR.BAIRD *is about fifty, a bit stout, balding. He has a pleasant voice and man-ner. He wears a tie and suit, the coat of which rests across his knees.*)

HENRY: We asked you to come out here because we don't want to get her all upset unless there's a real reason . . . unless you can really help her.

BAIRD: I wish we could have done this four years ago . . . Remember, when you first moved to town, I said . . .

HENRY (*Sharply*): I know. We're not asking you to remind us of any-thing. We did what we thought was best for her . . . The question is, what can you do now?

BAIRD (*Not taking offense*): I'll tell you what I want you to do. Take her to a specialist—a Dr. Keller, in the city. I've worked with him before.

HENRY: What will he do?

BAIRD: That's for Dr. Keller to say after he makes a thorough exam-ination. He may want her to wear braces. It may mean an operation.

GRACE: But you think he can help her?

BAIRD: Yes, I think . . .

(*Suddenly we hear children's laughter and sounds of running. A boy about twelve runs through from the kitchen across the living room and out the screen door. This is* DICK, *the neighbor boy. Close after him comes* JENNY, *limping, but running at a good clip.* HENRY *reaches out and stops her.*)

HENRY: All right, just hold on a minute, young lady. Jenny, do you remember Dr. Baird?

JENNY: Uh-huh. When I got an infection, he lanced my ear. That hurt!

BAIRD: I'm sorry to leave a bad impression on you, Jenny. You're a good patient.

HENRY (*Putting arm around her*): Jenny, we've been talking about you . . . Would you like to take a trip to the city? To see about your foot?

JENNY: What for?

GRACE: To . . . to change it. To make it like your other one.

(JENNY *is not sure how to take all this. She senses that the adults are all very serious. Too serious. She looks around and settles on* DR. BAIRD *as the instigator. She addresses him.*)

JENNY: What would they do to it?

BAIRD: Perhaps give you a brace. Maybe a little operation.

JENNY (*Shaking head*): Huh-uh. It'd hurt.

BAIRD: Not so much.

JENNY: I don't wanna go t'the hospital. Or wear an old brace . . . This is summer vacation!

HENRY: Wouldn't you like your foot to be . . . (*Painfully*) . . . like everybody else's?

CLOSE SHOT—JENNY

JENNY (*Emphatically*): No . . . I don't mind it. Lord Byron had a club foot and he swam the Hellespont.

BAIRD: Do you like Byron, Jenny?

JENNY: He's my favorite. Especially the one that goes:
   "Maid of Athens, ere we part,
   Give, oh give me back my heart."

(*Her delivery is slightly sing-song, but she has a genuine feeling for the poem, and has not learned it merely by rote.*)

INTERIOR LIVING ROOM—MEDIUM CLOSE SHOT—JENNY, DR. BAIRD

BAIRD: That's very pretty. Do you know this one?
  "She walks in beauty, like the night
  Of cloudless climes and starry skies.
  And all that's best of dark and bright
  Meet in her aspect, and her eyes."

> (*He speaks the lines with a surprising sensitivity.* JENNY *listens with rapt admiration.* DR. BAIRD *has just risen about a thousand percent in her estimation.*)

JENNY: That's beautiful . . . (*Defensively*) And he had a club foot.
BAIRD (*Gently*): If Lord Byron were to live now . . . instead of long ago . . . do you think he'd keep his club foot, by choice? (JENNY *regards the doctor solemnly. This is a whole new question. Camera moves in on her as she considers.*)

DISSOLVE TO

EXTERIOR FALLGREN FRONT PORCH—EVENING—MEDIUM SHOT—JENNY, DICK

> (*They are sitting in a large, old-fashioned wooden porch swing, hung from the porch ceiling by chains, one of which squeaks gently as they rock slowly back and forth. They sit toward opposite ends of the swing. Lighting is very low key.*)

JENNY: She walks in beauty, like the night of cloudless climes and starry skies . . . Isn't that beautiful?
DICK: It's okay . . .
JENNY: I've decided where we're going to live after we get married.
DICK: Oh?

> (*They speak without looking at each other, not out of embarrassment, of which they feel none at all, but because their friendship establishes a deep communication which does not require the ogling tactics of adults.*)

JENNY: Right here in Oakville . . . What's wrong with that?
DICK: I can't be a pilot *here*. We'll have to go some place they've got a big airport, where the mainliners land.
JENNY: Did you tell your folks that we decided to get married?
DICK: Ummm.
JENNY: I told mine. They said that was fine. (*Remembering his evasive mumble*) Did you tell yours?

DICK: Yeah. Who was that guy that was here today?

JENNY: Dr. Baird . . . What did your parents say?

DICK: Nothin'. Grown-ups are crazy anyway. Who's Dr. Baird?

JENNY: Just a doctor. He wants me to go to the city about my foot.
(DICK *looks at her, suddenly interested.*)

DICK: You gonna do it?

JENNY: I don't think so. It's okay . . . Besides, it'd hurt.

DICK: Maybe you oughta . . .

JENNY: Why?

CLOSE SHOT—DICK

> (*He is uncomfortable. He carefully examines a skinned place on the back of one knuckle while he speaks.*)

DICK: Aw . . . when I told my folks we were gonna get married, they laughed.

JENNY: Did you tell 'em we didn't mean *now?*

DICK: Sure . . . I told 'em I was gonna be a pilot and you were gonna be a stewardess.

TIGHT TWO SHOT—JENNY, DICK

JENNY (*After pause*): Well?

DICK: They said they never saw a stewardess with a club foot. (*They look at each other for a moment, very serious about this one cloud in their otherwise beautiful future.*)

DISSOLVE TO

CLOSE SHOT—DAY—JENNY'S LEGS AND FEET

> (*Her left foot is turned inward, with the toes curled inward. Her left calf is considerably thinner than her right one—an effect achieved by the use of a cosmetic stocking on the right leg.*)

INTERIOR DOCTOR'S TREATMENT ROOM—MEDIUM SHOT—JENNY, GRACE, DR. KELLER

> (JENNY *sits on the edge of the treatment table, her legs extended before her, while* DR. KELLER *examines them.* GRACE *is seated in a chair to one side.* DR. KELLER *is around forty, tall, slender.* JENNY *holds a thin book in her hands, the object in point from story opening.*)

JENNY (*Holding up book*): Dr. Baird gave me this. It's a book of poems . . . by everybody.

KELLER (*Continuing his examination*): Dr. Baird's a pretty nice guy.

JENNY: Do you have a favorite poem?

KELLER (*Looking up*): I'm afraid I've always been too busy reading textbooks . . . All right, Jenny, you can go out in the office with Miss Nelson for a while. (JENNY *slides off the table, standing.*)

JENNY: It's all right. You can talk in front of me.

KELLER (*Laughing*): I'm sure we can. But I'm sure you'd find your poetry book much more interesting.

GRACE: Run along, Jenny. We won't be long.

JENNY: Okay. (*She exits, closing the door behind her.* DR. KELLER *turns and crosses over to a position nearer to* GRACE.)

INTERIOR TREATMENT ROOM—ANOTHER ANGLE— GRACE, DR. KELLER

KELLER: First of all, I'll say that we *can* help her . . . but it would have been so much easier if we had seen her years ago . . . Why didn't you take her to someone when she was a baby?

GRACE: Well, until she was six, we lived in the Midwest, on a little farm way out in the country. We hardly ever saw a doctor.

KELLER: When did you first notice her foot?

GRACE: Not till she started to walk, really . . . I mean, it was always turned in, but all babies' feet are turned in. She limped as soon as she started to walk, but her grandmother—my mother, that is—said that it was nothing, that she'd grow out of it.

CLOSE SHOT—DR. KELLER

(*As he very forcefully—but without anger—makes this point.*)

KELLER: Mrs. Fallgren . . . that one phrase has caused a lot of pain, a lot of suffering . . . "They'll grow out of it." (*Shaking his head*) I don't know how many times doctors hear that . . . You can *never* grow out of a deformity. It will only become harder and harder to correct.

CLOSE SHOT—GRACE

GRACE: I suppose we did wrong . . . but by the time we could see that it wasn't getting any better, we had all just accepted the situation. Jenny never seemed hampered . . . She got around as quickly as anyone, and she was happy. People in the country are used to things like that. Everyone just said that she had a club foot, and let it go at that . . . We didn't even know that something could be done.

MEDIUM CLOSE SHOT—DR. KELLER

(*As he moves to a wall chart showing the bony structure of the leg and foot. He uses appropriate gestures as he explains to* GRACE.)

KELLER: Mrs. Fallgren, I wish we could make everyone in the country understand what I'm about to tell you . . . Because what you call "club foot" is a very common condition. It's just a lay term for any kind of foot deformity. Some turn out, some turn in. With some the bone structure is shortened, and so on. Many of these cases are very mild, hardly noticeable . . . (*With emphasis*) But all of them can be corrected. Almost always it can be done without surgery . . . if the baby is taken in time. Before the child is a year old.

GRACE (*Surprised*): Before one year?

KELLER: That's right. The earlier, the better. You see all these bones in the foot, here. While these are still soft and pliable, they can be wedged into a normal shape quite easily with braces and special shoes. The older the child gets, the more solidly the bones set . . . and the more difficult, and expensive, it becomes to make any improvement.

INTERIOR TREATMENT ROOM—MEDIUM SHOT— DR. KELLER, GRACE

(GRACE *looks very disturbed at the mention of surgery.*)

GRACE: But you said you could help Jenny . . . She's not too old for the braces, is she?

KELLER: She's twelve, isn't she?

GRACE: That's right . . . be thirteen this December.

KELLER (*Shaking head slightly*): I doubt that braces would do the job . . . We can try, if you like. But at this age, it would be a long, difficult process, with no assurance of success.

GRACE: How long?

KELLER: Years . . . In her case I'd say that an operation would be better—both quicker and more certain. Is she greatly afraid of the idea of surgery?

GRACE (*Attempting a smile, little success*): Not nearly so much as I am. What kind of operation do you do for club foot?

KELLER: There again it depends on the foot . . . on the individual case. Sometimes it's just the matter of cutting a tendon that's too short.

GRACE: But in Jenny's case?

KELLER: In Jenny's case, the operation is called an arthrodesis. It's a fusion of the bones into a normal position.

GRACE: Is it very expensive?

KELLER: Not terribly . . . considering the amount of good it accomplishes. I'll tell you this, however—it will cost many times more than it would have to correct the condition when she was a baby.

> (GRACE *is resigned to the idea of the operation, but she cannot keep herself from continuing to raise small objections.*)

GRACE: I'll have to call my husband. He couldn't get away from work to come with us.

KELLER: By all means, call him and discuss it with him.

GRACE: What are the chances of success? In the operation, I mean.

KELLER (*Smiling*): Excellent.

GRACE: Will it hurt her? Will there be a lot of pain?

CLOSE SHOT—DR. KELLER

KELLER: During the operation, she'll feel nothing. There will be a certain amount of soreness afterward, till the healing is well started.

GRACE: We've always hated to have her hurt in any way.

KELLER (*Gently*): I'd say that the operation will be much less painful than spending even one evening on the sidelines at a high-school dance.

INTERIOR TREATMENT ROOM—MEDIUM SHOT—
DR. KELLER, GRACE

> (As JENNY *opens the door and thrusts her head through.*)

JENNY: Hey, you said you wouldn't be long.

GRACE: Come in, honey. We're all through. (JENNY *enters and crosses to her mother's chair. It is near the window. We are apparently in a tall building, for the view is unobstructed; perhaps a rooftop or two in sight*) Dr. Keller says your foot can be fixed . . . good as new. But you'll have to have an operation.

JENNY: Now . . . in summer vacation?

GRACE: I'm afraid so.

> (JENNY *is very disappointed and alarmed at the interruption of her vacation, and by all the fears that the operation calls up. She and* GRACE *and* DR. KELLER *regard each other silently for a moment. Gradually, we become aware of the sound of a plane flying overhead. It grows louder, obviously a multi-engined passenger plane on its run. It passes overhead as*

JENNY *moves to the window, craning her neck upward to get a glimpse of it. Gradually, the sound fades.* JENNY *looks back into the room, first at her mother, then at* DR. KELLER.)

JENNY (*Simple acceptance*): Okay.

DISSOLVE TO

MONTAGE—JENNY'S PRE-OPERATION EXAM

A. MEDIUM CLOSE SHOT—JENNY UNDER X-RAY MACHINE

B. CLOSE SHOT—JENNY'S ARM AND BLOOD-PRESSURE GAUGE

(*As the tubing around her arm is inflated and the needle of the gauge jumps up to indicate her blood pressure.*)

C. MEDIUM CLOSE SHOT—DR. KELLER

(*As he studies the x-ray plates of* JENNY's *foot.*)

DISSOLVE TO

INTERIOR HOSPITAL ROOM—DAY—MEDIUM SHOT— JENNY, GRACE, HENRY

(JENNY *lies on a gurney, ready to be wheeled to surgery.* GRACE *and* HENRY *are doing their best to be bright and cheerful, but their faces and manners reveal their anxiety.* JENNY *seems much the calmest of the three.*)

HENRY: Dick says to tell you you're not missin' anything. The filtering plant broke down and they closed the swimming pool for a while.

GRACE: And Marlene says not to worry about your goldfish. She feeds them every day . . . (*Weak effort at humor*) In fact, I think she feeds them three times a day. They're getting fat as little whales. (*This effort amuses no one, and the conversation lapses into silence.* HENRY *massages one ear vigorously.* GRACE *examines the floor with great interest.* JENNY *regards them fondly.*)

JENNY: Don't worry.

GRACE (*Looking up quickly*): Why, we're not worried, honey . . . There's nothing to worry about.

JENNY: Dr. Keller's funny. I taught him my poem, you know, by Lord Byron . . . So he learned one and taught it to me. You wanta hear it?

HENRY: Sure, punkin'. (*As* JENNY *starts to recite, a* NURSE *enters and starts to wheel the gurney out into the hall.*)

JENNY:
>   "Timothy Fry could fly without wings,
>   But he went around knocking down chimneys and things."

>   (JENNY *is wheeled through the door,* HENRY *and* GRACE *following. Camera pans with* JENNY *to the door, then holds on the empty doorway as* JENNY's *voice fades down the hall.*)

JENNY (*Voice fading*):
>   "He lived in a belfry, with a number of bats;
>   'Cause they hung upside down they could never wear hats."

DISSOLVE TO

INTERIOR SURGERY—MEDIUM SHOT—ARTHRODESIS
  OPERATION

DISSOLVE TO

CLOSE SHOT—JENNY

>   (*As she struggles to wake from the anesthetic. She is in a hospital bed. Her eyes are closed.*)

JENNY (*Faintly disconnected*): Timothy fire-fly . . . without any rings . . . (*Abruptly her eyes pop open. She struggles for an instant to focus them. As she succeeds, a smile breaks through.*)

CLOSE SHOT—GRACE, HENRY

>   (*Their faces are close together. Camera shooting from* JENNY's *point of view. The image shimmers for a moment, then comes clear. They are both smiling happily.*)

GRACE: Jenny . . . Jenny, it worked fine. The operation was fine.
HENRY: Dr. Keller says your foot will be just like normal.
JENNY (*Faintly*): Thank you . . . Timothy.

>   (GRACE *and* HENRY *exchange smiles. They are weeping with happiness.*)

DISSOLVE TO

EXTERIOR FALLGREN FRONT PORCH—CLOSE SHOT—
  PORCH RAIL

>   (*As a boy's baseball bat collides with it, then is withdrawn, collides, and is withdrawn again. With the rhythmic thump of the bat is alternated the squeak of the chain supporting the porch swing. Together the sounds make a sleepy summer music.*)

EXTERIOR FALLGREN PORCH—MEDIUM SHOT—JENNY, DICK

(As they rock back and forth in the swing, DICK using the baseball bat against the porch railing to keep them in motion.)

DICK: I'll bet it didn't hurt as much as when I fell off the horse and broke my arm.

JENNY *(Shrugging)*: Maybe not . . . I didn't feel anything when they did it. They told me to start counting, and I never even got to four . . . I just felt all dreamy.

(DICK regards her with interest. He is just a little jealous of her dramatic experience. He would like to cap her experience with one of his own, but at the moment JENNY holds all the advantages. The evidence—her foot still encased in a cast— rests on the swing between them. DICK cannot help looking at it with respect. With the baseball bat he very gently and tentatively taps on it.)

DICK: That hurt?

JENNY: Huh-uh. It wouldn't hurt if you did it ten times that hard.

DICK: How long you gonna wear it?

JENNY: Three months.

DICK: Gee, you get to go back to school in it. *(JENNY nods. Her manner indicates she finds this prospect a happy one. The cast will be a great attention-getter at school.)*

JENNY: Maybe it'll be four months. I go to see Dr. Keller in three months, and he'll take x-rays to see whether to take it off then.

DICK: And your foot's gonna be just like anybody's?

JENNY: Uh-huh . . . My leg won't, though. Not for quite a while, anyway. 'Cause the muscles haven't developed . . . but it's just got to be ready by Halloween . . .

DICK: Why?

JENNY: 'Cause you're going to take me to the party at school.

DICK: Oh . . . sure . . .

JENNY: You thought up your costume yet?

DICK: Why? It's still four months away.

JENNY *(Seriously)*: We have to plan for the future, Dick.

DICK: Oh, well, I guess I'll go as a pilot.

JENNY: That isn't Halloweeny at all!

DICK: Doesn't matter. And you can be a stewardess.

JENNY (*Thoughtfully*): I don't know if I want to be a stewardess any more.

DICK (*Worried*): You mean—not ever?

JENNY: Unh-unh . . . I think maybe I'm going to be a dancing teacher.

DICK (*Surprised*): But what about me?

JENNY: What *about* you? Why don't you be a dancing teacher too?

MEDIUM CLOSE SHOT—JENNY, DICK

> (*We see only their faces and upper bodies as they confront this moment of crisis.* DICK'*s nose wrinkles as he considers this heretical suggestion as to his future.*)

DICK: Dancing teacher! (*Then*) Naw . . . you can do what you want. But I'm gonna be a pilot.

JENNY: Well . . . I guess you can do what *you* want to . . . (*A silence begins to grow . . . Finally, he rises.*)

DICK: Well . . . good-bye, Jenny.

JENNY (*Surprised*): You going?

DICK: Yeah . . .

JENNY: But I thought you were going to stay for the afternoon . . .

DICK: Oh . . . well . . . I got these things to do and think about . . . and . . . (*Pause*) I brought you a present. (*He gives it.*)

JENNY: Me? What is it, Dick?

DICK: Oh, just something—well, so long . . .

JENNY: So long. (*He goes. She opens her present.*)

INSERT: STEWARDESS' "WINGS"

DISSOLVE TO

INTERIOR FALLGREN LIVING ROOM—NIGHT—MEDIUM SHOT—HENRY, GRACE, DICK

> (GRACE *and* HENRY *are seated, reading the evening paper.* DICK *squats on the floor. He is dressed in partial masquerade for a Halloween party. He holds a Halloween noisemaker in his hand, examining it. Finally, he gives it a trial whirl, shattering the silence.* GRACE *and* HENRY *look up.*)

HENRY (*Slight irony*): That's a good one.

DICK (*Glancing upward*): Why doesn't she hurry up?

GRACE: Girls are always late, Dick. You'd better get used to it.

HENRY: You've got plenty of time yet. I can drive you over there in five minutes. What time's the party over?

DICK: Ten o'clock.

HENRY: You phone up if it's going to be any later than that. I don't want to drive over there and sit in the car for half an hour.

GRACE: What've you been doing with yourself the last few weeks, Dick? You haven't been around after school very much . . .

DICK (*Softly, after a difficult pause*): I've been—taking dancing lessons. (GRACE *and* HENRY *exchange an amused look.*)

HENRY: You like it?

DICK (*Not so sure*): Yeah—it's all right.

> (*Suddenly we hear the off-stage sound of* JENNY *descending the stairs, which are off stage. She is wearing heels, and they click steadily, rhythmically, perfectly spaced, as she descends. All eyes in the room are turned to follow her.*)

CLOSE SHOT—BOTTOM OF STAIRWAY

> (*As* JENNY'S *legs and feet walk into shot and turn toward the living room. The high heels she wears are those of her mother, slightly too big for her, but they reveal a pair of perfectly normal feet.*)

INTERIOR LIVING ROOM—MEDIUM SHOT—ANOTHER ANGLE

> (*Showing the stairs, with* JENNY *standing at the bottom of them, the other three looking at her. She wears a party dress, the stewardess wings are conspicuous instead of a brooch.*)

DICK (*Brief laugh*): Boy, do you look funny in those shoes.

JENNY (*Unperturbed*): I know it. I just wore them down here to show off. (*She steps out of the high heels and pads over to the end of the couch, where her own shoes are resting. They are a pair of ballet slippers which she quickly slips on.* DICK *clambers to his feet first, then* GRACE *and* HENRY *rise.* JENNY *picks up her coat.*)

DICK: C'mon, let's get goin'. (JENNY *kisses her mother good-bye, then walks across the front door with* DICK, *moving without the trace of a limp.* DICK *opens the front door.*)

HENRY: The car's out front. Run and get in it . . . I'll get my coat.

> (JENNY *and* DICK *exit, closing the door behind them.* HENRY *gets his coat from the closet, and* GRACE *helps him to put it on. As they turn toward the door,* GRACE *bends and picks up the high-heeled shoes.*)

MEDIUM CLOSE SHOT—GRACE, HENRY

    (*As they regard the shoes.*)

HENRY: It won't be long before she doesn't look silly in them. (*Happy smile*) What's that Lord Byron poem she's always spouting?

GRACE (*Returning smile*): She walks in beauty ...

FADE OUT

Paper Foxhole

by JAMES ELWARD

(Honorable Mention)

CATEGORY:

Television Comedy

(ONE HOUR OR MORE)

PAPER FOXHOLE

by JAMES ELWARD

Paper Foxhole
was first presented on the Kraft Television Theatre
on April 4, 1956,
under the direction of William Graham,
with the following cast:

GEORGE HARRIS · Hal March
PFC. HARRY MC CALL · Joe Mantell
COLONEL CARMODY · Kenny Delmar
CPL. CLIFF EVANS · Felix Munso
M/SGT. BATES · Jack Weston
1ST LT. MARVIN FENTRISS · John Fielder
COMMANDANT · John Gibson
ANDREW J. FOGARTY · Norman Lloyd
PVT. JOHNSON · William Duell
PVT. ADAMS · Joseph Elic

© Copyright, 1956, by James Elward

ACT ONE

Fade in on a tight shot of the cover of a copy of Event *magazine, a publication out-ranked only by* Life *and* Look. *The camera pulls back to show the table it rests on and the men seated around this small paneled conference room. Four men sit around the table:* ANDREW J. FOGARTY, *the publisher of* Event, *and three of his editorial staff.* FOGARTY *is a portly man in his fifties; the others are younger but only a shade less pompous. They are* MACAULEY (Editor of National Affairs, *according to the sign by his place*), SANDERS, (Editor of European Affairs) *and* FERGUSON, (Editor of Baltic Affairs). *One place remains vacant at the table: the* Editor of Far-Eastern Affairs. *A pretty young stenographer is seated away from the table, ready to take notes. It is obvious* FOGARTY *and his staff are waiting with no great patience for the last, late member of the conference.* FOGARTY *checks his watch and then the clock on the wall behind him. The time is* 12:03. *Over the clock hangs the magazine motto: "Each moment is an event." The other men and the* SECRETARY *immediately check their watches too. Aware of* FOGARTY's *impatience, the* SECRETARY *rises and goes to close the conference room door. As she reaches it, the final editor enters. At first glance,* GEORGE HARRIS *looks much like the others. But the hornrimmed glasses, the flannel suit and the slight softness in the waistline do not completely hide the fact that* GEORGE *is still only in his middle thirties and will never, at any age, be as solemn as an* Event *editor should be. He slides into his chair apologetically as the secretary closes the door.*

DISSOLVE TO EXTERIOR OF DOOR

It is marked: Staff Editors Conference Room. *Beside the door is a bulletin board on which is listed:* OPERATION RETURN, STAFF EDITORS, CONFERENCE ROOM. FOGARTY 12:00 NOON.

DISSOLVE TO INTERIOR OF CONFERENCE ROOM

The clock behind FOGARTY *is now at* 12:12. FOGARTY *is standing, all the others are taking notes.*

FOGARTY: So that is what Operation Return is about, gentlemen. A whole issue of *Event* devoted to the late world war. The five years that for our world, our country and our magazine were, if you'll forgive me, our most "Event-ful" ...

(He pauses for effect as the camera (his eyes) pans around listening men. Each responds with a somewhat forced smile. The third man is GEORGE, *who remains staring straight ahead. The camera goes on to the next man, and then snaps back to* GEORGE, *who belatedly smiles. It is obvious he hasn't the faintest idea what he is smiling about.)*

FOGARTY: Our battlefields . . . and what the years have done to them! It can be sensational. It *will* be sensational! Now this map has the principal campaigns . . .

(He spreads a huge map over the table. The men rise and gather around him. GEORGE *rises with them, trying to find a particular spot on the far corner. We see the tiny speck in the South Pacific he is looking for.)*

. . . and we'll need the old team spirit. So think. What stories did you cover? Of course, only George was an official soldier . . . (GEORGE *is seated now, doodling on a pad in front of him*) . . . but we all had our battles, even here on the home front. So now, let's all get into the proper spirit. 1945! Where were we then?

(Close shot of the pad on which GEORGE's *hand is writing* 1945 *over and over again. We hear* GEORGE's *thoughts as he remains off-camera.)*

GEORGE: I can tell you where I was in 1945. And 1944. And '43. And most of '42. I was on an island in the South Pacific, that's where I was . . . *(Dissolve to calendar hanging on the wall of an army squad tent. The date is* 1945. *The camera starts to pan around the dirty, sagging, weather-beaten tent.)* It wasn't the sort of island they make musical comedies about. It was a hot, sandy, wet thumb of coral five miles long and two wide. *(Camera pans over to entrance of tent and the makeshift desks of orange crates by the opening.)* I wrote those little fill-in paragraphs you used to see in your newspapers . . . "3 Local Boys in Pacific." Remember? *(We get a closer view of the desks now, loaded with government forms, a helmet, etc., small sign:* Public Information, 33rd. Inf. Regt.) . . . Sergeant George Harris, Public Information. Oh, there were heroes in the South Pacific. Only we never saw them. We were Division Rear. Very rear, and very safe. *(Pan to* HARRY *sleeping in his cot.)* For three years we lived together, we ate together, we worked together . . . *(We see all three of the desks now. A faint breeze ruffles the government forms.)* But in our own way, I guess we were soldiers, too.

Only our weapons were typewriters, and our foxhole was made of paper.

> (*Bugle sounds reveille. Over the public-address system box which hangs on a tent pole comes the voice of* M/SGT. BATES.)

BATES (*Yelling*): All right, fellows! Get up!

> (HARRY *doesn't move a muscle. A new voice comes over the box. The sound of it sends* HARRY, *a meek mild little fellow, out of his bed and hurrying into his uniform.* HARRY *is in his early twenties but seems older. The uniform is that of a private first class.*)

FENTRISS (*Box*): This is 1st Lieutenant Marvin H. Fentriss. Every man will fall out of his sack on the double. Guards will spot check quarters for failure to comply. Morning exercise, commence!

HARRY: George. Get up.

FENTRISS (*Box*): First exercise: Forward Bend, touch toes. Count is two. A one . . . A two. A one . . . A two! Hit those toes! Come on there . . . hit them!

HARRY (*Exercising*): I'm trying, aren't I? George, you've already got *two* DRs.

> (GEORGE, *in his bunk opens his eyes slowly. This is* GEORGE *as he was eleven years ago. No glasses, and thinner than when he entered the* Event *conference room. He is wearing army shorts and a tee shirt. He has a faint hangover.*)

GEORGE: That's right. Look on the bright side. (*We see what* GEORGE *is looking at . . . a sign at the end of his bunk saying* "Kill or Be Killed.") What a way to start the day!

FENTRISS (*Box*): Now the Indian Squat. On your toes! And down to the floor . . . squat! Up . . . Down . . . Up . . . Down!

GEORGE: When does he give the weather report?

FENTRISS (*Box*): You're getting soft, all of you! Soft! Up . . . Down!

> (GEORGE *covers the box with his field jacket, and finishes putting on his uniform. He is a Technical Sergeant.* FENTRISS *is no longer heard.*)

HARRY: If he catches you . . .

GEORGE: I go today. After three years, four months and twenty-seven days, what more can they do to me?

HARRY: Just think . . . it'll be quiet in the mornings again.

GEORGE: I'll miss you too.

HARRY: At home I used to have people trained not to say anything
until I had coffee ... Sometimes I wouldn't even have it at breakfast, I'd wait till lunch. But no talking till I had it.

GEORGE: I'll have to see your Edith when I get home. There must be
a better life for her *some place*. I understand they're taking on people
in the steel mills.

HARRY: She understood me. Don't forget to turn in your bedding.

GEORGE: Later.

HARRY: Don't leave it for us.

GEORGE: No *esprit de corps!*

HARRY: No. Whatever that is.

GEORGE: Wouldn't last a day in the Foreign Legion.

HARRY: What do you think I'm in now? Turn it in yourself. (GEORGE
pulls out an army canteen) What's that?

GEORGE: Last night you claimed it was native scotch.

> (*He takes a healthy swallow, choking a bit over it.* CLIFF
> *enters in full uniform.* CORPORAL CLIFF EVANS *is in charge of
> special services for this division rear. An ex-actor, he is a tall,
> bony fellow in his late twenties with a somewhat jaundiced
> sense of humor. The Army will never make a soldier out
> of him.*)

CLIFF: Lushes!

> (CLIFF *goes directly to his bunk and starts peeling off the
> equipment he has stood guard in. It stays where it falls.*)

GEORGE: I gather we did not make Colonel's Orderly last night?

CLIFF: We did not. We also did not make interior guard. We ended
up on that blasted hill again.

GEORGE (*Judiciously*): We must learn to be a better soldier.

> (CLIFF *pulls a cocoanut from his littered bunk.*)

CLIFF: Must have been quite a party.

GEORGE: My farewell to the troops.

> (CLIFF *climbs into his bunk.*)

CLIFF: Well, don't wake me when you leave. (*And he is asleep.*)

HARRY: You sure can tell this war's over.

GEORGE: Not for you, Harry. Not for Cliff. Just for Papa here.

HARRY: Thirty-six more days! Thirteen for Cliff. Then *home!* (*The
field phone on his desk rings.* HARRY *answers*) Bottleneck Rear, Pfc.
McCall speaking ... What? ... When? ... Thanks, Hal ... (*He
presses the button down, and rewinds the phone.*)

GEORGE: What's up?

HARRY: Fentriss! (GEORGE *moves quickly into action. He shakes* CLIFF *a couple of times, and then finally, in desperation, rolls him out of his cot.* HARRY *is still on the phone*) Charlie? . . . Harry . . . Fentriss . . . Inspection! . . . Pass it on!

(*By the time he rings off,* CLIFF *is on his feet. The three men start cleaning up the tent faster than seems possible. What can't be hidden goes into the mosquito nets bunched over the cots. Clean shirts are put on.* CLIFF *then takes a broom and sweeps the dirt floor.* HARRY *is at the desks, shoveling papers, bottles, odd equipment, etc., into the foot lockers that line the tent walls. When finished he pulls out the first three pages of official paper he finds, placing a page on each desk.* GEORGE, *meanwhile, is trying to get rid of the liquor bottles and beer cans. They too end up in the nets, which are beginning to sag a little. A discarded shirt is tossed from man to man for dusting purposes.*)

(*This is in no sense a "scrambled" scene. These men have been facing spot checks together for over three years. They move quickly and efficiently, with no wasted motion. Not a word is spoken. All three slide into the chairs behind their desks at approximately the same moment. In one uninterrupted move they sit, pick up the work pages and assume positions of vast concentration. After a long silent moment in which they remain frozen, an awful thought hits* HARRY.)

HARRY: Boots! (*He raises his feet, as do the others. Their boots are filthy.* CLIFF *pulls a small can from his pocket.*)

CLIFF: Rifle oil! (*He pours some over his shoes, shoves the can on to* HARRY *who does the same, and then passes it on to* GEORGE. *The oil is spread by rubbing the boots against the back of their trouser legs. Then, from outside the tent:*)

FENTRISS: 'Ten-shun!

(*The trio snap to attention. The tent flap is raised.* FENTRISS *enters.* LT. FENTRISS *is still quite young for his rank, a fact both he and the Army regret. He makes up for this by adding as grave a manner as he can to his bearing. Any Prussian regiment on the parade grounds of the First World War would recognize him immediately.*)

FENTRISS: At ease!

(*They stand at ease. The camera, as the eyes of* FENTRISS, *pans around the tent carefully. It appears spotless. The* LIEUTENANT *cannot resist a faint surprise.*)

FENTRISS: Well! Hard at work. And in the morning!

GEORGE (*As ranking non-com*): Ready for inspection, sir.

FENTRISS: We'll see, Sergeant. (*He wanders about the tent, the men following him with their eyes. He glances at the P.A. box.* GEORGE's *jacket still hangs over it*) What's that? (GEORGE *takes his jacket down immediately.*)

GEORGE: Sorry, sir. I was packing last night.

FENTRISS: Oh. So *that's* what it was.

HARRY: We gave a little party, sir.

FENTRISS: Sounded like Custer's Last Stand. And you'll be pleased to know the Medics report a record demand for aspirin.

GEORGE: You see, sir, I'm rotating . . .

FENTRISS: Aren't we all? But not today. Not for some time.

GEORGE (*Faint panic in his voice*): Sir . . . I'm on orders. . . .

FENTRISS: You were. They've been changed. That's why the Army uses P.A. boxes, Sergeant. For announcements. Your points were based on this being a combat zone. Well, it isn't any more. Instead of four points a month, we're a Grade B zone at two. Retroactive.

CLIFF (*The only one who can talk*): But that means we're only . . .

FENTRISS: Halfway through. I don't like it either, gentlemen. I had postwar plans too. (*He wanders about the tent again. This time he uncovers signs of the hasty preparation. The men are stunned. The last thing* FENTRISS *touches is one of the nets, which promptly overturns and sprinkles him with bottles, cans, dirty shirts, a rifle, a broom, etc.*) And what's all this? Sergeant, I asked you a question!

GEORGE (*Absently*): Go away!

HARRY (*Quickly*): He didn't say anything, sir. Cliff, did you hear him say anything?

FENTRISS: You could get a DR for that, Sergeant. And each Disciplinary Report subtracts four points.

CLIFF: He's still in shock, sir.

FENTRISS: This tent's a disgrace! And look at yourselves! Discipline, that's what you need. You're soft! I'm going to have improvement around here, gentlemen. Considerable improvement! 'Ten-shun! (*He strides out, with* CLIFF *right behind him.*)

GEORGE: It's a dream, that's what it is. A bad dream. Wake me up, Harry. Wake me up!

HARRY: 1949. I won't get home till 1949.

GEORGE: I'll never make it. I'll crack up, that's what I'll do. Three more years! We'll never get off this island! We'll never get out of the Army! Never!

HARRY: I wonder if Edith will marry again.

GEORGE (*Figuring*): Three more years . . . 1,096 days . . . Oooh!

> (CLIFF *re-enters.*)

CLIFF: No DRs, and we keep our stripes.

HARRY: How?

CLIFF: Guess who handles the officer's beer ration? (*He points modestly to himself*) Special Services. Two weeks' guard duty instead. Any questions?

GEORGE (*Remembering*): I've got to go today! I've got two DRs already!

CLIFF (*As he figures*): That's minus eight points . . .

HARRY (*Awed*): Four more months.

GEORGE: We'll fight back. That's what we'll do!

CLIFF: We'll show 'em. We'll resign.

HARRY: I suppose it's fair . . . (*The others stare at him*) In a horrible kind of a way. I mean we've been here three years, safe and sound . . .

CLIFF: Would you rather face Fentriss or the Japs?

HARRY: I didn't get any choice. . . .

GEORGE: None of us did. Didn't matter what *we* wanted.

HARRY: We could have transferred.

GEORGE: I put in for transfer the day after Fentriss arrived. Rejected. My newspaper experience was too valuable right here. (*And that brings him right back to his problem*) Darn it . . . there must be some way out!

CLIFF: Have you considered hara-kiri?

HARRY: I don't even know what a Grade B zone is.

CLIFF: It means you're close enough to the enemy to have to stand guard, and far enough back that you have to police the area.

GEORGE (*Talking to himself*): Somebody drop a bomb, they'd make this a combat zone fast enough!

HARRY: George, the war's been over two months. Nobody's going to drop a bomb.

CLIFF: Except Fentriss.

GEORGE: If only it could be a combat zone for just a little while. There must be plenty of people who hate this army.

HARRY: Just us, George. Just us. (*A great beaming smile spreads over* GEORGE's *face. The idea tinges his voice with awe*) Harry, you're a genius! The solution!

HARRY: What I say?

CLIFF: No, George. Whatever it is. No.

GEORGE: You haven't even heard it!

CLIFF: Look, George . . . we lived through the time you tried to distil cocoanut juice. And the time you invented the magnetic field alarm for approaching officers. And the time you tried to get compassionate leave to Australia. Not again.

GEORGE: You want to get off this island?

CLIFF: Alive? Yes.

GEORGE: If it works, we'll all get off. And *soon*.

HARRY: And if it doesn't?

GEORGE: Nothing. Oh . . . a Section 8 for nerves maybe. What can you lose?

CLIFF: We'll waive that for the moment. Go on.

GEORGE: Only one thing keeps us from going home . . . red tape. Right? So all we have to do is make this island a combat zone again. And how, you ask?

HARRY: The natives revolt?

GEORGE: No. No. *We* do!

CLIFF (*Shaking his head*): You've been in the Pacific too long.

GEORGE: What's to prevent us from firing off a few shots every night we stand guard? Do you know how fast word would spread there were guerrillas out there?

CLIFF: Who've been waiting till now? No, George.

GEORGE: Who knows when they arrived? There aren't any; they can't be questioned.

CLIFF: Just the three of us? That's a little fishy, George. Even for the Army.

GEORGE: You know what it's like on guard. A shot goes off . . . you get jittery, you fire.

HARRY: At what?

GEORGE: Nothing. But when the Officer of the Day comes around, who's going to admit he was just nervous?

CLIFF: No one.

GEORGE: Exactly. Somebody was firing *at* them. And we've got two whole weeks. The natives don't go out at night, so we won't hit anybody. Why, we'll be a combat zone before we know it! It's foolproof!

HARRY: It'll have to be . . . if we're going to do it.

CLIFF: So if the mountain won't come to Mohammed . . . You know, it might just work!

HARRY: They won't make it a combat zone for that.

GEORGE: They changed it once. They can do it again.

HARRY: I don't know, George . . .

GEORGE: You want to see Edith again, don't you?

HARRY: Sure, but . . .

GEORGE: Look at it this way. You want to listen to me every morning for the next three years?

CLIFF: That did it. What do we do?

GEORGE: First we draw up plans . . .

> (*Dissolve through film shot of flag being lowered into long shot of guard standing retreat in the parade compound that evening.* GEORGE, HARRY *and* CLIFF *are standing together in the ranks. They are equipped for guard as* CLIFF *was on his first entrance.*)

HARRY: Suppose we don't get perimeter guard?

CLIFF: With the rust you've got in that rifle, you'll be lucky you don't get the stockade.

> (M/SGT. BATES *is in front of detail, as sergeant of the guard.*)

BATES: Guard detail . . . the Officer of the Day! 'Ten-shun! (*He does a smart about face*) All present and accounted for, sir.

> (*And we see the Officer of the Day,* FENTRISS.)

FENTRISS: Thank you, Sergeant.

HARRY (*Shuddering*): No. Not him! I won't do it!

GEORGE: "Ours is not to reason why."

CLIFF: "Ours is but to do or die."

HARRY (*Quoting the line that precedes*): "Someone blundered!"

FENTRISS: Men, I've noticed a general letdown in this unit recently. Now you all know the rules for a military appearance . . . Clean shaves . . . (*Close shot of* CLIFF. *It's practically a beard*) . . . polished boots . . . (*Close shot of* GEORGE, *panning down to his boots. They are covered with mud*) . . . neat, well-fitting uniforms. (*Close shot of* HARRY. *He never looked more like a laundry bag*) I expect these things of a soldier. The Army expects them. And if you can't live up to it . . . Well, I understand perimeter guard is not the most desirable place to spend an evening. Sergeant, commence inspection! (*Dissolve to long shot of* FENTRISS *and* BATES *passing along the ranks. Close shot of* FENTRISS *in front of* CLIFF. *He grabs his rifle and inspects it*) Just as a matter of curiosity, Corporal, what have you got in this rifle barrel?

CLIFF: Didn't have time to clean it, sir.

FENTRISS: I thought maybe it's where you were keeping your laundry. (FENTRISS *moves on to* HARRY) Look at yourself, soldier. You *are* on our side, aren't you?

HARRY: Yes, sir.

FENTRISS: Perimeter guard, Bates. (*He passes on to* GEORGE *who looks, if possible, worse than the other two*) Perimeter guard for all three of them, Sergeant. Let's see if that does anything. (*He moves on.* CLIFF *and* GEORGE *in frame.*)

GEORGE: Plan one.

CLIFF: Check!

> (*Dissolve to jungle path, that night. The guard detail moves along casually. The last two men are* GEORGE *and* CLIFF. *They move in a semi-crouch. Rifles ready in their hands.* BATES, *walking upright, is behind them.*)

BATES: What's the matter with you guys? What are you bending for?

GEORGE: Listen! Did you hear something? (BATES, *without thinking, automatically crouches a little.*)

BATES: What? (*He straightens up*) You guys are crazy. Come on, I haven't got all night. (*He strides off.* CLIFF *and* GEORGE *exchange glances.*)

CLIFF: Plan two.

FADE OUT

> (*Fade in on* HARRY *in position. The jungle is black behind him, and he starts nervously at every sound. There is a noise in the bushes behind him.*)

HARRY: Who . . . who's there?

> (GEORGE *creeps in to the clearing.*)

GEORGE: Put that thing down, it's me.

HARRY: I thought you were Fentriss.

GEORGE: He wouldn't be out here. Now remember, when I fire, follow right away. We don't want any separate shots. You know how to fire, don't you?

HARRY (*Unhappily*): I guess so. It's been so long since Basic. Where do I aim?

GEORGE: Straight out. Up in the air. Any place.

HARRY: Why don't we wait till tomorrow?

GEORGE: *Tonight!* And remember your story . . . (*He hears something and crawls back into the bushes.* FENTRISS *comes into the clearing.*)

FENTRISS: Who were you talking to, McCall?

HARRY: Just myself, sir. You know how it is . . .

FENTRISS: You're on guard! I could have knocked that rifle out of your hands.

HARRY (*Miserably*): Yes, sir.

(*Fade in on* GEORGE *in another part of the jungle. He sees* FENTRISS *approaching.*)

GEORGE: Halt! Advance and give the password!

FENTRISS: You know me.

GEORGE: Password! Lieutenant! Sir.

FENTRISS: "Lulu." And put that thing down. I wouldn't trust any of you with a loaded weapon. Everything all right?

GEORGE: Well ... kind of ...

FENTRISS: What do you mean?

GEORGE: Don't you get a funny feeling out here, Lieutenant? Like somebody was watching you, somebody not friendly? Out there in the darkness, with a gun . . . watching and waiting . . . until that one moment when he will raise his rifle, and aim, and then . . .

(*Without thinking,* FENTRISS *is almost caught in the spell. With great effort he breaks it.*)

FENTRISS: But there isn't anybody out there.

GEORGE: Seems kind of silly to have a guard then, doesn't it?

FENTRISS: Sergeant, are you being insolent? (*Pan to* CLIFF, *sneaking up on them. He sees* FENTRISS *and starts to retire, but is caught by the scene*) Answer me!

GEORGE: Sir?

FENTRISS: You've been asking to be taken down a peg. All right, you can just ...

(GEORGE *sees* CLIFF *over* FENTRISS' *shoulder. He signals frantically with his head for* CLIFF *to fire.*)

GEORGE: Just what, sir?

FENTRISS: Stop bobbing your head like that! All right, Sergeant, you'll report ... (*Cut back to* CLIFF. *He's in a horrible predicament. In a moment* FENTRISS *will have* GEORGE *on his way to the guardhouse, yet he hates to be the one to start the shooting. Finally, in desperation, he raises his rifle straight up in the air, closes his eyes, and fires. Cut to* GEORGE *and* FENTRISS, *crouching on the ground. More and more rifle shots sound around them*) What was that?

GEORGE: It must be ... guerrillas! Over there, sir.

(*He starts firing.*)

FENTRISS: Stop that!

GEORGE: But I saw them! Defend yourself, sir. (*And he commences firing again.*)

(Dissolve to a nearby clearing in the jungle. BATES *and two other privates on guard,* ADAMS *and* JOHNSON *listen to the shots. They are company clerks.)*

BATES: Now what's all that?

JOHNSON: An attack! *(He starts shooting gleefully into the dark.)*

BATES: Knock it off. *(Yells)* Who's out there?

*(*FENTRISS *staggers in, pistol in hand.)*

FENTRISS: It's me. I. Lt. Fentriss. Get back to camp, Bates. Sound Red Alert.

BATES: What's going on out there?

FENTRISS: Unexplained shooting. Report that. And bring up the rest of the detail. No, maybe I'd better go back. You stay here.

BATES: Sure, sir. But what are they firing *at?*

FENTRISS: We don't know. Could be guerrillas.

BATES: Guerrillas? *Here?*

FENTRISS: Escaped Japanese . . . anything. Don't be dense, Bates.

BATES: Better let me take a look . . . *(The firing starts up again.* FEN-TRISS' *cap goes sailing off.* BATES *yells into the dark)* Knock it off, you guys! Look, sir, they're just jumpy . . .

*(*FENTRISS *picks up his cap. It has a hole in it.)*

FENTRISS: I could have been killed! I'm reporting this, Bates. We're in trouble. Tell the men to dig in.

BATES: Yes, sir, but . . .

FENTRISS: I'll be back. Don't . . . don't give up the ship! *(He disappears rapidly.)*

JOHNSON: Can we shoot now, Bates?

BATES: At what?

ADAMS: Who cares?

(The firing starts up again. Close shot of GEORGE *and* CLIFF *in nearby brush, listening. They look at each other, shake hands solemnly, and turn back to their shooting. The noise of the gunfire continues to the fade out.)*

(Dissolve through exterior view of squad tent with sign planted in the mud before it, saying "HEADQUARTERS COM-PANY COMMANDER" *into interior view of squad tent. A very bored and relaxed colonel in his fifties,* COLONEL CARMODY, *is listening to* FENTRISS. CARMODY *looks very little like a colonel, and much more like a Kansas real-estate salesman forced to*

*play soldier. Which is what he is. On his desk, where at the
moment he is resting his feet, is a sign: "Hqs. Co. Comm.
Col. Carmody.")*

FENTRISS: . . . and fifty rounds of ammunition. And machine-gun fire.
   And I think I saw some artillery up in the hills.
CARMODY: No aircraft carriers?
FENTRISS: I couldn't see the sea, sir.
CARMODY: I thought they might be coming over land.
FENTRISS: I know it sounds fantastic, sir. But there *was* an attack!
CARMODY: I don't hear anything.

   (They both listen for a moment. Not a sound.)

FENTRISS: Maybe we've been wiped out.
CARMODY: By what? The tsetse fly? Fentriss, there couldn't be any
   Japs here. We're three thousand miles from Tokyo. The same dis-
   tance as Pocatello, Idaho.
FENTRISS: I don't know what an enemy is doing here, but they *are* here.
CARMODY: The war's over. We're not even a combat zone any more.
   Unfortunately.
FENTRISS: And my cap? We were taught to take these things seriously
   at R.O.T.C.
CARMODY: Of course I only sold real estate in Topeka. And yet I'm a
   colonel and you're a lieutenant. No justice, is there, Fentriss?
FENTRISS: No, sir. What will you do now?
CARMODY: Drink that beer. If you'll hand it to me.
FENTRISS: And the attack? Don't we report it?
CARMODY: What? That the natives want our paper clips?
FENTRISS: Even a lieutenant can have a superior officer charged with
   neglect of duty . . . *sir!*
CARMODY: You really are an unpleasant type, aren't you? All right,
   Fentriss. If it'll make you happy, submit a report. I don't exactly
   know where I can forward it to, but you'll think of *something.*
FENTRISS: Thank you, sir.

   *(Dissolve to jungle path, immediately afterwards. The detail
   that has been on guard is coming off duty: GEORGE, HARRY
   and CLIFF with them. BATES is at the end. FENTRISS, bare-
   headed still, comes in with their relief.)*

FENTRISS: Any more activity, Bates?
BATES: No, sir. Guess the men were just restless.
FENTRISS: Take your shift to my tent. We're making out a report.

(BATES *stares at the soldiers with* FENTRISS.)

BATES: And what happens to these guys?

FENTRISS: From now on we have perimeter guard twenty-four hours a day.

(CLIFF *turns to* GEORGE *and says quietly.*)

CLIFF: My buddy.

BATES: We never did that before.

FENTRISS: We do now. Detail, Forward . . . March!

(*The two groups pass each other. The outgoing guards move stealthily, crouching, rifles in their hands. The incoming men still move in the casual way they did before.*)

CLIFF: What happens now? When nothing happens?

GEORGE: Even guerrillas sleep some time.

(*Cut to close shot of* FENTRISS.)

FENTRISS: Move along, men. That report has to get out today.

(*And he puts on his newly acquired helmet and moves after them.*)

FADE OUT

(*Fade in on interior of officer's squad tent, a few minutes later.* CARMODY *is not present. The first guard shift mills around as the lieutenant questions them.* ADAMS *is giving his story.*)

ADAMS: . . . then I saw these flashes of light in the jungle. And heard the noise. So I started firing too.

FENTRISS: *After* you heard the bullets singing over your head?

ADAMS: Singing?

FENTRISS: Whistling. Flashing. You *did* hear the bullets going over you, didn't you?

ADAMS: Yes, sir. I guess I did. But I wasn't afraid . . . (*He starts to become carried away by his story*) I hit the dirt, my M-1 coughing its bullets out into the dark. I thought of Mom's apple pie. I don't know how long I was there, lying in the mud. Seconds? Minutes? Hours?

(GEORGE *and* CLIFF *stand nearby, listening.*)

CLIFF (*Quietly*): Weeks? Months?

(ADAM'S *story is getting pretty good now.*)

ADAMS: Nothing but darkness and bullets all around me. I was tired. I felt I couldn't take much more . . .

> (GEORGE *nods to* CLIFF *sympathetically.*)

GEORGE: Battle fatigue!

ADAMS: I guess that's all, sir.

> (CLIFF *applauds politely.*)

FENTRISS: You there! Yes, you!

CLIFF: Me, sir?

FENTRISS: You're next. What did you hear?

CLIFF: Nothing, sir.

FENTRISS: No bullets? No attack? *Nothing?*

CLIFF: Some rifles went off. I didn't pay much attention.

FENTRISS: Of course not. Special Services never consider themselves soldiers, do they? All right. You can go.

CLIFF: Am I still on guard, sir?

FENTRISS: From now on, we're all on guard. All the time. What's the matter?

CLIFF: Nothing, sir. (*He looks at* GEORGE *with a faintly worried expression*) I just hope we all know what we're doing!

FADE OUT

ACT TWO

> (*Fade in on the trio's squad tent the following morning.* GEORGE *is at the tent opening, looking out into the compound.* SGT. BATES *is calling out the morning exercises over the P.A. box, and* HARRY *and* CLIFF *are doing them,* CLIFF *rather leisurely. The exercise is to spread the arms out and touch the toes of one foot with the opposite hand.*)

BATES (*Box*): Come on, it's the last exercise. Put something into it! Left toe! Right toe! Left toe! Right toe!

CLIFF (*To* GEORGE): Anything happening?

GEORGE: Not that I can see.

HARRY (*Hopefully*): Everybody's probably forgotten it by now.

BATES (*Finishing the count on box*): Left toe, right toe and UP! Attention to the following announcement . . . (HARRY *is making his bunk,* CLIFF *has drifted over to his desk*) Helicopter will be taking mail back to Battalion Headquarters on the carrier at 0900. Repeat:

0900. So get it in, we won't wait for it. Corporal Evans will report to Headquarters. That is all.

(GEORGE and HARRY stand frozen.)

HARRY: They've found out. Already!

GEORGE: Now don't worry, Cliff. Just deny everything!

CLIFF: What a bunch of conspirators! They just want the movies that are going back . . . (He lifts up the cans of movies, reads the title of one) "The Bowery Boys Over Berlin." Hm, I wondered where Adams got that story.

GEORGE: Maybe it's a trap . . . trying to separate us.

CLIFF: Relax, George. Nobody cares about the shooting. I could have told you that.

GEORGE: With everybody on guard? Don't you feel the tension mounting?

(CLIFF lifts a finger as if to determine the direction of a breeze.)

CLIFF: Nope. Don't feel a thing.

GEORGE: I tell you it's like back home, on the first day of the deer season. Those guys out there will fire at anything!

(Dissolve to officer's tent. FENTRISS is standing watching CARMODY read his report.)

FENTRISS: I think it covers the situation clearly.

CARMODY: Practically in glorious Technicolor.

FENTRISS: Those are eye-witness reports, Colonel.

CARMODY: All right, Fentriss. Let's not go through that again. Now what do you expect me to do with it? (He looks longingly at the wastebasket by his desk) Because I have a suggestion.

FENTRISS: Why, forward it!

CARMODY: Where? Battalion? Division? Tokyo? They'd laugh me off this island. Which might not be a bad idea.

FENTRISS: I believe that's what's known as a calculated risk, sir.

(Dissolve back to squad tent. HARRY and GEORGE are alone now.)

HARRY: Come on, George, let's just forget about it.

GEORGE: It's too late, Harry. You could drop a lightbulb right now, and seventeen rifles would go off.

HARRY: After one night? George, please . . .

(GEORGE looks at him and then casually goes over to the hanging light cord, and unscrews the bulb. Without a word *he moves to the opening of the tent and heaves the bulb out into the compound. The crash of the bulb is heard clearly. It is followed immediately by several rifle shots which continue as the camera cuts to the officer's tent.* CARMODY *and* FENTRISS *listen to the shots: the colonel's hand frozen as he holds the report over the wastebasket.*)

FENTRISS: Well? (*He takes the report from the colonel*) I'll see this gets on the mail plane.

(*He exits.* CARMODY *stares after him.*)

CARMODY (*Muttering*): "Cry Havoc! And let loose the dogs of war!"

FADE OUT

(*Fade in on a close shot of* FENTRISS *putting the report into the mail pouch. The report is quite thin, and has a distinctive cover.* FENTRISS *closes the bag, which is marked* Official.)

(*Dissolve through film shot of helicopter landing on aircraft carrier deck.*)

(*Cut to* SAILOR *unpacking the pouch. He takes out the report. He looks up at off-camera helper.*)

SAILOR: Take over, Joe. I'd better get this up to the Commandant.

(*Camera moves in on close shot of report. It stays on it as he exits. Dissolve to close shot of door marked* Battalion Commandant. SAILOR *knocks on the door, opens it and walks in. A* COMMANDANT, *obviously one with many years spent doing paper work, is seated at a desk. There is a porthole behind him.*)

COMMANDANT: Yes?

SAILOR: This just came in with the mail from Bondagroupa, sir.

(*The* COMMANDANT *takes the report, opens it and starts to read. Then he looks up at the* SAILOR.)

COMMANDANT: Get my staff up here at once, sailor!

SAILOR: Yes, sir!

(*The* COMMANDANT *flips through the few pages of the report. As he reaches the last one . . . Dissolve to same scene, only now a* MAJOR *and a* CAPTAIN *are standing beside his desk.*)

COMMANDANT: Well, there it is, gentlemen.

MAJOR: What do you think of it, sir?

COMMANDANT: I think . . . (*He edges closer to them, his voice dropping with the seriousness of the situation*) that this report is either accurate . . . or it isn't.

MAJOR and CAPTAIN (*Together*): Yes, sir!

COMMANDANT: It may mean nothing. Then again it may not.

CAPTAIN: Commandant, you really think it's an attack?

COMMANDANT: Captain, it's not our place to think.

MAJOR: No, indeed!

COMMANDANT: We do our duty!

CAPTAIN: Yes, sir!

COMMANDANT: And pass it on to higher authority. Type up my endorsement.

(*The camera closes in on the report.*)

(*Dissolve through film shot of plane in flight to film shot of Tokyo and the exterior of the Dai Itchi building.*)

(*Fade in on tight shot of a military desk. On it sits the report. It is growing fatter. Weighing down the last page is a corncob pipe. And we hear a brisk voice:*)

VOICE: You know what to do with this, gentlemen?

2ND VOICE (*Unemotional*): Yes, sir. Usual endorsements.

(*And, as a khaki-covered arm picks up the report . . .*)

(*Dissolve to a close shot of a definitely thicker report, with the same cover, being placed in a small important-looking pouch. The bag is padlocked and stood up. The bag is marked: "Top Secret."*)

(*Dissolve to film shot of Washington, D.C., view from the air. The shot includes the Pentagon.*)

(*Cut to a close shot of an officer's shoulder. The wearer is a brigadier general (one star). The camera pulls back and we see he is seated at a desk which carries the sign:* General Phipps, Far Eastern Affairs. *Phipps is a thin, middle-aged man who looks far too shy to be a general. He appears faintly puzzled by the report which he is now reading, but when he finishes it, he sighs, and taking the report with him, rises.*)

(*Cut to tight shot of second military shoulder. This is a major general (two stars). The camera pulls back. The sign on this desk says:* General Ames, Far Eastern Affairs. Island Bases.)

(PHIPPS *stands behind* AMES, *who is much more assured-looking than he, and watches him finish the still-growing report. When* AMES *does, he looks at* PHIPPS, *with the gravity of the situation. Without a word, they pick up the report which is still growing, and move quickly off-camera.*)

(*Cut to tight shot of third military shoulder. This belongs to a lieutenant general* (three *stars*). *The camera pulls back. The sign on this desk is:* General March, Pacific Island Bases, Task Strategy. *The report* GENERAL MARCH (*A florid man in his fifties*) *is reading is even thicker, and he reads it with growing astonishment.* PHIPPS *and* AMES *stand behind him, watching him nervously. When* MARCH *finishes the last page he looks at the other two. He rises silently. All three faces are incredibly grim.*)

(*Dissolve through exterior of door marked "War Room" to a tight shot of a fourth military shoulder . . .* GENERAL SMITH *is a full general* (four *stars*). *He is the oldest of the quartet, the most florid, and the most serious.*)

(*The camera pulls back and we see the other three generals clustered with* SMITH *around a cluttered table. The scattered maps and overflowing ashtrays are witnesses that the generals have been at it for some time. The report is in the center of the table, fatter than ever.*)

SMITH: Could very well touch off a ticklish situation.
AMES: If they take Bendagroupa, they'll be within striking distance of Belunegra. And its sister islands!
MARCH (*Horrified*): Belunegra!
PHIPPS: What's on Belunegra?
MARCH: Nothing. But even so . . .
PHIPPS: Couldn't we just forget about it?
AMES: Phipps, this could be important.
PHIPPS: Just a few rifle shots.
SMITH: Gentlemen, we're public servants. The public wants this war *over.*
PHIPPS: It is *over.* Isn't it?
AMES: Only one thing to do.
SMITH (*Nodding*): Pass it on.
PHIPPS: But there's no place left!
MARCH: Phipps! Have you lost your senses?

(Dissolve through film shot of exterior of White House to close shot of man playing the piano. We see only his back, square, solid, graying hair, etc. He is having a little difficulty with The Missouri Waltz. A door opens and closes off-camera, and GENERAL PHIPPS comes up to the piano with a bulky volume the size of the Manhattan phone directory. The piano player stops playing as PHIPPS hands him the report.)

PHIPPS: Sorry to disturb you, sir, but you'd better see this right away. At least, that's what everybody seems to think.

(As the man at the piano reaches for the report, cut to a tight shot of a newscaster in the process of broadcasting. His tie is tugged down from his neck, his hat perches rakishly on his head, and he hugs the microphone with enthusiasm.)

BROADCASTER: . . . and inside sources say the tiny island of Bendagroupa and sister islands are under constant guerrilla attack from undefeated, unsurrendered Japanese forces. It is time the great white light of public concern turns on our gallant soldiers of these islands for whom the war shows no signs of being over . . .

FADE OUT

(Fade in on a close shot of the light cord hanging in the squad tent. There is no bulb to replace the one GEORGE threw into the compound. It is afternoon, three days later. The camera pans down to show HARRY at his desk, typing. GEORGE is seated alongside, head cradled in his arms, asleep. After a moment, HARRY nudges him.)

HARRY: George?

(GEORGE sits up quickly.)

GEORGE: Just closed my eyes, sir! *(He realizes where he is)* Oh, I thought we were on guard again.

HARRY: Not for another half hour. You got a typewriter ribbon?

GEORGE: No.

HARRY: You got a fountain pen?

GEORGE: No.

HARRY: I can't write Edith in pencil. It's unromantic.

GEORGE: What have you got to write her about?

HARRY: Nothing.

GEORGE: Then why write?

HARRY: That's right . . . be grouchy. You need more sleep.

GEORGE: I was trying to get it. Sometimes I think Sherman was right.

HARRY: Maybe this wasn't such a good idea.

GEORGE: Harry, do you know how many times you've said that?

HARRY: What does it matter? You never listen.

> (CLIFF *enters in full guard uniform—helmet, rifle, etc.—carrying a roll of barbed wire. His expression is pained, to say the least.*)

GEORGE: What's that?

CLIFF: Barbed wire.

HARRY: What?

CLIFF: For all tents in the compound. Orders.

GEORGE: What do we do with it?

CLIFF: It's to go on the other side of the sand bags, just behind the slit trenches.

HARRY: *What* sandbags?

CLIFF: The ones *we're* going to make out of the dirt from the trenches *we're* going to dig. (*He nods his head toward the tent opening*) Take a look. (GEORGE *heads quickly for the tent entrance*) Only don't go out like that. DR for anyone caught outside quarters without a helmet and rifle.

GEORGE: They believe it! They really believe it!

CLIFF: Some trick . . . selling a war to the Army!

GEORGE: Don't you see? It's working!

CLIFF: So are we.

HARRY: And we're still not a combat zone. Everybody'll be home. Out of service. And here we'll be . . . standing perimeter guard.

GEORGE: What do you expect in three days? It was people like you that laughed at the Wright Brothers.

CLIFF: Do you know how long it took the Wright Brothers to get off the ground? Twenty-seven planes, that's how long. I'd have laughed, too.

HARRY: We got to go through this twenty-seven times?

CLIFF: No, Harry. We're quitting, right now. Couple of quiet nights . . . everybody'll calm down . . . they'll send out search parties . . . and that will be *that*.

GEORGE: You can't stop now!

CLIFF: Look, George . . . we'll pass over the moral question of whether you had any right to do this, and get down to a simple basic fact. We're tired.

GEORGE: A couple of more nights . . .

CLIFF: Do you know they sent that report to Washington? "Mom's apple pie" and everything? Do you know what could happen? We could be back at war again. And frankly, George, I don't think you're worth it!

GEORGE: It's probably filed away in somebody's desk. Have a little faith, fellow. Have I ever given you a wrong steer?

HARRY: Yes.

GEORGE: Look at the way things are run here. And the further back it gets, the longer it takes. You know that. Harry, *you* know that.

HARRY: I promised Edith. I wouldn't get into any trouble.

GEORGE: All that can happen is a little interest might come our way.

CLIFF: Do you know what *interest* in the Army means? The Inspector General! Is your office ready for inspection? Because mine isn't!

GEORGE: I tell you, nothing can happen! Except we'll get off this island.

CLIFF: You know, Alcatraz is an island, too!

FADE OUT

> (*Fade in on* COMMANDANT, MAJOR *and* CAPTAIN *seated around the* COMMANDANT's *desk on the carrier, the porthole behind them, maps strewn all over the desk, etc.*)

COMMANDANT: There it is, gentlemen. Plan operations. Troops will land at 1900 hours this evening . . .

> (*Dissolve to a tight shot of the carrier's P.A. box, hanging in the wardroom.*)

VOICE (*Over P.A. box*): Flight groups A, D, F and G will leave carrier at 1900 hours. Exact location of bomb target will be radioed from the advance infantry unit . . .

> (*Dissolve to a close shot of the* SAILOR *seen previously, tapping out a message by Morse code in the carrier's signal room. The* SAILOR *speaks the message as he sends it.*)

SAILOR: To all fleet ships: attention! Commanders will assemble their vessels at south side of Bondagroupa, this date, 1900 hours . . .

> (*Dissolve to the interior of the officer's squad tent. A very confused* COLONEL CARMODY *is listening to* FENTRISS.)

FENTRISS: . . . the first wave lands at 1900 hours, off-shore ships covering the landing with heavy fire. The air support will arrive at approxi . . .

CARMODY: Air support for *what?* Fentriss, do you realize the United States Government is sending a full invasion force to the south part of this island tonight, and there's going to be no one there? Absolutely *no one?* Do you know how much money this is costing? How much time? How much energy? And do you know what's going to happen to me when they find no one there? I may want to get out of the Army. But not *this* way!

FENTRISS: Sir, we have a responsibility . . .

CARMODY: I know, I know . . . you can't wait to show the Regular Army what a hero you are.

FENTRISS: There've been three nights of guerrilla fire . . .

CARMODY: Three nights. In which none of our men have been killed or wounded. The Japs have better aim than that.

FENTRISS: We're experienced troops . . .

CARMODY: At what? Changing typewriter ribbons?

FENTRISS: And my cap?

CARMODY: All right, Fentriss. Let's not talk about it any more. I'll march the men south tonight till we meet these guerrillas of yours. We may reach the sea first, but we'll keep right on marching. But Heaven help you if there's no one there! Heaven help you!

> (*Cut to exterior of the officers' tent, heavily covered with barbed wire.* GEORGE *comes up and starts to knock when he is caught by what* CARMODY *and* FENTRISS *are saying. He stands there appalled.* FENTRISS *comes out.*)

FENTRISS: What do you want, Harris?

GEORGE: I just wondered about guard . . .

FENTRISS: We're all on it. It's "over the top" tonight.

> (*As he strides off, we see the growing horror on* GEORGE'S *face.*)

FADE OUT

> (*Fade in on the interior of the trio's squad tent.* HARRY *and* CLIFF *are busy tying up some sand bags. A pale, frightened, jittery* GEORGE *enters.*)

CLIFF: Hi.

HARRY: We left the west trench for you. We figured that was your share . . .

GEORGE: Fellows . . . I'm sick.

CLIFF: Won't work, George. You've still got to dig it.

GEORGE: They're invading tonight . . .

HARRY: What?

GEORGE: There's going to be ships . . . and troops . . . and air support . . . and the colonel's going to lead us . . . and we're all in the first wave . . .

CLIFF: Harry ... the bottle!

(HARRY *disappears, bringing back a bottle of whiskey.*)

CLIFF: Drink this, George. (GEORGE *tries to gulp it down*) I said *drink.* Not drown. Now, what is all this?

GEORGE: You were right. They're taking it seriously. They're forming the counter-offensive right now. The colonel and everybody. And if they don't find the enemy ...

HARRY: *I* need a drink.

CLIFF: I *told* Orville it wouldn't fly. (*He hands* HARRY *the bottle*) You mean they're sending a whole task force out here to clean up our snipers?

HARRY: And there won't be anybody there! (*He giggles a little over his next drink*) Not *anybody!*

CLIFF: Now look ... not you, too!

GEORGE: Beat me, fellows. I deserve it. Shoot me.

CLIFF: The Army'll take care of that.

(HARRY *laughs happily to himself.*)

HARRY: *Nobody* there!

CLIFF: Put down that bottle!

GEORGE: What are we going to do? Cliff?

(CLIFF *looks at him for a long moment.*)

CLIFF: Give ourselves up.

HARRY: *No!*

CLIFF: They're bound to find out. At least we'll have stopped this invasion. That's something.

GEORGE: What'll we get? Twenty years? Thirty? Life?

CLIFF: If I know Fentriss, he won't want to make an idiot of himself. We tell him everything, and he calls the deal off. Then he'll have to go easy on us.

HARRY: Couldn't we just tell the Chaplain?

(FENTRISS *enters in full battle dress.*)

FENTRISS: 'Ten-shun! Better get started, men. We're having bayonet drill before guard mount.

HARRY: Yes, sir!

FENTRISS: And don't forget to pick up your extra ammo for tonight.

CLIFF: George? Haven't you something to tell the lieutenant?

GEORGE: Sir ... Maybe you'd better sit down first.

FENTRISS: What's the matter, Sergeant? I haven't got all day.

(GEORGE *takes a deep breath, and plunges in.*)

GEORGE: Sir . . . there aren't any Japs out there. We fired those shots.

(FENTRISS *sits suddenly on a chair.* CLIFF *moves up just in time.*)

CLIFF: I thought you'd need it.

FENTRISS: You mean . . . there's no guerrillas out there?

CLIFF: Not with guns.

FENTRISS: No Japs? No snipers? *Nothing?*

CLIFF: Mosquitoes.

HARRY: We only wanted it to be a combat zone again, sir. So we could go home.

FENTRISS: And the hole? In my cap?

GEORGE: People get reckless.

FENTRISS: And you did it all! What are you anyway? Saboteurs, or something?

GEORGE: We didn't mean any harm . . .

FENTRISS: Do you know what they'll do to me? I might have had a career in the Army. Washed up! Finished! I'll be selling real estate in Topeka with the colonel. If he'll have me!

CLIFF: We were only trying to be helpful.

FENTRISS: What were you going to do next? Poison the water?

GEORGE: We thought we should tell the colonel.

FENTRISS: *No!* Tell him nothing! Understand?

HARRY: But, sir . . .

FENTRISS: *Nothing!* I'll handle that.

GEORGE: What do you want us to do?

FENTRISS: You're under arrest. You're broken to recruits. You're fined every penny of pay coming to you. You're court-martialed. You're everything I can think of . . .

(M/SGT. BATES *enters in full battle-dress.*)

BATES: Sir? The colonel wants you.

FENTRISS: I'm sick, Sergeant. Tell him I'm sick.

BATES: Yes, sir. I think he expected you to lead the troops tonight.

FENTRISS: Where? To the U.S.O.?

(BATES *is puzzled by this, but gets back to his original errand.*)

BATES: Come on, you guys. You're on guard.

(GEORGE *turns to* FENTRISS.)

GEORGE: Sir?

FENTRISS: Go along. I'll take care of you when you get back. *If* you get back. *Alive.* It might be better if you don't!

FADE OUT

(*Fade in on tight shot of wrist watch on* COLONEL CARMODY'S *arm. It is 20 minutes before 1900 hours. (7:00 P.M.) The* COLONEL *is standing with a group of soldiers in full battle dress (as is he) in the compound. He is briefing them on the attack.*)

CARMODY: . . . then once contact is made, we'll radio Headquarters the exact location. This'll be transmitted to off-shore reinforcements. They'll take it from there. Any questions?

BATES: Sir . . . what if there's nobody out there?

CARMODY: Any other questions? Now I'll want three men to act as scouts. Any volunteers?

(*Nobody moves.*)

BATES: Aw, come on, fellows! Johnson!

JOHNSON: Sir, I'm a Company Clerk. My glasses fog up.

CARMODY: Never mind, Sergeant. I'll take those three men who've been on guard these last five nights.

(*For the first time in this scene, we see* GEORGE, HARRY *and* CLIFF. *They have not spent much time and effort on looking like sharp eager guards.*)

CARMODY: If anybody knows where these snipers are, it should be you three. Shouldn't it?

GEORGE: Well, sir . . . you see . . .

CARMODY: Uh huh . . . Just what I figured. Let's get started!

(*And the men commence to file off,* GEORGE, HARRY *and* CLIFF *reluctantly in front . . . the* COLONEL *right behind them.*)

FADE OUT

ACT THREE

(*Fade in on a section of the jungle. We hear wild thrashing about. Finally* GEORGE *appears. He looks around carefully, and then signals behind him.* CLIFF *appears.*)

GEORGE: Okay . . . we've lost them.

(*The bushes part and* CARMODY *appears.*)

CARMODY: Any sign?

GEORGE (*Wearily*): Must be further along, sir.

CARMODY: Let's keep going then.

> (*They all head back into the brush. Dissolve to another section of the jungle.* GEORGE *and* CLIFF *are crawling along together.*)

CLIFF: How much longer do we keep this up?

GEORGE: I don't know. You don't think he's doing this for revenge, do you?

CLIFF: If he is, it's working. Let's rest a minute.

GEORGE: Cliff . . . do you think Fentriss didn't tell him?

CLIFF: I'm not thinking *anything* at the moment. Of all the silly things I've done in my life, crawling through an empty jungle heads the list.

GEORGE: I'd better tell the colonel . . .

CLIFF: George, for once in your life, keep your mouth shut! What time is it?

GEORGE: It's five minutes to . . .

> (CARMODY *crawls into the frame.*)

CARMODY: *Now* what?

GEORGE: Well, sir, we're outside the perimeter guard . . . It's kind of hard to remember just where the shots came from.

CARMODY: *Do* try. We've an invasion force, a fleet and four squads of airplanes waiting.

GEORGE: Yes, sir. Well now. I think some of them came from over there . . .

> (*He points to the left.*)

CLIFF: Yes, sir . . . over that way . . .

> (*He points to the right.* CARMODY *stares at them with heavy resignation.*)

CARMODY: All right. We'll just keep going straight ahead.

> (*He crawls off again.* CLIFF *and* GEORGE *prepare to follow him.*)

CLIFF: "Off we go, into the wild green yonder . . ."

> (*Dissolve to another jungle clearing.* BATES *is seated with the walkie-talkie.* ADAMS *and* JOHNSON *sit beside him.* CARMODY *comes out of the brush.*)

CARMODY: Anybody see anything?

JOHNSON: Something moved over there.

BATES: You had your glasses off.

ADAMS: Seems to me it was further along.

JOHNSON: Maybe it was up in the trees.

CARMODY: We can't have lost them *again!* Forward!

> (*Cut to close shot of* HARRY *and* CLIFF *crawling through the darkness.*)

CLIFF: Why do we have to crawl? That's all I want to know.

HARRY (*Thinking desperately*): Suppose I fired a shot or two?

CLIFF: Harry, this guy isn't Fentriss. I wouldn't put it past him to count our ammo when we get back.

HARRY: What'll we do? Just keep crawling forever?

CLIFF: We'll hit the beach in another half mile. It'll be all over then.

HARRY (*Looking at his watch*): One minute to 1900. Cliff . . . do something!

CLIFF: We're a lost cause, Harry.

> (CARMODY *crawls up once more.*)

CARMODY: *Now* what are you stopping for?

CLIFF: Sgt. Harris has gone on ahead, sir.

HARRY (*It's a feeble imitation of* GEORGE *in the first act*): Colonel, don't you get the feeling that out there in the darkness people are watching us . . . raising their weapons . . . taking aim . . .

CARMODY: Yes. And they're on our side. Keep moving. We'll see the ocean from the top of this ridge.

HARRY: Yes, sir.

FADE OUT

> (*Fade in on the top of the ridge. Off-camera we can hear the sound of the sea. After a moment,* GEORGE *crawls up into view. He reaches the top of the ridge, but before he looks over he crosses his fingers. Finally, he gets up enough courage to look. He obviously sees nothing. He shrugs his shoulders. The ever-present* CARMODY *appears. He also looks.*)

CARMODY: Well, Sergeant?

GEORGE: Nothing, sir.

CARMODY: Don't want us to swim out a way? Just to make sure?

GEORGE: No, sir.

CARMODY: All right. Clear your weapon. We'll start back. (GEORGE *takes the ammo clip from his* M-1) Barrel clear?

GEORGE: Yes, sir. See? (*He squeezes the trigger. One shot goes off.*)

CARMODY: Good Heavens, man! Didn't anyone ever tell you that one round stays in the chamber?

GEORGE: Sorry, sir . . .

 (*But whatever he is trying to say is lost in the rifle fire starting up around them.*)

CARMODY: Now you've got the rest of them started. (*Yelling*) Stop that firing, you idiots! Stop it! (*He plows off down the hill.*)

 (*Dissolve to the jungle clearing.* BATES *and* JOHNSON *are alone with the walkie-talkie.*)

JOHNSON: There they go!

 (BATES *winds up the walkie-talkie.*)

BATES: CHQ! CHQ! Come in . . . come in . . . Bottleneck Forward . . . enemy has been sighted at the end of the island.

 (JOHNSON *looks at his watch.*)

JOHNSON: 1900 . . . right on the nose. (*He looks suddenly glum*) Darn it . . . I should have brought my camera!

 (*Dissolve to the* SAILOR *receiving the message in the carrier's signal room. Dissolve through film shots of PT boats landing on the shore with infantry men piling out and up on to the beach to a film shot of planes circling, guns firing, dropping bombs, etc. Fade in on the top of the ridge.* GEORGE *and* CLIFF *are watching the scene. Judging from the noise, all hell is breaking loose on the beach.* HARRY *has his eyes covered with his hands.*)

CLIFF: Look at that!

HARRY: I can't.

GEORGE: Now there's *no* need for bombs.

CLIFF: Never have so many done so much for so little. They can put that over our graves.

 (HARRY *is looking at the scene now too.*)

HARRY: Must be six ships out there.

CLIFF: Hundreds of troops . . .

HARRY: Shouldn't somebody say something? To the colonel, I mean?

CLIFF: What would you suggest? "Happy Fourth of July?"

 (CARMODY *crawls up.*)

CARMODY: Quite a show, isn't it?

GEORGE: I suppose the Government will look on it as maneuvers. I mean if ...

CARMODY: If what? If there's nobody down there?

GEORGE: Well, it's good practice. And everything.

CARMODY: I'm afraid it'll take a much more serious view than that. Are you all satisfied now?

CLIFF: Satisfied?

CARMODY: I think it's about time we stopped this little game ...

(BATES *crawls up, and without stopping yells:*)

BATES: All right, there. Up with your hands!

CARMODY: Oh, stop it, Bates.

BATES (*Bewildered*): Where's the enemy?

(CARMODY *turns to the rear and yells.*)

CARMODY: Cease fire! Bates, place these troublemakers under arrest.

(HARRY *is watching* CLIFF, *who has his eyes closed.*)

HARRY: What are you doing?

CLIFF: Praying. What else is there? (*A shot passes over his head. He ducks automatically, and then looks up to where he had been aiming his prayers*) That isn't what I asked for!

HARRY: There's another one!

(*He ducks.* CARMODY *and* BATES *hit the dirt behind them.*)

CARMODY: They're firing at us now! Can't they see where they're aiming? (*He crawls up to the top of the ridge again and stands*) Cease fire! The exercise is over.

(*Another shot whistles past him.* GEORGE *pulls him down.*)

GEORGE: They sure got in those caves in a hurry.

CARMODY (*Shouting*): Don't you men understand English? I said, "Cease fire!" (*Three more shots go over their heads. The battle is becoming noisier.* BATES *is in the rear, struggling with the walkie-talkie*) Bates, contact those ground troops. Tell them to stop firing at once!

BATES: I can't, sir. They're still pinned down on the beach.

CARMODY: Then who's down there?

(*He doesn't quite get to finish this as a series of shots goes over their heads.* GEORGE *scratches his arm. He moves his hand away. It is wet and sticky.*)

GEORGE: Holy Cow! *Real* blood! (*To* CARMODY) I hate to ask this, sir. But may we fire back?

(CARMODY *looks highly confused.*)

FADE OUT

(*Fade in on officers' squad tent.* FENTRISS *is asleep in his chair, his legs propped up on the table before him. The sound of gunfire off-camera awakens him. He rises, stretches slowly and moves to the opening of the tent. There is not much rifle fire now, but what there is sounds nearer.* FENTRISS *reaches the tent opening. He cannot believe what he sees in the compound.*)

FENTRISS: No. No ... no ... NO! (*The camera pulls back and we see the men returning from the patrol. In front of each of their rifles walks a small ragged Japanese soldier: hands clasped above the head. There is quite a bit of laughter among the soldiers ... both the Japanese and the Americans.* BATES *comes up to* FENTRISS *wearily*) What is this, Bates?

BATES: Sir, I'm just an ignorant country boy. I know there isn't anybody out there. There couldn't be.

FENTRISS: But these captives!

BATES: Well, sir, *you* know it. And *I* know it. But *they* don't know it.

(GEORGE *comes up, a temporary bandage on his arm.*)

GEORGE: Just wanted to let you know we found them all right, sir.

FENTRISS: Found them ...

GEORGE: The guerrillas. Over a hundred of them, living in the caves. Been there for weeks. Didn't even know about the peace. Colonel's still down there.

(HARRY *hurries up.*)

HARRY: Come on, George. Those guys'll have that submarine stripped by the time we get back.

GEORGE (*To* BATES *and* FENTRISS): That's how they got here. Bates, can I borrow your ammo? (BATES *hands it to him silently*) Thanks. You know, sir, you *do* look sick. You'd better lie down again.

(*And* HARRY *and* GEORGE *dash back to their war.*)

BATES: He was wounded too. Some guys have all the luck.

FENTRISS: Sergeant, you live in Topeka, don't you? (BATES *nods*) Ever think of buying some real estate?

FADE OUT

> (*Fade in on exterior of squad tent later that evening. Off-camera we can hear* GEORGE, HARRY *and* CLIFF *approaching. They are singing* "Onward, Christian Soldiers." *They appear with their souvenirs of the war . . . a Japanese sword, a flag, etc. As they go into the tent, dissolve to interior of the tent. What can be seen appears empty.* GEORGE *enters last, his arm neatly bandaged. The other two have seen something when they entered that quiets them.* GEORGE *doesn't see it at first.*)

GEORGE (*Entering*): Good-bye, cruddy tent! Good-bye, lousy chow . . .

> (*And we see* FENTRISS, *sitting and waiting.*)

FENTRISS: Well. Back from the Front!

GEORGE: We missed you, sir.

FENTRISS: Why did you say it was a fake? That's all I want to know. Why?

GEORGE: Well, sir . . . you'd been on guard so many times. You looked tired. And you would have wanted to go . . . and . . . well . . .

HARRY: Yes, sir. You would have wanted to go.

CLIFF: It just seemed best.

FENTRISS: Do you realize you've cheated me out of the only combat experience I could have had in this war? Do you know what that means on a promotion list? When I think of your tricks . . . your lies . . .

> (CARMODY *outside the tent yells:*)

CARMODY: 'Ten-shun! (*He enters*) Where's my boys? You here, Fentriss?

FENTRISS: Yes, sir.

CARMODY: Thought you were sick. Mustn't shirk action, Lieutenant. Looks bad.

FENTRISS: Sir . . .

CARMODY: Now, young men, I have a proposition. I must admit I didn't believe you about those snipers. Didn't seem possible, did it, Fentriss?

FENTRISS: I always said . . .

CARMODY: Yes. Well, we're back as a combat zone. So you can either stay on with your friends and comrades, and be put up for medals . . .

GEORGE: Same . . . officers too, sir?

CARMODY: No, most of us have enough points to rotate. But Fentriss here . . . no combat experience . . . he'll be staying.

HARRY (*Gently*): And the other choice?

CARMODY: That report of the lieutenant's brought us a troop ship, headed for the States. You can rotate tonight. If you can get ready in time.

CLIFF: We're ready.

FENTRISS: They have to go through medical inspection, Colonel.

GEORGE: We could do that on board.

CARMODY: Of course you could. I'll be there to sign the papers.

FENTRISS: There's equipment to turn in ...

CARMODY: Don't be an old fuddy-duddy, Fentriss. It isn't every day the Army provides door-to-door service. Too bad about the medals, though ...

CLIFF (*Modestly*): That's all right, sir.

FENTRISS: Colonel . . . suppose I told you these men cooked up the whole scheme just to rotate?

CARMODY: Why then we'd have to have them punished. That is, if there hadn't been an enemy out there. And I'd have to have you disciplined as an over-imaginative, hysterical officer who jumped at the sound of a little gunfire. I don't think any of us would like that. Would we, Lieutenant?

FENTRISS (*He's licked*): No, sir.

CARMODY: See you on board, men. (*He turns to leave and then stops and stares at the three of them. It's very hard for him to keep a straight face while looking at them*) The things soldiers think up when they're bored! (*And he exits. The men immediately begin their preparations.*)

GEORGE: Now that cot doesn't belong to Supply, Lieutenant. It's Pfc. Winkler's in Headquarters Company ...

CLIFF: The magazine ration arrives every other Wednesday. Forward it to the units in that green box ...

HARRY: I sort of got behind on the Morning Reports. But it shouldn't take you long ...

GEORGE: This typewriter's a little tricky. No w, use two v's instead. And the zero is the capital o. And if anything sticks, well, I always hit it here ...

FENTRISS: Pretty clever soldiers, aren't you?

GEORGE: No, sir. Just average civilians.

(*The camera moves in on a tight shot of* FENTRISS.)

FENTRISS: There'll be a day of accounting. You'll see! We don't live in a peaceful century, gentlemen. And the Army never forgets. Someday...

FADE OUT

> (*Fade in on the* Event *conference room and a close shot of* ANDREW FOGARTY. *The clock behind him is at* 12:47.)

FOGARTY: Someday, gentlemen, we knew the time would come for accounting. That day is now. As for your assignments ... (*The men at the* Event *table start to rise, gather up their copious notes, pick up their coats and put them on. As each man passes* FOGARTY *on his way out, he shakes his hand*) Well, Ferguson, it's back to Africa ... Sanders ... I hear Berlin looks very different now ... Macauley, Washington again, eh? And Harris ... where are you, George?

> (GEORGE *comes up, his overcoat already buttoned up, his glasses firmly in place, hat in hand.*)

GEORGE: Here, sir.

FOGARTY: Back to Bandagroupa. Remember that guerrilla campaign? Made every front page.

GEORGE: Yes, sir. Couldn't I trade with somebody else?

FOGARTY: You don't like OPERATION RETURN?

GEORGE: It's not that ... it just has unpleasant associations.

FOGARTY: It'll be different now, George. You'll be going back as an officer.

GEORGE: In the Army?

FOGARTY: It's still a military outpost ... rotation points got cut to one a month. But you'll be an acting First Lieutenant. That should take care of any problems.

GEORGE: I guess so.

FOGARTY: Get in touch with their PIO officer. Fentriss, his name is. Captain Fentriss. (*There is a look of doom about* GEORGE) And let us hear from you now and then, George ... (*With an eloquent look of despair,* GEORGE *nods and heads for the door.*)

FADE OUT

The Penny

by STANLEY NISS

CATEGORY:

Radio Series

(ANY LENGTH)

THE PENNY

by STANLEY NISS

The Penny
was first presented on the 21ST PRECINCT program, on CBS,
under the direction of Stanley Niss,
on January 20, 1956,
with the following cast:

CAPTAIN · James Gregory
SERGEANT · Harold Stone
LIEUTENANT · Ken Lynch
JOHN · Mandel Kramer
SHIRLEY · Elspeth Eric
POP · Ralph Camargo
MERCADO · Ralph Camargo
KANE · John Sylvester
MAN · Frank Marth
BAILEY · Frank Marth

SWITCHBOARD BUZZER—PLUG IN CORD

SERGEANT: Twenty-first Precinct, Sergeant Waters.—Who? Who's fighting there?—Well, who is it? His wife? What's the address? What apartment number? (*Fade under on cue*) What's the matter? Can't you stop them? Oh, yeah? Yeah? Is that so? Where are you calling from? Oh. I see.

CAPTAIN (*Cue*): You are by transcription in the muster room at the Twenty-first Precinct. The nerve center. A call is coming through. You will follow the action taken pursuant to that call from this minute until the final report is written in the 124 Room at the Twenty-first Precinct.

SERGEANT (*On mike*): All right. I'm sending the officers right over there. Yes. That's right. They'll be right there. Okay.

SWITCHBOARD BUZZER—PLUG OUT AND SNAPS BACK—BUZZER OUT

ANNOUNCER: Twenty-first Precinct. It's just lines on a map of the City of New York. Most of the 173,000 people wedged into the nine-tenths of a square mile between Fifth Avenue and the East River wouldn't know, if you asked them, that they lived or worked in the Twenty-first. Whether they know it or not, the security of their homes, their persons and their property is the job of the men of the Twenty-first Precinct.

CAPTAIN: The Twenty-first. One hundred and sixty patrolmen, eleven sergeants, and four lieutenants of whom I'm the boss. My name is Cronin. Vincent P. Cronin. I'm Captain in command of the Twenty-first Precinct.—I was doing night duty, 4 P.M. to 8 A.M. The weather had been extremely cold and, although this creates harder working conditions for policemen, it keeps troublemakers off the streets. As a result, the four to twelve was a quiet tour. I turned out the platoon for the late tour at midnight, and, among those men who marched out the front door to take over their posts was Patrolman William Kane assigned to Post No. 7. He marched with the men assigned to posts east of the station house, and broke ranks at Third Avenue to continue toward his post alone. There he relieved Patrolman Anthony Giordanno and began his first round, checking the door of every business establishment on the post as required. At 12:35 A.M. he was walking through a darkened block on East 95th Street, past a row of old-law tenements, toward First Avenue.

STEPS ON SIDEWALK—WIND—TRAFFIC WAY IN BACKGROUND—OPEN DOOR—OFF

POP (*Off*): Policeman.

> (*Stop steps.*)

KANE: Yeah?

POP (*Off*): Policeman! He's killing her.

> (*Fast steps on sidewalk.*)

POP (*Fading in to half off*): He's killing her. Hurry.

KANE: All right. I'm coming.

> (*Up stone steps.*)

POP (*Fading in from half off*): Hurry. Hurry.

> (*Few steps on flat.*)

POP (*Fading in*): He's killing her.

KANE: Where?

> (*Step through door.*)

POP: Upstairs. In the hall.

STEPS ON WOOD—TAKE TRAFFIC OUT

POP (*Fading out*): She's screaming bloody murder.

> (*Start upstairs.*)

SHIRLEY (*Off*): Help. Police. Police!

KANE: All right, lady.

POP (*Fading out from little off*): Do you hear her?

SHIRLEY (*Off*): Help.

> (*Fast steps on flat.*)

KANE: Okay. I'm here.

SHIRLEY (*Fading in to half off*): Help! Police! Police!

> (*Beating on door.*)

SHIRLEY (*Fading in*): Somebody get the police.

> (*Slow down steps.*)

KANE: What's the trouble, lady?

> (*Stop steps.*)

SHIRLEY: He's killing me.

> (*Beat on door.*)

SHIRLEY: He's killing me.

KANE: Who's killing you? I don't see anybody.
SHIRLEY: He's in there.

(Beat on door.)

SHIRLEY: He threw me out.
KANE: All right. Stand away from the door and tell me what it's all about.
SHIRLEY: He's killing me.
KANE: Come on, lady.

(Little movement.)

SHIRLEY: I'll show him.
KANE: Yeah.
POP *(Half off)*: All right? Is everything all right?
KANE: Yeah, Pop. Everything's fine. Thanks.
SHIRLEY: You're not going to let him kill me.
POP *(Half off)*: Can I do something?
KANE: You just better get back inside your flat.
POP *(Half off)*: Okay.
SHIRLEY: You're not going to let him get away with killing me.
KANE: You're not dead yet, lady. What's the trouble here?
SHIRLEY: What's the trouble? I'll tell you what's the trouble. He threw me out. He picked me up and threw me out in the hall.
KANE: Who's he? Your husband?
SHIRLEY: Yeah. My husband. He picked me up and threw me out the door.
KANE: That's no reason to yell out in the hall you're being killed.
SHIRLEY: He was killing me. Before he threw me out he knocked me around. You should have seen him. He hit me with his fist. Do you want to see how? I'll show you.
KANE: All right. Never mind. I know. What do you want me to do about it?
SHIRLEY: What do you mean what do I want you to do about it? It's not safe with a wild man like that loose. I want him arrested. I want him in jail.
KANE: I can't arrest him, lady.
SHIRLEY: What do you mean you can't arrest him? What are you for?
KANE: But if you want to make charges against him I'll take you both down to the station house.
SHIRLEY: Will they put him in jail?
KANE: If you make the charge.

SHIRLEY: I make the charge. Oh! That animal, that beast! He belongs in a zoo, not in jail. In a zoo. A wild man.

(*Open door—half off.*)

MAN (*Half off*): Hey, why don't you knock it off so somebody can get some sleep? What's going on?

SHIRLEY: Go on and get to sleep! Who's stopping you?

MAN (*Half off*): You're waking up the whole building.

SHIRLEY: If you want to sleep, take a pill!

MAN (*Half off*): Listen, I'm going to come out there...

KANE: All right. That's enough. Get inside your flat and close your door. (*Pause*) Close the door.

(*Close door—half off.*)

SHIRLEY: Neighbors. You could be getting murdered and you don't hear from them. Make a little sound and they can't sleep.

KANE: All right. Knock on your door.

SHIRLEY: Do you think he'll answer? I don't.

KANE: Knock.

(*Steps to door.*)

SHIRLEY: All right.

(*Knock on door.*)

KANE: He slugged you, huh?

SHIRLEY: With his fists. With his closed fists.

(*Knock on door.*)

SHIRLEY: John! Open up the door!

JOHN (*Dead side*): I told you to get out of here. Now get out before I come out there and throw you down the stairs myself.

SHIRLEY: You see? You see that?

(*Knock on door with night stick.*)

KANE: All right. This is the police. Open the door.

JOHN (*Dead side*): Shirley? Did you call the cops on me?

(*Another knock with night stick.*)

KANE: Open up.

JOHN (*Dead side*): Did you call the cops on me?

SHIRLEY: Sure. I called the cops. What did you expect me to do? Stand here and get murdered?

KANE: Open up in there.

JOHN (*Dead side*): Why'd you call the cops?

(*Unlock and open door.*)

JOHN: I'm your husband. I'm your own husband.

SHIRLEY: I'd call them a million times.

(*Step through door.*)

KANE: All right.

JOHN: Haven't you got sense enough to keep something like this in the family?

SHIRLEY: Why should I keep it in the family if you're killing me?

JOHN: Okay. I'll kill you good.

SHIRLEY: And you're just the man to do it, huh?

KANE: All right. Cut it out.

JOHN: Yeah, I'm just the man to do it.

KANE: Okay. That's enough. (*Pause*)

KANE: Now let's get this straightened out. You've got half the neighborhood up already. You don't want to wake up the other half, do you?

SHIRLEY: Nobody in the neighborhood cares for me, why should I care for them?

KANE: All right. Just cut it out.

SHIRLEY: Don't tell me to cut it out.

JOHN: Go ahead. Go ahead make him mad enough to slug you, too. Make him mad enough. You see. You see what she does. She needles. She twists. You could kill her. Go ahead. Go ahead. Make the policeman mad enough to slug you, too. You see what I've got to live with?

SHIRLEY: Look who's talking what he's got to live with. What do you think I've got to live with? An animal.

KANE: All right.

JOHN: An animal?

KANE: Okay.

SHIRLEY: The worst kind. A hyena.

JOHN: I'll bat you one!

SHIRLEY: You see. You see that.

KANE: Now stop it, will you? You, sit down there.

SHIRLEY: Me?

KANE: Yeah. You. Sit down. And you stand over there. Now let's get this straightened out.

SHIRLEY: I'll get it straightened out. I want him arrested. I want him taken to jail. That's what I want.

JOHN: I supported you for eleven years, and you want me taken to jail. Is that the appreciation I get?

SHIRLEY: Supported me? Do you call this supported?

KANE: Now, that's enough. Okay. What's this all about?

JOHN: I didn't want to do it but she got me so mad that I . . .

SHIRLEY: What do you mean you didn't want to do it?

KANE: All right. Now, cut it out! What's your name, Mister?

JOHN: John Howick.

KANE: What's your first name, Mrs. Howick?

SHIRLEY: Shirley.

KANE: All right, Mrs. Howick. You tell me what happened.

JOHN: Oh, you'll get some story all right.

KANE: Now, look. Let her talk. You'll get your chance. What happened?

SHIRLEY: Midnight he comes home. How do you like that? Midnight and not a word from him. Not a word from him. He's supposed to be home at five-fifteen and he came home at midnight. I'm supposed to say, good evening, John. Come in and sit down and have supper. You look so nice tonight. I'm not supposed to ask him where he'd been or what happened or who he's been out with.

JOHN: I was out with nobody!

KANE: Okay. I told you you'd get your chance. Go ahead, Mrs. Howick.

SHIRLEY: All I did was ask him a couple of questions. I asked him where he'd been and who he was with. And he slammed into me. He slammed me across the room. And he threw me out in the hall. Threw me out and locked the door. What am I supposed to do?

KANE: Is that all?

SHIRLEY: Except, you see? You see where he hit me right in the chin? It's black and blue, isn't it?

JOHN: It's nothing.

SHIRLEY: He told you to shut up.

JOHN: Aw . . .

KANE: Just sit there.

SHIRLEY: And on my arms. Look on my arms. Bruises. See the welts? With his fists. And he threw me out and locked the door. Where am I supposed to go with no coat? With nothing?

JOHN: You go away from me like you came to me. With no clothes, nothing. Like I got you.

SHIRLEY: I came to you with plenty.

KANE: Okay.

SHIRLEY: I came to you with youth and beauty.

JOHN: What beauty?

KANE: All right now! What's your story, Mr. Howick?

JOHN: There's no story. My boss asked me to work overtime.

SHIRLEY: Hah!

JOHN: What're you "hahing"?

SHIRLEY: Your boss asked you to work overtime.

JOHN: Officer, would you kindly give me the same privilege you gave her? Make her let me tell my story.

KANE: She'll let you tell your story. Go ahead.

JOHN: My boss asked me to stay and work overtime. So I came home at midnight, dog tired. Tired out. I went to work at eight o'clock this morning and I didn't get off till eleven. I was forty-five minutes on the subway. I'm tired, I'm hungry and she gives me a hard time. She says where was I. Who was I out with? What was I drinking? She needles and she twists and finally I couldn't stand it any more. I slammed her across the room. That doesn't stop her, so I slammed her again. That still doesn't stop her and I threw her out. What do you want me to do? Do you want me to sit here and take it after what I've been through all day, working for fifteen hours on my feet almost? From her? I took enough from her already.

SHIRLEY: Admit it. You were out with a woman! Go ahead. Go ahead, don't lie about working like that.

JOHN: You see?

SHIRLEY: You were out with a dame and you got drunk. Loaded.

JOHN: You see, Officer.

SHIRLEY: That's what he does. He lies about working.

JOHN: You can't reason with her. You've got to slam her.

KANE: Okay, now. Let's cut it out.

SHIRLEY: Hit me. I dare you.

KANE: All right now. Just sit down, Mrs. Howick. Did you have anything to drink tonight, John?

JOHN: Nothing. Not a drop. I swear. Not even a beer. Nothing.

SHIRLEY: Don't believe him.

JOHN: I swear. Nothing. I was working.

KANE: Now, look. You don't want to have him arrested, do you? It's just a family argument. You'll get it straightened out.

SHIRLEY: It's not a family argument, because the family is ended. Finished. It's done.

JOHN: That's the way you feel about it, huh?

KANE: Okay, folks.

SHIRLEY: That's the way I feel about it.

KANE: Now, look. Both of you are going to be sorry about this in the morning.

SHIRLEY: I won't be sorry.

KANE: If you have him arrested it's nothing but a lot of trouble, believe me. And you'll regret it.

SHIRLEY: Regret it? Why should I regret it? He tried to kill me. He belongs in jail, don't he?

JOHN: I didn't try to kill you. I only tried to shut you up.

KANE: All right.

JOHN: But maybe the only way to shut you up would be to kill you.

SHIRLEY: There, you see? He admits it. He admits it. You heard him. You heard him.

KANE: You want him arrested?

SHIRLEY: You bet your life I do.

KANE: All right. Let's go to the station house.

JOHN: Shirley, I'm warning you. I'm warning you if you have me arrested that's the last you're going to see of me. That's the last. I swear. I had it. I'm done. I'm finished.

SHIRLEY: Well, what do you think I am? Nobody slams me around and gets away with it. I've got feelings.

JOHN: What do you want? The purple heart? I'll give it to you.

SHIRLEY: I'll tell you what I want. I want you in jail. I want him in jail right now.

KANE: Okay, lady. If you say so, that's where he's going. (*Pause*)

CAPTAIN: Much of a police officer's time is spent quieting, mediating, and settling family fights. Through experience he knows that it's wise to talk the quarreling parties out of carrying their troubles away from the home. In ninety-five percent of the instances where arrests result, the aggrieved persons have a change of heart by the time they are due to appear in court. The action is dismissed and the only result is a waste of time in court by the police officer, loss of work by the husband, and a crowded docket. But, as in this case, it is sometimes impossible to get the matter settled, or, the case may be serious enough to warrant its attention in Home Term Court, one of the magistrates courts of the City of New York. Then, it is the duty of the police officer to inform the aggrieved party— invariably the wife—that she may arrest her husband and that he, the police officer, will accompany them to the station house. Patrolman Kane did just that. At five minutes after one A.M. with John and Shirley Howick, he walked into the Muster Room where Sergeant Waters was sitting in as desk officer.

MUSTER ROOM SOUNDS—STEPS

KANE: All right, folks. Step right up to the desk there.
SHIRLEY: Just keep him away from me, that's all.
JOHN: Who wants to get near you?
KANE: Okay.

> (*Stop steps.*)

KANE: That disorderly conduct arrest, Sergeant.
SERGEANT: Yeah. Move in a little closer, huh?

MOVEMENT—SWITCHBOARD BUZZER—HALF OFF

SERGEANT: You're man and wife, is that right?

PLUG IN BUZZER—HALF OFF

MERCADO (*Half off*): Twenty-first Precinct. Patrolman Mercado.
SHIRLEY: But not for long.
JOHN: You said it.
MERCADO (*Half off*): Okay. Seventeen.
SERGEANT: How long have you been married?

BUZZER AND OUT

SHIRLEY: Eleven years.
SERGEANT: That's a long time.
JOHN: Too long.
SERGEANT: What happened over there, Kane?
KANE: Well, Sergeant, I was walking post on the block and some neighbor in the building yelled out to me on the street: "He's killing her," or something like that. I ran upstairs and found her screaming in the hall. She said he slapped her around, threw her in the hall, and locked the door.
SHIRLEY: Locked me out of my own house.
JOHN: It's my house. I pay the rent.
SERGEANT: All right. Let the officer tell the story.
KANE: I got him to open the door. It seems he was due home at five-thirty and didn't arrive until midnight.
SHIRLEY: Ten after.
JOHN: Will you let him tell it? Stop sticking your big nose in.
SHIRLEY: Whose big nose?
SERGEANT: Okay.

KANE: All right. Cut it out now! Didn't we have enough of this?

SERGEANT: Yeah? And?

KANE: He said he was working overtime. She claimed he was out with a woman drinking. That caused the fight.

SERGEANT: Were you drinking?

JOHN: I didn't have a drop. I swear.

KANE: It didn't seem like he had any, Sergeant.

SHIRLEY: He was loaded.

JOHN: Since when are you an expert on the subject?

SHIRLEY: Since I married you.

SERGEANT: Okay!

JOHN: Oh, I could murder her.

KANE: Now stop it. The war's over.

SERGEANT: You want to have him arrested, is that right? You know you're going to be sorry in the morning, don't you?

SHIRLEY: Who? Not me.

SERGEANT: You don't want to go to court. You can get this settled between you. He'll have to spend a night in a cell. You wouldn't want him to do that.

SHIRLEY: Why not?

JOHN: How do you like that?

SHIRLEY: A man don't come home when he should. And when he does come home he slaps me around. He belongs in jail.

JOHN: And you know where you belong, don't you?

SERGEANT: Okay.

JOHN: You belong in the—

SERGEANT: All right! (*Pause*) You can yell and scream at home. But we're going to have some quiet here. Do you understand that?

JOHN: That's all I want is some quiet. And if it takes jail to get it, it's okay with me.

SHIRLEY: It will have to be okay with you.

JOHN: It's fine with me.

SERGEANT: All right. It's fine with me, too. Mercado.

MERCADO (*Half off*): Yes, sir.

SERGEANT: Bailey went upstairs to the Detective Squad. Ring up there for him. I've got a prisoner.

MERCADO (*Half off*): Yes, sir.

BUZZER AND OUT—HALF OFF

SERGEANT: What's your name, Mister?

JOHN: Howick. John Howick.

MERCADO (*Half off*): This is Mercado on T.S. Is Bailey up there?
SERGEANT: How do you spell the last name?
MERCADO (*Half off*): Tell him we're booking a prisoner.
JOHN: H-o-w-i-c-k.
MERCADO (*Half off*): Okay.
SERGEANT: How old are you, John?

BUZZER AND OUT—HALF OFF

JOHN: Forty-two.
MERCADO (*Half off*): Bailey's on the way downstairs, Sergeant.
SERGEANT: Okay. What's your address?
JOHN: 738 East 95th Street.
SERGEANT: What's your occupation?
JOHN: Shipping clerk.
SHIRLEY: Assistant shipping clerk. Tell the truth.
JOHN: Shipping clerk.
SERGEANT: That's good enough. Place of occurrence was 738 East 95th
   Street at 12:35 A.M.
KANE: That's right, Sergeant. Okay, let me look in your pockets, John.
   Keep your hands on the railing. (*Starts to search him.*)

FADE IN STEPS

BAILEY (*Fading in*): You want me, Sergeant?
SERGEANT: Yeah. We've got a prisoner, Bailey.
BAILEY: Yes, sir.
SHIRLEY: Where did you get all that money?
JOHN: What do I have to do? Give you a written report.
SHIRLEY: Payday was last Tuesday. Where did you get all that?
JOHN: The woman you said I was out with gave it to me.
KANE: All right. That's enough. Fight it out in court.
SERGEANT: Put all that stuff back in your pocket, John.
SHIRLEY: The money, too? Are you going to let him keep all that
   money?
JOHN: It's mine, isn't it?
SERGEANT: All right, John. You're charged with disorderly conduct,
   violation of Section 722 penal law. Bail is five hundred dollars.
JOHN: Who needs bail? I'll be happy for a little privacy.
SERGEANT: Okay. Mrs. Howick, you be in Manhattan arrest court,
   455 West 151st Street at 9 A.M. You've got to make a complaint.
SHIRLEY: With bells on. With bells on I'll be there.
BAILEY: Okay, John. Let's go on back.

START STEPS

SHIRLEY (*Fading out*): This'll teach you.

STOP STEPS

JOHN: I don't need this to teach me. I learned a long time ago.
KANE: Okay, John. Go ahead.

STEPS—TAKE DOWN MUSTER SOUNDS

JOHN: How do you like it? I'm going to get locked up and I feel free as a bird.

MUSTER ROOM SOUNDS OUT

BAILEY: Well, don't start flying, John. Get the door, Kane, huh?
KANE: Yeah.

STOP STEPS—OPEN DOOR

BAILEY: Go ahead, John.

STEP THROUGH—SOME ECHO

JOHN: No other customers?

CLOSE DOOR

BAILEY: No. You're it tonight. That way.

STEPS

JOHN: Then I didn't need to make a reservation.
BAILEY: Go ahead. Inside.

STEP INTO CELL

JOHN: She doesn't know how lucky she is I'm getting locked up. If I was out I could really murder her.

CLOSE CELL DOOR

JOHN: Officer, thanks. I know I give you a hard time. But do you blame me? She makes me so mad. So mad!

LOCK CELL DOOR

KANE: It doesn't pay to get mad, Mister.
JOHN: I'm happy. I'm tickled to death. I'm at peace with the world.
BAILEY: Well, keep your little world in there clean. I'll see you.

START AWAY

JOHN: Listen.

BAILEY: Yeah.

JOHN: If you see her out there, tell her I said she did me a great big favor. I'm in heaven.

KANE: Well, you better make the most of it, John. The judge will bring you down to earth in the morning.

CUT

ANNOUNCER: You are listening to Twenty-first Precinct. A factual account of the way police work in the world's largest city.

CAPTAIN (*Cue*): Once the prisoner was lodged in his cell, Patrolman Kane went back to the Muster Room and was directed by Sergeant Waters to return to his post. He was instructed to report at the Station House at 5 A.M. to go on reserve duty in order to get a few hours sleep prior to his appearance in court in the case. I was out on patrol of the precinct paying particular attention to traffic conditions on the East River Drive where early-morning speeding by motorists bound for the Bronx and Queens had resulted in several serious accidents during the last few weeks. As the 12 to 8 tour is invariably the least busy, the desk officer on duty during that time had the task of completing, collating and filing or routing all reports, forms and communications that had accumulated during the previous twenty-four hours. At 2:40 A.M. Sergeant Waters was so engaged and Patrolman Mercado was still on telephone switchboard duty.

MUSTER ROOM SOUNDS

SERGEANT: Mercado.

MERCADO (*Half off*): Yes, sir.

SERGEANT: Give me those aided cards, will you?

FADE IN STEPS

MERCADO (*Fading in*): Yes. Sure, Sergeant.

FLIP THROUGH FILE CARDS

MERCADO: Here you are.

PILE CARDS ON DESK—OPEN DESK—HALF OFF

MERCADO: Oh-oh. Here comes your friend, Sergeant.

CLOSE DOOR—HALF OFF

MERCADO: The lady whose husband is locked up.

FADE IN STEPS

SHIRLEY (*Fading in*): Can I talk to you a minute?
SERGEANT: That's what I'm here for.
SHIRLEY: Well, it's about my husband.
SERGEANT: Yeah.

BUZZER—HALF OFF—FADE OUT STEPS

MERCADO (*Fading out*): Excuse me.
SHIRLEY: I got home, and I thought the whole thing over.

PLUG IN—BUZZER OUT—HALF OFF

SHIRLEY: I don't know. Maybe he was right. Maybe he was working like he said.
MERCADO (*Half off*): Twenty-first Precinct. Patrolman Mercado.
SHIRLEY: He could have been telling the truth.
MERCADO (*Half off*): Okay. Take your meal now, huh?
SHIRLEY: I give him the benefit of the doubt.
MERCADO (*Half off*): Where'll you be?
SHIRLEY: He was probably lying, but I give him the benefit of the doubt.
MERCADO (*Half off*): Okay.

BUZZER AND OUT—HALF OFF

SERGEANT: Didn't he slap you around like you said?
SHIRLEY: Oh, yeah. But that's nothing.
SERGEANT: And throw you out of the flat?
SHIRLEY: Well, I'm willing to let bygones be bygones.
SERGEANT: All right. Tell it to the judge in the morning.
SHIRLEY: I want him to come home now.
SERGEANT: I'm sorry, Mrs. Howick.
SHIRLEY: What do you mean you're sorry? Let him out. Let him out so we can go home.
SERGEANT: I can't do that.
SHIRLEY: Who says you can't? I want him out.
SERGEANT: I can't turn him out. It's up to the magistrate now. You had him arrested.
SHIRLEY: If I can have him arrested, I can have him unarrested.
SERGEANT: Look, Mrs. Howick. When the officer came up there he tried to get it straightened out. He tried to tell you not to bring him over here and have him arrested. You insisted that that's what you wanted to do. When you got here I told you I thought we could get it straightened out. You wouldn't listen to me. You wanted him in jail. All right. That's where he is.

SHIRLEY: This is a fine thing. You can't keep him locked up if I don't want him locked up.

SERGEANT: You talk to the judge in the morning.

SHIRLEY: I want him released now. Let him out. Go on. I want him to come home with me.

SERGEANT: I'm sorry, Mrs. Howick. It's up to the court.

SHIRLEY: Isn't there something that can be done?

SERGEANT: Well, what time is it? Quarter to three? He'll be out in five or six hours.

SHIRLEY: I want him out now.

SERGEANT: I'm sorry, lady.

SHIRLEY: You've got no right to hold him.

SERGEANT: I'm holding him because you arrested him.

SHIRLEY: Well, what's this about bail? You said something about bail.

SERGEANT: You don't have five hundred dollars in cash, do you? That's what the bail is. Five hundred dollars.

SHIRLEY: What does that mean? Bail?

SERGEANT: It's just a bond to insure his appearance in court.

SHIRLEY: Five hundred dollars?

SERGEANT: Yeah. You post five hundred dollars bail and he'll be released.

SHIRLEY: Well, I don't have five hundred dollars. Where am I going to get five hundred dollars?

SERGEANT: You don't need bail if you'll just wait until the morning. The magistrate will release him.

SHIRLEY: I don't want to wait until the morning. I don't want him to spend another minute in there. I can't stand my husband in jail. I can't stand him to spend a night in jail like this. There are people who make a business out of putting up bonds, aren't there? Aren't there people in business like that?

SERGEANT: Yeah. Professional bail bondsmen.

SHIRLEY: Well, what do they charge.

SERGEANT: The legal rate is five dollars a hundred.

SHIRLEY: You mean for twenty-five dollars I could get him out? I've got the money. I've got twenty-five dollars. I've got more.

SERGEANT: It'll be another hour before the bondsman can get here. That's four o'clock. He'll be in court at nine o'clock. That's only five hours.

SHIRLEY: That's not the point. I want him home. Where do you get one of these professional bondsmen?

SERGEANT: There's lots of them around.

SHIRLEY: Well, do you know one? Who could I call?

SERGEANT: Mrs. Howick, we're not allowed to make any recommendations along that line. Go look in a classified telephone index under bail bondsmen. Call the closest one.

SHIRLEY: Will he come?

SERGEANT: Well, look for one that says twenty-four hours service. They always keep somebody on the job around the clock.

SHIRLEY: All right. Where can I use the telephone? Have you got a classified book?

SERGEANT: Mrs. Howick . . .

SHIRLEY: Can I use the telephone, please?

SERGEANT: The public's not allowed to use the telephone in here.

SHIRLEY: Well, that's a fine thing. A citizen isn't allowed to use the telephone. Don't you have a public phone?

SERGEANT: There's no public phone in the station house. Go down to the corner of Third Avenue there. You'll see an all night luncheonette. You can use the telephone in there.

SHIRLEY: All right. (*She starts to go.*)

SHIRLEY: Oh.

SERGEANT: Yeah?

SHIRLEY: I know he didn't have any cigars with him. He's never at home without a cigar. I brought some along. Can I give them to him? I'd like to go back there and give them to him.

SERGEANT: Well, you can't go back there, Mrs. Howick. Besides, he's probably asleep.

SHIRLEY: Oh, no. He wouldn't be asleep. He couldn't sleep any place but home. That's his nature.

SERGEANT: Well, you give me the cigars. I'll have the attendant take them back to him.

SHIRLEY: All right. (*Cigars in cellophane.*)

SHIRLEY: You'll be sure he gets them.

SERGEANT: Yeah. He'll get them.

SHIRLEY: Thank you. Right away?

SERGEANT: I'll ring for the attendant now.

BELL—WAY OFF—FADE OUT STEPS

SHIRLEY (*Fading out*): I'll go make the telephone call.

SERGEANT: All right. He'll be here.

OPEN AND CLOSE DOOR—HALF OFF

MERCADO (*Little off*): Well, it figured, huh, Sergeant?

SERGEANT: Yeah. It figured.

MERCADO (*Little off*): It happens every time.

FADE IN STEPS

BAILEY (*Fading in*): Yes, Sergeant?

SERGEANT: That Mrs. Howick was in. She left some cigars for her husband.

BAILEY: Did you examine them? They could be loaded.

SERGEANT: Nope. She wants him out now. She's on her way to get a bail bondsman.

BAILEY: No kidding.

SERGEANT: Is he asleep?

BAILEY: He wasn't the last time I looked.

SERGEANT: Okay. Take these on back to him. (*Hands him cigars.*)

BAILEY: Okay, Sergeant.

SWITCHBOARD BUZZER—START STEPS—BUZZER FAD-
ING OUT—PLUG IN—BUZZER OUT—HALF OFF

MERCADO (*Fading out from half off*): Twenty-first Precinct. Patrolman Mercado.

CONTINUE STEPS—FADE DOWN MUSTER ROOM
SOUNDS—STOP STEPS

BAILEY SIGHS—OPEN DOOR—SOME ECHO—STEP
THROUGH—CLOSE DOOR—FEW STEPS ON CONCRETE

JOHN (*Fading in*): Listen, what's the matter? Can't you stay out of here and let a guy get a little sleep? I'm trying to fall asleep.

BAILEY: I've got something for you.

FADE IN STEPS

JOHN (*Fading in a little*): Yeah. What?

BAILEY: Your wife left some cigars for you.

JOHN: My wife?

BAILEY: Yes. She was just out talking to the Sergeant. She left the cigars.

JOHN: What was she doing back here?

BAILEY: She wants to bail you out. She's looking for a professional bondsman.

JOHN: Oh, she is, is she? Well, supposing I don't want to get bailed out.

BAILEY: That's your problem.

JOHN: I'm going to stay right here. There's nothing can stop me from staying right here, is there?

BAILEY: Look, Mister. I don't care what you do.

JOHN: Are you married?

BAILEY: Yes. Sure.

JOHN: Have you got troubles?

BAILEY: No.

JOHN: You're a liar. This is the most peace I ever had. In eleven years, the most peace. I'm staying. You tell her I'm staying. And there's not a thing she can do about it.

BAILEY: Look, it's enough you fight with your wife. I don't want to fight with her, too. (*Pause.*)

CAPTAIN (*Cue*): It was five minutes to three when I returned to the station house. I got out of Sector Car No. 2 in which I was on patrol and I instructed the operator, Patrolman Nelson, to pick up his partner who had been relieved for his meal. And to resume patrol. I walked in the front door and headed around behind the desk to sign the blotter.

MUSTER ROOM SOUNDS—STEPS—FADE IN SWITCH-BOARD BUZZER—PLUG IN—BUZZER OUT

MERCADO: Captain.

CAPTAIN: Hello, Mercado.

MERCADO (*Fading out*): Twenty-first Precinct. Patrolman Mercado.

CAPTAIN: Sergeant.

SERGEANT: Hello, Captain. (*Sits down. Signs blotter.*)

MERCADO (*Little off*): Yeah. Listen, take a walk around to 340 there. A man called in here twice about somebody honking an automobile horn in the block. See what there is to it. Okay.

BUZZER AND OUT—LITTLE OFF

CAPTAIN: What's doing, Sergeant?

SERGEANT: Nothing much, Captain. Pretty quiet.

OPEN DOOR—HALF OFF

SERGEANT: How's the weather? Is it warming up any?

CLOSE DOOR—HALF OFF

CAPTAIN: It doesn't seem like it is.

FADE IN STEPS

SERGEANT: The paper said it was going to.

SHIRLEY (*Fading in*): Well, I got hold of the bondsman. He's coming over. He said he'd be here in a half hour.

SERGEANT: All right, Mrs. Howick. You just wait over there till he comes.

SHIRLEY: This is terrible. I don't see why I have to spend twenty-five dollars to put up bail for him. If I want him out I should just be able to get him out.

SERGEANT: I told you what the story is. You had him arrested. It's up to the court to discharge him.

SHIRLEY: I should be able to discharge him myself. That's what I say.

CAPTAIN: What's the trouble, Sergeant?

SERGEANT: She had her husband arrested on a disorderly conduct charge. Now she wants him out. I told her before I booked him she might change her mind and they ought to go home together. She insisted on having him in jail.

SHIRLEY: A woman's entitled to change her mind, isn't she?

SERGEANT: Yeah. But you changed yours a little bit late, Mrs. Howick.

SHIRLEY: To spend twenty-five dollars for nothing.

FADE IN STEPS

BAILEY (*Fading in*): Listen, Sergeant. I've got a little problem back there.

SERGEANT: Yeah. What is it, Bailey?

SHIRLEY: John's all right? Nothing happened to my husband?

BAILEY: He's all right. Yeah. When I went back there before I told him his wife wanted to bail him out. He said he didn't want to get bailed out. Now I just made another round. Do you know what he did?

SERGEANT: What?

BAILEY: He took a penny out of his pocket and stuck it in the keyhole. When I came through there he pointed it out to me. He said, I'm not going to leave here now. I tried to open the cell door. I can't even get the key in the lock.

SHIRLEY: You mean he's not going to get out. Even with a bail bondsman?

BAILEY: It doesn't look like he will for a while, lady. Looks like he wants to stay.

SHIRLEY: Well, how do you like that?

CAPTAIN: Did you tell him that he could refuse to be bailed out?

BAILEY: The question never came up, Captain. He never asked me.

CAPTAIN: All right. Let's go have a look.

START STEPS

SHIRLEY: I'm going to go, too.
SERGEANT: No, you stay here.

STOP STEPS

CAPTAIN: Oh, Mercado.
MERCADO (*Half off*): Yes, sir.
CAPTAIN: Is Lieutenant King upstairs?
MERCADO (*Half off*): Yes, sir. I think so.
CAPTAIN: All right, ring up there! Tell him to come down and take a look. Come on, Bailey.

START STEPS

BAILEY: Yes, sir.
SHIRLEY (*Fading out a little*): Why can't I go?
SERGEANT (*Fading out from half off*): You've got to stay here.
CAPTAIN: Lieutenant King's pretty good with locks and keys.
BAILEY: He was with the Safe and Loft Squad, wasn't he?

SWITCHBOARD BUZZER FADING OUT FROM HALF OFF

CAPTAIN: Yeah, for a long time.

SEVERAL MORE STEPS—OPEN DOOR

BAILEY: Go ahead, Captain.

STEP THROUGH—SOME ECHO

JOHN (*Half off*): What're you gonna do?

STEPS

JOHN (*Fading in*): I fixed her, didn't I? Didn't I fix her?
BAILEY: It looks like you fixed yourself, John. This is Captain Cronin.
CAPTAIN: What did you do here?
JOHN: I didn't want to go out so I stuck a penny in the lock. Right in the keyhole there. See. You can't get the key in. You can't get the key in!
CAPTAIN: Didn't you know you could refuse to be bailed out if you wanted to?
JOHN: Could I?
CAPTAIN: If you didn't want to go.
JOHN: Why didn't somebody tell me that?
CAPTAIN: Well, you know it now. Let's see that key, Bailey.
BAILEY: Yes, sir.

KEY—TRY TO GET IT IN KEYHOLE

JOHN: You're wasting your time. It won't go in. He tried it for ten minutes.

CAPTAIN: Did you try to fish the penny out?

BAILEY: Yes, sir. I couldn't get it. I couldn't even reach it. It's got to be grabbed and turned. I tried a pair of tweezers. Nothing helps. I get hold of it, but then I always dropped it.

JOHN: Boy, this is some joke on her, isn't it?

CAPTAIN: It may turn out to be a joke on you.

OPEN DOOR—HALF OFF

LIEUTENANT (*Half off*): Captain.

CAPTAIN: Come in, Matt.

STEP THROUGH—HALF OFF

JOHN: I didn't mean any harm.

CLOSE DOOR—HALF OFF—FADE IN STEPS

JOHN: I just wanted to stay here, that's all.

LIEUTENANT (*Fading in*): What've you got, Captain?

BAILEY: He pushed a penny into the keyhole, Lieutenant. We can't get the cell door open.

LIEUTENANT: Let's see the key, huh?

BAILEY: Yes, sir. (*Tries to get key in keyhole.*)

JOHN: It's not going to work. I guarantee it. It's not going to work.

LIEUTENANT: Let me get in it there from that way.

BAILEY: Yes, sir.

LITTLE MOVEMENT—TRY KEY AGAIN

JOHN: All I wanted to do was stay here. I just wanted to guarantee that I'd stay here. I didn't want to get bailed out and go home with her. Not tonight. I don't know whether I ever want to go home with her. I don't think I could live through it.

LIEUTENANT: Well, it looks like you're going to be here for a while.

JOHN: I didn't know I could refuse to be bailed out. I didn't know that. Why don't somebody tell me these things?

LIEUTENANT: The plate's got to be burned off, Captain. That's the only way I can see to get the penny out. See those four rivets. If they get burned off the front part will come right off.

CAPTAIN: All right. I'll get the Emergency Squad. Stay here with him, Bailey. Don't let him put anything else in there.

JOHN: I wouldn't. I swear I wouldn't.

START STEPS

BAILEY (*Fading out*): All right. You just go back to the cot and lie down, John.

LIEUTENANT: Who is he, Captain?

OPEN DOOR

CAPTAIN: His wife had him locked up.

STEP THROUGH DOOR—ECHO OUT

CAPTAIN: She changed her mind, and wanted him bailed out.

CLOSE DOOR—STEPS

CAPTAIN: But he decided he wanted to stay.

LIEUTENANT: Well, that's just about par for the course, isn't it?

CAPTAIN: Yeah. Just about.

STOP STEPS

CAPTAIN: Thanks, Matt.

LIEUTENANT: For what? I couldn't do anything.

START UP STEPS

LIEUTENANT (*Fading out*): Tell Sergeant Waters to let me know when the Emergency Squad gets here. I'd like to see them burn that face off.

CAPTAIN: Okay, Matt.

STEPS—BRING UP MUSTER ROOM SOUNDS

SHIRLEY (*Fading in*): Well, how is he? Is he all right? Is he going to be all right?

CAPTAIN: Yes, he's all right, lady. He'll be in there a while.

SHIRLEY: I've got a bondsman coming. If he can't get out, do I have to give the bondsman the twenty-five dollars anyway? Will he want his money?

SERGEANT: Yeah. I imagine he will. But you don't have to pay him.

SWITCHBOARD BUZZER—HALF OFF

SHIRLEY: That's good. All I want is my husband home. That's all I wanted in the first place. I'm sorry I put him in. I'm very sorry. I'll never do it again.

MERCADO (*Half off*): Twenty-first Precinct. Patrolman Mercado.

CAPTAIN: Well, from the way he talks, don't know whether he's going to give you the opportunity to do it again.

SHIRLEY: You mean he's not coming home at all?

MERCADO (*Half off*): Okay. Eleven.

CAPTAIN: You'll have to talk to him about that.

SWITCHBOARD BUZZER AND OUT—HALF OFF

SHIRLEY: This is terrible. If he won't come home with me, it's awful. It's terrible.

CAPTAIN: It'll be worse. Wait'll you get the bill from the city for the lock.

PAUSE—SWITCHBOARD BUZZER—PLUG IN—BUZZER OUT

SERGEANT: Twenty-first Precinct, Sergeant Waters. Yeah. Yeah. How many women? What is it, a bargain sale there? Well, what do they want? Yeah. Yeah. Hasn't he opened up the store yet? Well, get them back from the glass there. You don't want it broken. Yeah. Yeah. Oh, is that so? All right. I'll send a car around there. Right away. Yeah. Okay.

SWITCHBOARD BUZZER—PLUG OUT AND SNAPS BACK—BUZZER OUT

CAPTAIN: And so it goes. Around the clock, through the week, every day, every year. A police precinct in the City of New York is a flesh and blood merry-go-round. Anyone can catch the brass ring. Or the brass ring can catch anyone.

FADE OUT

Decision for Freedom

by ROBERT S. GREENE

CATEGORY:

Radio Documentary

(ANY LENGTH)

DECISION FOR FREEDOM

by ROBERT S. GREENE

Decision for Freedom
was first presented on NBC,
under the direction of Andrew C. Love,
on October 9, 1955,
with the following cast:

JEFF CHANDLER · NATALIE MASTERS
LARRY DOBKIN · BYRON KANE

FULL PERSPECTIVE—THE EXTERIOR SOUND OF
IDLING PLANE ENGINE—HOLD HIGH LEVEL
BEHIND

NARRATOR (*On mike, above engines*): We are going to take a journey.
There is an empty seat waiting for you. You will learn our destination once you are aboard. However, you should know this. There
is no guarantee that you will return feeling the same way that you
left. For the duration, you will *be somebody else!* Any takers? Good!
Come aboard! (*The hatch door is closed.*)

SWITCH TO INTERIOR OF PLANE IDLING

NARRATOR: OK ... Fasten your seat belt.

INTERIOR—START RACING ENGINES—GO INTO TAKE-
OFF AND INTO CLIMB—DROP LEVEL BUT HOLD BE-
HIND FOR MUSIC

MUSIC: UP ... AND SEGUE BACK TO INTERIOR
PLANE FLYING

NARRATOR: You are flying west, along the Great Circle. Our speed is
as fast as thought itself. Already we are over the flat rich farmlands
of the Western Plains. Ahead lie the jagged peaks of the Rockies
... and beyond them the Sierras. Let's go higher.

INTERIOR—AS PLANE CLIMBS, BACK DOWN FOR:

NARRATOR: That blue patch before you is the Pacific Ocean. We'll be
over it in a minute!

CHANGE FILTER ON ENGINES, TO GIVE DIFFERENT
QUALITY

NARRATOR: There. We have just left the continental limits of the
United States. The Pacific stretches out before us. Hold on to your
seat belts and we'll cut ourselves a patch of sky!

INCREASE SPEED OF ENGINES. ON VARIABLE SPEED
TABLES PUSH FASTER A NOTCH

NARRATOR: No eagles fly here ... and the fishing boat below us can see
our path only by the scratch of white we make against the blue
enamel of the sky. There, out to the left, is Wake Island. Up north
thin shadows on the curve of earth are the islands of Japan. But our
destination is farther south. Come on!

ENGINES RACE—DOWN FOR:

NARRATOR: We're over the China Sea now. We're getting closer. And
there's the mainland of Asia. Now ... let's lose some altitude.

ENGINES REACT ACCORDINGLY

NARRATOR: Good. We are over Indo-China. It is our destination. That huge "S" cutting down from the north is an off-shoot of the Yun-Nan range, and those twisting lines of silver following it are the rivers of the Mekang and the Song-Koi. (*Projecting to* PILOT) All right, take her down! (*Plane descends*) We are in North Viet Minh . . . the northern section of Indo-China ruled by the Communists. We'll touch down in a minute. (*Plane lands, bumps, steadies, taxis a moment, and then stops. Keep motors running*) OK . . . Unfasten your seat belt. Come on . . . (*Hatch opened*) There . . . we're done with the plane. (*Hatch shuts. Plane guns and takes off. Lost in perspective*) Pretty quiet, eh. Now listen. (*Sneak the call of the violet kingfishers*) This is the valley of the Song-Koi. That group of thatched huts over there is your village. The field you're standing in is your field—a rice field. And that woman standing beside you is called Mai . . . and she is your wife. This is your whole life—here in the village, with the coconut palms and the crimson flamboyants and the flat rice paddies with the mountains behind them. Forget that you've ever heard of the U. S. A. Your new name is Ta Hai. These huts—this field you stand in—are all you've ever known.

MUSIC: IN QUIETLY—DOWN FOR:

(*The kingfishers call from up high.*)

NARRATOR: You're watching the mountains, watching two violet king-fishers winging their way toward the Yun-Nans. They are flying farther and faster than you shall ever dream of traveling. Mai watches you for a moment, and then follows your gaze.

MAI: I see them.

TA HAI: Look how they wheel through the air.

MAI (*Quietly*): Ta Hai?

TA HAI: Yes?

MAI: Would you fly as the kingfishers?

NARRATOR: You look down at her. She is so much like a child, and yet so very much a woman. And you answer her.

TA HAI: If you flew beside me.

MAI (*Quietly*): That is as I should wish it.

NARRATOR: She touches the ring of coral you gave her. She longed for it for over a year, and one day you bought it from a trader from the south . . . and ran all the way home to give it to her. You remember what she said then as she put it on her finger.

MAI: Of all those who walk in the valley of the Song-Koi, I am glad you choose me. I am happiest when I am near you. I bear thee much love, Ta Hai.

NARRATOR: You look down at her, and she reads your heart, and her fingertips brush yours.

TA HAI: Come . . . It is late . . . We shall go back to the house.

NARRATOR: You live with the Old Woman, your mother. She is many years now and you worship her. For you are content. But there are some things that you do not understand. For there has been fighting in the villages around you, and you do not know why. The soldiers come from the north and they call themselves by a strange word— Communists. You have learned that there has been a great battle in a town not far from you called Dien Bien Pu, and that the French have been defeated. You do not know what this will mean, but this very week a man from the north has come to your village. They call him the Can Bo—the Communist. And on this very day he has made a speech.

CAN BO (*Slightly on echo, projecting*): The war of liberation is over. The village of Son La is now free! Rejoice at the coming of the New People's Republic. The conspiracy against you is ended. Freedom and democracy have come to the village of Son La!

NARRATOR: You do not like this Can Bo. You knew that this morning when you heard him speak . . . And yet his words sounded brave and exciting. Perhaps it is his face, with his fat cheeks, or his plain tunic buttoned up to his throat, or the way his belly sticks out before him. You do not know. But as you enter the hut now, with Mai at your side, you see him sitting there. And in the corner, the Old Woman your mother sits silently, watching him.

CAN BO: Dong-chi, Ta Hai. Dong-chi.

TA HAI: I bid you welcome to this house.

NARRATOR: He begins to talk. He calls you Dong-chi—comrade—and yet you hardly know him. He inquires about your health and he congratulates you for your fine rice field. And then he says something.

CAN BO: Ta Hai, each village must have a leader among the people. Why should it not be you?

TA HAI: I do not know what you say.

CAN BO: One who can be trusted—one who will mix with his neighbors —and let us know of those who are backward in their thinking and who are in need of teaching of the new ways.

TA HAI: My neighbors are my friends.

CAN BO: Exactly, Dong-Chi. And they must be friends of the new People's Republic too. We must know what they feel . . . and say . . . and think. (*He rises*) Consider well what I have spoken. It will go well for you.

NARRATOR: He rises, puts both hands on your shoulders, calls you Dong-Chi again, and departs. And you are left with an unquiet feeling, for these are strange words he has said.

MAI (*Coming on*): I do not like this Can Bo, Ta Hai. I think he speaks with two tongues.

TA HAI (*Slowly*): The words of my neighbors are like the flowers of the tree. This man wishes me to be—a locust.

NARRATOR: You look down. Mai is standing beside you, small and close. Suddenly she looks up at you, and you put your arm around her.

MAI: I am afraid, Ta Hai, I am afraid.

MUSIC: COVER SOFTLY—DOWN FOR

NARRATOR: You do not sleep well that night. And the following day a truck appears in your village from the north, and on it are many boards of fine white wood. (*Truck pulls in*) And then, a space is cleared in the center of the village and a big building is put up. It is the largest building you have ever seen. Three wooden steps lead to the door, and above the door are printed the letters: "Peace Center." You are not sure of the meaning of all this, but it looks important. And in spite of yourself, you cannot help feeling a bit proud that your village should now have such a magnificent building. When it is finished, Can Bo stands on the three wooden steps, his tunic buttoned up to his throat, and the men cheer. (*The cheer*) And that night, when you come back from the field, Can Bo is sitting in your thatched hut again, talking with Mai. He rises as if he were host in your own home.

CAN BO: Good evening, Dong-Chi. I have come to learn the answer to my request. We have need of you.

NARRATOR: You look at Mai, and her lips are tight. The Old Woman your mother sits in the far corner of the hut, her shawl around her, her eyes closed as if she is asleep. But you know she is not.

CAN BO: Well, Dong-Chi? You have thought of what I have offered?

NARRATOR: You can't answer because you don't think you can make him understand. Suddenly there are no words. You can't find them. You look at him helplessly. And then you say what came into your head before.

TA HAI: I will not be a locust!

NARRATOR: You turn away, but you know his eyes are boring into you.

CAN BO: It will not go easy with you, Ta Hai, to be unreasonable.

NARRATOR: You don't turn. There is nothing to say. The eyes of the Old Woman your mother are still closed. There is not a sound. And then, finally, Can Bo speaks.

CAN BO: It is a pity. They will not be pleased in Hanoi. But we will find other work for you here.

NARRATOR: You hear his steps and he walks out of the hut. And now you notice that your mother has opened her eyes. And then . . . She spits upon the floor! (*Old Woman spits*) You're cold and you're trembling, for somewhere there is a kind of terror that you're caught up in, and you've never felt this before. Perhaps it is that the words in this hut will go to Hanoi—and it will be the first time a word has ever left the hut. Suddenly the world has grown larger and more frightening.

MUSIC: IN—DOWN FOR

NARRATOR: Later that night, when you and Mai are lying on your mats, you turn and place your arm around her, and her head is very close to yours.

TA HAI: This afternoon—before I came in—when you and Can Bo were talking—of what did he speak?

MAI (*Trembling*): He wished that I might inform him of your doings, as he wished you would inform of your neighbors.

MUSIC: TOUCH

NARRATOR: Her body shakes a little, and you notice her cheek is wet. And yet, how silently she cries. She moves closer . . . You feel her tremble and your arm tightens around her shoulder.

TA HAI (*Very softly*): Mai. Sleep. Sleep now.

MUSIC—WIPE IT OUT GENTLY

NARRATOR: But you don't sleep, and the next morning one of the soldiers comes to your hut.

SOLDIER: In the interest of the new Republic, you will work three hours today, repairing roads which have been destroyed in the fighting.

TA HAI: But I have no time for such a thing. I must be in my field.

SOLDIER: You will report at the Peace Center.

NARRATOR: They give you a pick, and march you five miles in the hot sun outside the village . . . and for three hours you break your back and the sweat runs down your sides until you're soaked. And then, a whistle blows. (*Whistle blows.*)

SOLDIER: You have given your time to the People's Republic. You will learn that this is a privilege and to be grateful for it.

NARRATOR: And you come back—dead tired—and there is still the field to attend to. Mai has rice for you when you return. She says little, but there is a look on her face you have not seen before, except on an animal when it is being hunted.

MAI: Here. Eat. You will feel better.

MUSIC: IN—DOWN FOR

NARRATOR: It happens again. First, Can Bo.

CAN BO: You have considered my request?

TA HAI: Locust! (*Whistle blows.*)

SOLDIER: You will dig till sundown.

NARRATOR: And it happens again and again. And gradually you begin to understand. That to say "No" to the orders of Can Bo means punishment . . . to say "yes" means reward. It is the beginning of a pattern . . . and you can't forget it. And it makes you feel like a small boy again. And, somehow, way back in your mind, you realize that this is what they wish you to feel. And then you begin hearing the grumblings of your neighbors. (*Low murmur of voices.*)

MAI: It is said that they may not listen to the priest any longer, Ta Hai. Why do they forbid it?

TA HAI: I think it is because he says "no" to them.

MUSIC—TOUCH

NARRATOR: It goes on—little by little. Your friends look at you and you look at them, and you realize that you are now afraid of them. For which one has Can Bo spoken to and which one has said "yes." Suddenly your village is not your village any longer—the coconut grove has lost its beauty . . . There is nowhere to turn. And one night you can bear it no longer. Suddenly you weep. (*Muffled sobs from* TA HAI.)

MAI: Ta Hai!

TA HAI: I cannot help it. I am sorry. I weep like a woman, but I cannot help it.

NARRATOR: She comes over to you, but you turn away, for you are ashamed.

MAI: It is all right, Ta Hai. It is all right.

TA HAI: Today on the road I thought I would kill the soldier. And then I thought I would be shot, and you would be alone. I cannot go farther, Mai!

NARRATOR: The Old Woman, your mother, sits in the corner, watching silently. And then she speaks.

OLD WOMAN: There is word from the other villages. (*Long pause.*)

TA HAI: What do you mean? How?

OLD WOMAN: There are the old ways of learning news. Point your ear to the east. No—*so!* Now listen. (*Very slowly, almost inaudibly, we hear the reverberations of a large wooden gong many, many miles away.*) All day the villages have been speaking. To the mountains the bells have been taken—away from the soldiers. And the wooden bells speak in the old way.

TA HAI: What do they say? Can you read them?

OLD WOMAN (*Slowly*): That our land is in two parts . . . and below, to the south, one may live as he wills.

TA HAI: You speak the truth?

OLD WOMAN: I speak only what the bells speak.

MUSIC—SNEAK

NARRATOR (*Fast pace*): Somehow the news has gotten around the village. You know nothing about a Geneva convention—or a 17th parallel or an agreement on the part of the Communists to let those who wish move to the south, where the old government still rules. But on every face this morning there is a new look . . . The bells have spoken. To the south! No one goes to the field, but in the air something stirs and gradually, without knowing it, you are drawn to the center of the village and to the steps of the Peace Center.

SNEAK CROWD BUZZ

NARRATOR: Around you stand almost all the men of the village, clamoring, milling about, so that the soldier on guard fingers his rifle nervously. And then, gradually, a word begins to float from mouth to mouth.

CAST (*Chant it, build it*): Can Bo . . . Can Bo . . . CAN BO . . . CAN BO!

NARRATOR: And then he appears on the wooden steps, his fat paunch sticking out before him, his jowls hanging heavy from his neck.

CAN BO: Go home! Go to your huts!

NARRATOR: The cry increases, and then finally he raises his hands for silence. (*Slowly the chant ceases, until all is still.*)

CAN BO (*Slightly on echo*): So you wish to go to the south and you blame me for having kept this from you. You are brave men. Yes, you are brave men to believe news your women tell you. You don't know who are your friends. You are greater fools than I thought!

CAST MURMUR UP—DOWN FOR

CAN BO: Do you not realize that all this is but a trap, that those in the south envy you and would destroy you from their envy?

NARRATOR (*Sotto voce*): You listen to him, and you can't know.

CAN BO: Do you know what will happen to you if you try to go? They will load you on a boat in Haipong like cattle, and then when they are out to sea, they will throw you overboard—those of you who have not already died from the disease they will spread among you.

NARRATOR (*Way down*): Could it be true? You can't tell. There's no way to tell.

CAN BO: And if any of you live through this voyage, before you arrive in the south, your hand will be cut off, so that all may know who you are. (*Beat*) Are you so eager to go now? (*Hold for beat of silence*) Here you have a chance to build a great new nation and be free. Your homes are here, your future is here. But perhaps you wish to be beggars in the south on the streets of Saigon! Go home! You make me sick! You are swine!

NARRATOR: He turns and goes inside. And slowly, you walk home. You don't believe what he said about the disease, about the death, the awful thing about the hand. And yet—how do you know it is not true?

MUSIC: TOUCH—DOWN FOR

NARRATOR: All day you try and make up your mind. You don't work in the field. You only think. And then you look up to the Yun-Nans, hazy and blue in the distance, and in your heart you know what you must do. When you come back, the Old Woman, your mother, reads your eyes.

OLD WOMAN: You choose well, my son. You choose well.

NARRATOR: There is a sadness in her eyes now, and suddenly you know she will not come with you.

OLD WOMAN: I am too old to start again. My home is here. You were born here and I shall die here.

NARRATOR: There is no use to argue, for you know she speaks the truth.

OLD WOMAN: The spirit you take from this house will always be with you. I am but a shadow. And as the shadow, I must remain behind.

MUSIC—COVER SOFTLY—HOLD UNDER

NARRATOR: That night you and Mai are very quiet. You lie on your mats and cannot speak. For suddenly you realize that you are leaving your home, and that you will never see it again. Your field. Your dream of the water buffalo. And you reach out and touch her hand beside you. And then you notice something!

TA HAI: Your ring of coral, where is it? (*There is a long silence*) Always you have worn that ring I bought from the trader. We were not married as Christians, and yet you wore it. What has happened?

MAI (*Finally*): I have hid it.

TA HAI: Hid it? But why?

MAI (*She pauses. Then quietly*): In case they take the hand, Ta-Hai, the ring will be safe.

MUSIC—COVER SOFTLY—AND DOWN BEHIND

NARRATOR: That night you dream about the violet kingfisher. You cannot remember this dream, but somehow the bird has come up to you, and is unafraid. And it waits by your side. When you awake, you turn to Mai, to tell her about this dream, but she is not on her mat. She is over in the hut, and you see she has gone out and cut a bamboo pole. It is very early. You look around you. Your straw mats, your few clothes—all that you and she own can be hung on it. And suddenly your throat becomes thick.

MAI (*Coming on*): I have cut the pole, Ta Hai.

NARRATOR: Nanoi and Haipong are a long way off, but you have heard that if you follow the waters of the Song Po, it will lead you there. And then the Old Woman, your mother, speaks.

OLD WOMAN (*Coming on*): It is time.

NARRATOR: You have your final tea with her. Mai stays outside, for she knows of this moment. The Old Woman sips from the cup, holding it by both hands. You know that never in your life will you see her again. You finish without speaking, and then you rise and look at her. Her eyes meet yours.

OLD WOMAN: Go, my son, and do not look back.

NARRATOR: And you turn and walk through the door. You do not look behind. And then you walk through the street of the village in the early morning. Mai walks behind you. The pole is between you. You do not look back. She does not speak. You have already passed your field, but you do not look back. And then you reach the outskirts of the village. You walk on. And you do not look back. And then, high above you, you hear something. The cry of the violet kingfisher. (*The kingfisher, high above.*)

MAI: Look, Ta Hai. Look!

MUSIC—A TOUCH—DOWN BEHIND

NARRATOR: You walk, and then presently you are joined by two more

from the village who carry their poles. And then there are four . . .
(*Build low voices as they join up*) . . . and eight, until soon there
are many. Without words between you, you have all reached the
same path. And you know that, when the sun is high, the village
will be nearly empty. And you think of the Old Woman, your
mother, but you do not look back. And then you begin to pass the
other villages. Van Nen and Na Phu. And others join you. You
walk by the waters of the Song Po, and those from Hoa Binh join
you. You walk and there are those from Ha Dong and Son Tay. The
road is full now and dusty. And you walk and walk. One day becomes
two, and two days become three, and you cannot walk any more.
And then you smell something. You cannot place it, for it is new to
you, but somehow you know what it is!

MAI: The sea, Ta Hai! The sea!

MUSIC—UP—DOWN FOR

NARRATOR: And then, finally, before you is the port of Haipong. And
there in the river without a shore lies the great iron boat.

MAI: It is like a dream.

NARRATOR: You think of what Can Bo said about the disease and the
death and how they will cut off your hand. But you do not look
back. You have not looked back once. And then you are faint from
the walk. Many things happen.

MUSIC—OUT

AMERICAN: Easy with that gangplank there. Steady. All right. Let 'em
come on!

NARRATOR: There are strange voices in a tongue you do not know. But
the men are fair and they smile at you and in spite of your fear, you
cannot help smiling back.

AMERICAN: Easy there, lady. Here, let me help you with that pole.
That's it . . . Up you go . . . There you are!

NARRATOR: You and Mai are on the great iron ship. There are many of
you. You stand and look at the water below you. It is so high it
makes you dizzy. Someone puts a box in your arms.

AMERICAN: Some soap and milk and towels and a blanket for you,
Johnny. And for the lady, too. That other stuff is chewing gum.
Don't swallow it!

NARRATOR: You stand on the deck, high above the water. You've come
a long way and you're going a longer way—down to Saigon and a
new life. But you don't know that now. All you know is that Mai is

standing beside you, small and sunburnt and dusty from the road. And then there is a great sound. (*Almost on mike. A great blast from the steamboat whistle*) The boat trembles beneath your feet. And as it does so, there is another sound from high above. (*The kingfisher calls, up high*) You look up into the clear blue sky and then you see it. The violet kingfisher high above the boat. And then it makes a great circle around the boat, as if to say farewell, and then dips back toward the land. Perhaps the boat has seen it too, for the kingfisher calls . . . (*Kingfisher calls*) And now the boat calls back. (*Almost on mike again. A great blast from the whistle*) Mai moves closer to you and then she looks up at you, and through her tired, smudged, dirty face she smiles for the first time. And it's the most beautiful sight you've ever seen. You reach down for her hand.

MAI (*Softly*): Ta Hai. Ta Hai.

NARRATOR: And then you feel sómething—the ring of coral. She has put it on again. And your eyes meet, and suddenly all the fear leaves. You've brought her with you and you're going to a new land—a free land, *your* land. And as her hand tightens on yours and the boat trembles again beneath your feet and slowly moves out to sea, suddenly you're proud. Very proud. You've made the decision for freedom!

MUSIC: COVER SOFTLY—BUILD—SUSTAIN—BUT IN-STEAD OF CONCLUSION, SEGUE TO AIRPLANE. EXTERIOR—COMING ON—SEGUE TO INTERIOR SOUND OF PLANE ENGINES . . .

NARRATOR (*Over engines*): All right, you've seen it. Maybe you've felt it. We're going home now, back across the Pacific. Take a last look at that transport below you, taking them down to the south . . . to freedom. Over to the west, the violet kingfisher is heading inland. And over to the east lies home. (*Beat*) Come on . . . Let's go!

BUILD PLANE ENGINES. SEGUE TO CLOSING THEME. BRING UP SOFTLY. BUILD. SUSTAIN AND OUT TO CONCLUSION

The Edgar Bergen Show

by SI ROSE

CATEGORY:

Radio Comedy

(ANY LENGTH)

THE EDGAR BERGEN SHOW

by SI ROSE

The Edgar Bergen Show
was first presented on CBS,
under the direction of Sam Pierce,
on November 27, 1955,
with the following cast:

EDGAR BERGEN · CAROL RICHARDS
GARY CROSBY · MELLOWMEN QUARTET
JACK BENNY · DR. FREDERICK WEBB HODGE
JACK KIRKWOOD

HIESTAND: From Hollywood—it's the new Edgar Bergen hour, with Charlie McCarthy.

MUSIC: SWELL AND OUT

CHARLIE: I'll clip you—so help me, Bergen, I'll mow you down!

MUSIC: THEME FULL AND FADE

HIESTAND: It's Sunday night and time again, transcribed for Edgar Bergen and Charlie McCarthy with Mortimer Snerd, Effie Klinker, Gary Crosby, Carol Richards, Ray Noble, Jack Kirkwood, The Mellomen, yours truly, John Hiestand . . . and our special guests . . . Dr. Frederick Webb Hodge, world's leading authority on the American Indian . . . *and* Jack Benny!

MUSIC: UP TO TAG

JOHN: Ladies and gentlemen, this past week-end, Edgar Bergen attached his trailer to the back of his car and he and Charlie were off to Palm Springs for a glorious and inexpensive vacation in the sun. As it turned out, it wasn't as inexpensive as they thought . . . But, to see what happened, let's look in on Edgar and Charlie as they approach Palm Springs, with Edgar behind the wheel . . .

MUSIC: TRAVELING MUSIC

SOUND: CAR MOTOR—ESTABLISH—THEN HOLD UNDER

CHARLIE (*Sings*): "Oh, in his black denim toupée and his high button shoes . . ."

BERGEN: Well, Charlie, how are you enjoying the ride?

CHARLIE: Okay, but can't you go a little faster?

BERGEN: Why, we're moving right along. After all, we just passed three cars.

CHARLIE: Yeah, but they were parked.

BERGEN: Never mind. Better check our trailer back there. How does it look?

CHARLIE: Like Elsa Maxwell doing a rhumba. Come on, Bergie, speed it up.

BERGEN: Just take it easy, Charlie, we're entering Palm Springs now.

CHARLIE: I know—a pedestrian just passed us.

BERGEN: My, isn't it beautiful here? Oh, Charlie, look over there— somebody left an old golf club lying in the sand.

CHARLIE: That's Frank Sinatra taking a sunbath.

BERGEN: Oh, yes, yes. You're right . . . Well, we better keep our eye out for the Blue Skies Trailer Park . . . that's the one Jack Benny owns—and, you know, he promised to give us a special rate. Oh, he's a tough man to tangle with over money.

CHARLIE: Yeah—you both throw around pennies like manhole covers. Heh, Heh.

BERGEN: That will do.

CHARLIE: Say, that must be Jack Benny's trailer park over there. Look at the sign in front—"Free Water, Free Electricity, also Free Violin Lessons—at slight extra charge."

BERGEN: That's the place, all right. I'll pull in.

SOUND: MOTOR UP—THEN CUT

BERGEN: Well, here we are, Charlie. That must be the parking attendant coming toward us.

BENNY: Park your car for two bits, sir?

BERGEN: Why, it's Jack Benny.

BERGEN: Jack, how come you're parking cars?

BENNY: Oh, I'll do anything to make a buck. Gentlemen, welcome to the Blue Skies Trailer Park—surrounded by swaying palm trees— and you're welcome to pick all the dates you can eat . . .

CHARLIE: Gee, that's swell.

BENNY: . . . for 69 cents a pound. Here, Edgar, have a date. I hope you don't mind if I take it out of your first pound.

CHARLIE: How do you like that? He's got all this and capital gains too!

BENNY: Don't knock it, Charlie. A man my age has to start thinking about his future.

BERGEN: Jack, what *is* your age? How about settling it once and for all —just how old are you?

BENNY: 39 . . . going on 38.

CHARLIE: Let's face it, Buster, the only way you'll see 50 again is on a speedometer!

BENNY: Hmmmmmmmm. (*To audience*) That's a nice line for a guest star. Hmmmmm!

BERGEN: Sorry, Jack, our trailer wasn't big enough to bring along any writers. But this is quite a trailer park you've got here.

BENNY: Well, I'm just running it as a sideline. After all, who knows, as a comedian I may not be able to go on forever.

CHARLIE: Haven't you already?

BENNY: Hmmmmm. (*To audience*) They did it to me again.

BERGEN: Well, anyway, Jack, we're here—and we'd like to check in.

BENNY: Gee, I don't know, Edgar . . . We have a certain standard to maintain . . . and your trailer is pretty old. Just look how thin those tires are . . . You can see right through the rubber.

BERGEN: You cannot . . . and please keep your hands off them . . . Jack, I said stop feeling those tires!

SOUND: LOUD BURST OF ESCAPING AIR AND POP

BENNY: I'm sorry, Edgar . . . I forgot about my hangnail.

BERGEN: Now what'll we do!

BENNY: I also fix tires . . . I'll do anything for a buck.

CHARLIE: Well, here's a dollar . . . go get a manicure.

BENNY: Thanks, but would you mind making it $1.25. I'm a big tipper.

BERGEN: Look, Jack, are you letting us in or not? I'm waiting.

BENNY: So am I . . . for the laugh. (*To self*) Now where can I put that junk heap? (*Up*) Edgar, tell you what I'll do. I'll put you way down at the end right next to the road.

BERGEN: Next to the road?

BENNY: Yes. Your trailer will be all right there . . . People will think it's just an accident.

CHARLIE: Come on, Bergie, let's take the spot and check in.

BERGEN: Okay. Where's the desk clerk?

BENNY (*Clears throat*): Care to register, sir?

CHARLIE: You mean?

BENNY: I told you—I'll do anything for a buck.

CHARLIE: At least we're saving on actors.

BERGEN: Well, Jack, you better tell us. What are your rates?

BENNY: Oh, you'll find me very cheap.

CHARLIE: Yes, we have!

BENNY: (*To audience*) He's a regular knotty-pine Fred Allen. I threw that in myself. They had me down for another "Hmmmm."

BERGEN: Jack, you still haven't told us what your rates are.

BENNY: Well . . . What would you say to . . . $9 a night?

BERGEN: Oh, come now, Jack, you wouldn't charge that much for poor little old me.

BENNY: Certainly. That's how I got to be rich little old me.

BERGEN: I won't pay a cent over $2. So I guess the deal's off.

BENNY: (*Panicky*) Now wait a minute . . . That was my first offer.

BERGEN: Jack, please, you're crushing my carnation.

BENNY: How about $8.75?

BERGEN: $2.25 is as high as I'll go.

CHARLIE: This is a battle of the titans, and two tighter titans I've never seen.

BENNY: $8.50 . . . and not a penny lower.

BERGEN: $3.50.

BENNY: $8.25.

BERGEN: $3.75.

BENNY: $8.00.

BERGEN: $4.00.

BENNY: $7.75.

BERGEN: Oh, Jack, what are we arguing about!

CHARLIE: Blood!

BENNY: I'll tell you what, Edgar . . . I don't want to quibble over a few bucks. Let's settle for $5.

BERGEN: Okay, it's a deal.

CHARLIE: Ladies and gentlemen, the preceding scene starring Edgar Bergen and Jack Benny was from the picture—"Money Is a Many-Splendored Thing."!

BENNY: I'll trade you that for the "Hmmm."

BERGEN: Well, it's all set then.

CHARLIE: Gee, it oughta be fun staying here at the Blue Skies Trailer Park . . . especially with you one of the owners, Mr. Benny . . . You're such a popular celebrity and such a good comedian . . .

BENNY: Oh, you're just saying that.

CHARLIE: No, if I was saying it, you wouldn't come out so good.

BENNY: I wonder what Don Wilson would charge to sit on him.

BERGEN: Now, Charlie, behave yourself. Jack, how about showing us around a bit?

BENNY: Sure, be glad to . . .

SOUND: FOOTSTEPS ON GRAVEL

BENNY: Now, over here is our swimming pool. Of course, you know there's a 25-cent service charge per person if you use the swimming pool.

BERGEN: Well, that sounds reasonable enough.

BENNY: When there's water in it, it's a dollar.

CHARLIE: If I know Bergen he'll take it dry.

BENNY: And then this is our lovely bathroom over here.

CHARLIE: Oh, no!

BERGEN: Charlie, what's the matter?

CHARLIE: I just took a peek inside—parking meters!

BERGEN: Charlie!

BENNY: (*To audience*) That time they didn't even give me a "Hmmmm." Oh, gentlemen, before I forget—we have another special service here at the Blue Skies Trailer Park . . . For a very slight extra charge you're furnished with entertainment.

BERGEN: What kind of entertainment?

BENNY: Oh, it's the best—really outstanding. I go from trailer to trailer playing requests on my violin.

CHARLIE: Gad, he will do anything for a buck.

BERGEN: Jack, if I may ask, how much does it cost *not* to have you play your violin?

BENNY: You couldn't afford it.

CHARLIE: Maybe we just oughta buy ear plugs.

BENNY: Young knothole . . . I'll have you know all my customers here just love my violin playing . . . And to think that as a violinist I've just scratched the surface.

CHARLIE: Scratched is right. Your playing reminds me of a magician sawing a woman in two.

BENNY: Well!!!! I'll show you how everyone here in the trailer park feels about my violin playing! (*Plays few bars on the violin.*)

SOUND: CAR MOTORS START UP AND CARS START LEAVING

CHARLIE: Hey, all the trailers are pulling out.

BENNY: They can't . . . Stop . . . No . . . I'll be ruined . . . No . . . Please . . . *Wait a minute*!!!!

SOUND: ALL CAR MOTORS OFF AT SAME INSTANT

BERGEN: Jack, what are you doing? You've stopped playing. You're putting your violin away.

BENNY: Yes, I'll do anything—even that—for a buck! (*Up*) Okay, come on back folks. Park your cars for a quarter . . . two bits . . . right this way . . .

MUSIC: PLAYOFF

BERGEN: Jack, I want to thank you for dropping in on us.

BENNY: I enjoyed being here, Edgar. It was a non-financial pleasure.

CHARLIE: Oh, yeah . . . Don't forget the seven times we mentioned Blue Skies Trailer Park.

BENNY: Thanks, Charlie. That makes eight. And I want to thank you on behalf of all my co-owners at the Blue Skies—Bing Crosby, Jerry Lewis, George Burns, John Wayne, etc.

CHARLIE: Say, that's quite a mob.

BENNY: Yes. In fact, we don't take in any customers—only partners. But drop in and see us anyway. Good night, Edgar, Charlie.

MUSIC: PLAYOFF

BERGEN: Well, Charlie, wasn't it wonderful of Jack Benny to drop in on us?

CHARLIE: Yeah, but that business of him being only 39 . . . Ha!

BERGEN: Charlie, please . . . We can't question it unless we have positive information.

CHARLIE: Well, I've got it. While he was here I took a peek at his driving license.

BERGEN: What did it say?

CHARLIE: "For Covered Wagons Only."

BERGEN: Now, Charlie, that's ridiculous!

GARY: (*Coming on*) Hiya, Edgar, Charlie.

BERGEN: It's Gary Crosby!

BERGEN: Well, Gary, we were just speaking to one of your father's partners at the Blue Skies Trailer Park.

GARY: I know. I just saw him drive off in his covered wagon.

CHARLIE: See!

BERGEN: Never mind. Tell me, Gary, how do you feel about trailer living?

GARY: I don't know, Edgar. I keep remembering the morning that woman woke up in her trailer and found her husband missing.

BERGEN: How awful!

GARY: Oh, it wasn't too bad. The next day she got a wire that said: "I didn't desert you, honey. I turned over in my sleep last night and I'm now on a Greyhound bus bound for Chicago."

BERGEN: Well, those things happen. But I've found that most people actually enjoy trailer living.

GARY: Yes, it's really a great life, Edgar, but . . . he said recognizing a song cue when he hears one . . . "But Not For Me."

MUSIC: GARY AND ORCHESTRA "BUT NOT FOR ME"

MUSIC: MORT THEME

MORTIMER (*Singing*): "I'll never smile again like I smole before."

BERGEN: Why such a sad song, Mortimer?

MORTIMER: Oh, I got the dismals.

BERGEN: The dismals?

MORTIMER: Yah, I'm sorta down in the humpty dumps.

BERGEN: Why?

MORTIMER: Well, I'm worried.

BERGEN: Worried about what?

MORTIMER: Wull, let me see now . . . How many guesses do I get?

BERGEN: Surely you must know what you're worried about.

MORTIMER: I'm worried about things back home on the farm. Everything is all topsy-turtle. We got sixteen new mouths to feed.

BERGEN: Well, are they pigs or chickens?

MORTIMER: No, my Uncle Sorghum and Aunt Busillas and their kids.

BERGEN: Uncle Sorghum and his family.

MORTIMER: I didn't even know I had an Uncle Sorghum and they're all moved in and living with me now—if you can call that living.

BERGEN: Are you sure they have that many children?

MORTIMER: Wull, let me see now—there is Vestibula, Twitchy, Narrowhead, Fungus and Grunion, Quagmire, Putrid and Slurp and the triplets, Myrt, Burt and Squirt . . . Oh, ya, and then there's the oldest sister, Groucho.

BERGEN: A sister named Groucho?

MORTIMER: Yah, they call her that because she has a mustache and smokes cigars.

BERGEN: Well, that must make things pretty crowded around your house.

MORTIMER: Yah, they sleep all over the place—in the kitchen, too.

BERGEN: And they don't mind that?

MORTIMER: Well, no . . . Except Cousin Twitchy. He ain't used to sleeping in a strange sink.

BERGEN: Well, they've made themselves at home, haven't they?

MORTIMER: Yah, they're even wearing my clothes . . . Jerkimer got up this morning and got right into my best suit.

BERGEN: Well, now that is annoying.

MORTIMER: Yah . . . What's more, he didn't even give me time to get out of it first.

BERGEN: They don't sound like very attractive people.

MORTIMER: No. They sure made a mess of the house.

BERGEN: I can imagine that.

MORTIMER: I didn't realize how dirty the house was until the dog came in and tried to bury a bone in the living room. We got wall to wall dirt now.

BERGEN: Well, how could they drag so much dirt into the house?

MORTIMER: Well, you know when the little kids go to sleep, you know, they play "this little piggy went to market."

BERGEN: That's nice.

MORTIMER: Yah, with real pigs they play it.

BERGEN: I know it must annoy you, but remember Mortimer, blood is thicker than water.

MORTIMER: Oh, yah, and then again what isn't?

BERGEN: Relatives certainly can be a problem. Do you know what Hubbard said about relatives?

MORTIMER: No, and I don't care to listen to that kind of language.

BERGEN: Oh, you've heard the saying of Elbert Hubbard "The devil gives us our relatives. Thank God we can choose our friends."

MORTIMER: No, how does it go?

BERGEN: It just went.

MORTIMER: I must have been lookin' the other way.

BERGEN: Mortimer, how do you handle the food situation? The meals must be a problem for so many.

MORTIMER: Oh, it's a regular madhouse at meal time. They go at it like they wuz mad at it.

BERGEN: You mean they all stab for the food at once?

MORTIMER: Yah, this morning I reached for a pork chop and I got my arm back so full of forks it looked like a porcupine.

BERGEN: Well, with so many around a table I guess they have to eat fast in order to get anything.

MORTIMER: You never saw such fast eaters. Why, they're eatin' their dessert before the echo of their soup has died away.

BERGEN: Mortimer, why on earth don't you get rid of that mob?

MORTIMER: Wull, it's kind of flatterin' havin' them around. They think I'm awful smart.

BERGEN: They do?

MORTIMER: Yah. They think I'm a regular Albert Epstein.

BERGEN: Oh, I see.

MORTIMER: Kinda a nice change to hear somebody say to me "How can you be so smart?" Ho! Ho!

BERGEN: So they think you're hot stuff. They really must come from the hills.

MORTIMER: Yah, they can't get over the new fandanglements in my house.

BERGEN: You mean your modern improvements?

MORTIMER: Yah, they can't get over the idea of having a water pump right in the kitchen.

BERGEN: Well, Mortimer, that's very nice, but if they're going to stay I think they should work and earn their keep, and also be a little neater around the house.

MORTIMER: Yah. I asked them why they didn't wear shoes and they says, "What do you think we are—horses?"

BERGEN: Well, maybe they'll get tired of you in a few days.

MORTIMER: I don't think they're ever going to leave.

BERGEN: What makes you say that?

MORTIMER: I happened to overhear Uncle Sorghum say, "We'll stay until he gets wise."

BERGEN: Mortimer, I'm beginning to see the light.

MORTIMER: Wull, turn it up a little brighter so I can see it too.

BERGEN: He's not your uncle. They're not your relatives. I think they're a bunch of impostors.

MORTIMER: Yuh?

BERGEN: Well, of course. How can you be so stupid?

MORTIMER: Wull, it comes easy after you reach the first plateau.

MUSIC: PLAYOFF

CAROL: Hello Edgar.

BERGEN: It's Carol Richards!

CAROL: I hope you'll excuse my coming out early. Edgar . . . But I've been anxious to meet Mortimer. He's so cute.

MORTIMER: (*Bashful giggle*)

CAROL: Mortimer, don't tell me you're a shrinking violet.

MORTIMER: Wull, not exactly . . . I'm more of a stinkweed type. Ho. Ho.

CAROL: Now, don't be afraid of me, Mortimer . . . I won't bite you.

MORTIMER: No teeth, eh?

CAROL: I think you're just adorable, Mortimer . . . and I'm going to give you a big kiss!

MORTIMER (*Struggles*): Oh, no, no!

SOUND: KISS

CAROL: There! How was that?

MORTIMER: Gosh, whizz . . . riggy-diggy . . . razzle dazzle . . . I guess I'm gonna get married after all.

CAROL: You're going to be married? To whom?

MORTIMER: Why, to you'm . . . you kissed me, didn't you?

CAROL: Yes . . . Well?

MORTIMER: Wull.

CAROL: Well, what?

MORTIMER: Miss Carol, us Snerds ain't cads!

BERGEN: I think you better sing, Carol.

MORTIMER: Yes, go ahead, wifie.

MUSIC: CAROL AND ORCHESTRA "THE TENDER TRAP"

JOHN: And now, ladies and gentlemen, here is where we take care of you do-it-yourself fans . . . as we proudly present our genius of all-trades—Professor Kirkwood and his Do-it-yourself Department!

SOUND: LOUD HAMMERING . . . ETC. . . . BUZZ SAW

KIRKWOOD: Owwwwwwwwwww!

BERGEN: Professor, at the rate you've been going with that buzz saw you must be down to about two fingers.

KIRKWOOD: How many?

BERGEN: Two fingers.

KIRKWOOD: Don't mind if I do—no chaser, please.

BERGEN: Professor, what is your subject for tonight?

KIRKWOOD: Tonight's subject will be "How to Make Money at Home" —with my "Print-it-Yourself" kit.

BERGEN: Now, just a second, Professor . . . This money you're going to show us how to print—it can't be genuine.

KIRKWOOD: So what . . . Listen, son, we're living in the age of "falsies" . . . teeth, hair, shoulders—and other things too humorous to mention.

NOBLE: Pardon me, old boy, but are you allowed to print money yourself?

KIRKWOOD: Why, certainly . . . Haven't you ever heard of "freedom of the press"?

NOBLE: That's right, I have.

KIRKWOOD: Well, there you are, boy. Now, stand by, it's time for our commercial. (*As announcer*) Folks, is money the one luxury you haven't been able to afford?

NOBLE: Would you like to be as rich as John's other Rockerfeller?

BERGEN: Would you like to have two Cadillacs—one for right turns and one for left turns?

KIRKWOOD: Then, buy Kirkwood's "print-it-yourself" kit . . . It's Kirkwood's answer to inflation.

NOBLE: Think of the fun you'll have sowing your wild notes.

BERGEN: With your own money you can not only look the whole world in it's face, but you can spit in its eye.

KIRKWOOD: Be rich beyond your wildest dreams . . . Have a yacht waiting for you when you're paroled.

BERGEN: Now, just a second . . . Let's stop this foolishness . . . Kirkwood, I'm sure it's against the law to print real money.

KIRKWOOD: Well, that's where we play it smart . . . We don't print real money. We just print counterfeit money.

BERGEN: Kirkwood, you should be ashamed . . . Always trying to do something illegal or put over some racket . . . What do you have to say for yourself?

KIRKWOOD (*Weakly*): I've been sick.

BERGEN: It's just awful. Don't you ever think of anything except money?

KIRKWOOD: Well, sometimes I think about women.

BERGEN: What kind of women?

KIRKWOOD: Women with money. (*Laughs*) Oh, I've got him coming and going.

BERGEN: All I can say to you is—money alone does not bring happiness

KIRKWOOD: No, but it sure makes your unhappiness awfully pleasant. (*Up*) Remember, folks, with all the money you can make on my printing press—why, every year you can spend six months in Europe, six months in Florida, and six months in California.

NOBLE: But I say old boy . . . that makes 18 months.

KIRKWOOD: Sure, see what you can do when you've got money.

BERGEN: No, Professor, I'm sorry I must disagree . . . There are no short cuts to easy money . . . Remember—real money doesn't grow on trees.

KIRKWOOD: Yours did, boy. (*Laughs*) Oh, I made a dummy out of him then!

NOBLE: I say, old chap, is this money you print any good?

KIRKWOOD: Let's put it this way. It's like the Hollywood Freeway—dangerous but passable. Which reminds me, Ray, I could use you . . . Do you think you could pass a twenty-dollar bill?

NOBLE: Certainly, old boy, if it will pull over to the right. Ho. Ho . . . er . . . you're not laughing.

KIRKWOOD: And that's the way it's gonna be.

BERGEN: Don't let him talk you into anything, Ray . . . I wouldn't touch his counterfeit money with a ten-foot pole.

KIRKWOOD: How about a nine-foot Roumanian? (*Laughs*) Oh, turn the fan on, Mother, I'm hot tonight!

BERGEN: I don't want to cool you off, but where did you learn to print money?

KIRKWOOD: Oh, this money-making skill runs in my family.

BERGEN: It does?

KIRKWOOD: Yeah, my father taught my brother how to make one-hundred-dollar bills and now he's got "Life with Father."

BERGEN: How about you, Kirkwood? Have you ever been in jail?

KIRKWOOD: (*Laughs*) Have I ever been in jail! (*Take*) The warden calls me by my first number, boy!

BERGEN: Been in that often, eh?

KIRKWOOD: Let me put it this way: I've been in stir more often than the paddles of a mixmaster.

BERGEN: Well, you certainly got the bowl for it!

KIRKWOOD: You're talking with that Lazy Susan back there! But to get back to the subject—How to Make Your Own Money . . .

SOUND: BANGING ON DOOR . . . POLICE WHISTLES . . . OFF

BERGEN: It's the police! Kirkwood, they're probably after you!

KIRKWOOD: Oh, wonderful!

BERGEN: You're happy about it?

KIRKWOOD: Of course. It's depressing if they don't come and get you once in a while ... Makes you feel sort of unwanted. So long boy!

BERGEN: Tune in next week folks when Professor Kirkwood's topic will be "How to engineer your own jail break"! Good night.

MUSIC: PLAYOFF

BERGEN: Ladies and gentlemen, I am extremely happy to be able to introduce to you once again our outstanding vocal group—The Mellomen. What are going to sing tonight fellows?

THURL: "Gilly Gilly Ossenfeffer Katzen-Ellen-Bogen-by-the-Sea."

BERGEN: Yes, but what are you going to sing?

THURL: "Gilly Gilly Ossenfeffer ..."

BERGEN: Never mind—just do it.

MUSIC: MELLOMEN AND ORCHESTRA "GILLY GILLY"

MUSIC: EFFIE THEME

JOHN: Ladies and gentlemen, once again we bring you one of the more popular portions of our program—our "How to Stay Young" Department ... And here to let us in on her secret of eternal youth is that all-time girl ... just back from a rejuvenation course with Ali Khan ... Miss Effie Klinker!

EFFIE (*Sings*): "Oh, I may be falling apart, but I'm young at heart ..."

BERGEN: My, you look lovely tonight, Miss Klinker.

EFFIE: Well, I believe in growing old gracefully ... or better yet—disgracefully! ... Whoopee!

BERGEN: I gather that you still like to have a little fling.

EFFIE: A little fling is all I can have ... The rest has all been flung.

BERGEN: I think it's wonderful how you've kept your youth.

EFFIE: How did you find out about George?

BERGEN: Never mind. Tell us, Miss Klinker ... Nowadays they give you shots for almost everything ... Are there any shots you can take to make you feel younger?

EFFIE: Yes, indeedy ... After a few shots of scotch you'd be surprised how young I feel!

BERGEN: Miss Klinker, don't tell me that you drink!

EFFIE: Well, the doctor said that for my health I should have just a wee drop before I go to bed.

BERGEN: I see.

EFFIE: You know, sometimes I find myself going to bed four or five times a night!

BERGEN: Effie!

EFFIE: Yes, siree, I really sleep tight!

BERGEN: I hate to say this, Effie, but drinking will cut your life in half.

EFFIE: Well, it comes out even ... You see twice as much ... Whoopee!

BERGEN: That will do. Right now it's time to answer some of your mail.

EFFIE: All right . . . But better hurry up, it's getting close to one of my bedtimes.

BERGEN: This first letter is from Minneapolis. (*Reads*) Dear Miss Klinker—I am 80 years old . . . Would it keep me young if I married a 20-year-old girl?

EFFIE: Sonny, it would probably kill you! . . . It's like buying a steak when you haven't got any teeth. Next.

BERGEN: Here is one from a listener in Cleveland. (*Reads*) Dear Miss Klinker—Would you say that too much romance shortens your life?

EFFIE: Oh, yes definitely ... But what a way to go!

BERGEN: This letter from New York says . . . Dear Miss Klinker—I am 35 and going with a used-car salesman . . . Should I marry him?

EFFIE: If you love him, what if he is used!

BERGEN (*Reads*): Dear Miss Klinker—What is the most important rule in staying young ... Besides lying, that is.

EFFIE: Good health is most important . . . People are too run down these days.

NOBLE: I say, old girl . . . Would you say that I looked run down?

EFFIE: Worse. You look run over.

BERGEN: Miss Klinker, I suppose you recommend exercise to stay young?

EFFIE: Oh, yes. Exercise is very important . . . The average woman spends most of her time sitting down—as the figures clearly show. (*Laughs*) Oh, I am catty tonight!

NOBLE: Speaking of exercise, only this morning I ran ten miles.

EFFIE: Doing road work?

NOBLE: No, you see my tie got caught in the door of the bus.

EFFIE: Oh, I've just got to go to bed again!

BERGEN: Please, Effie, you've still got one more letter to answer . . . (*Reads*) Dear Miss Kinker—Do you ever wear a sweater to attract men?

EFFIE: Me—wear a sweater—with my figure! Why, that would be like trying to flag down the Super-Chief with an empty can of sterno!

BERGEN: Thank you, Miss Effie Klinker . . . Our time is up, but before we go, do you have any last message to our audience?

EFFIE: Yes. All of you men out there—take care of yourself and heaven keep you—I wish I could afford to! Good night!

MUSIC: PLAYOFF

MUSIC: ORCHESTRA AND MELLOMEN—THEME

JOHN: Ladies and gentlemen, once again it is time for our weekly excursion into the realm of culture. Tonight, our forum of intellectual titans bring their great wisdom and perception to bear on the ever-continuing scholastic debate "Whither Literature." Here they are—Edgar Bergen and his End Table.

BERGEN: Thank you and good evening, panel.

PANEL: (*Ad libs hellos.*)

KIRKWOOD: Hiya, kid.

NOBLE: Crazy man.

BERGEN: Good evening, Professor Kirkwood . . . Professor Noble . . . and, well, if it isn't Mortimer Snerd.

MORTIMER: Well, if it isn't—the stork sure played a dirty trick on my mother.

BERGEN: That's enough!

MORTIMER: That's exactly what my parents said when they got their first look at me.

BERGEN: Gentlemen, our subject for tonight is "Whither Literature" . . . and I intend to base our discussion on the eternal argument of modern literature versus the classics. Do you all comprehend?

KIRKWOOD: Oh, Bergen, you're so full of it—knowledge, that is.

NOBLE: You had me quite nervous there, old boy.

BERGEN: Please, gentlemen. We must begin our forum. Now, to start the discussion—who would like to define the meaning of "literature"?

MORTIMER: Wull, in my opinion . . . (*Clears throat*) literature is the term applied to all printed matter developed by the processes of imagination and intended to serve artistic rather than utilitarian purposes.

BERGEN, NOBLE, KIRKWOOD (*In unison*): NOOOOOOOOO!

MORTIMER: Bunch of dopes!

BERGEN: Mortimer, I'm surprised. I didn't know you had such a literary mind.

MORTIMER: Oh, my mind is as littered as they come.

NOBLE: I say, chaps, I should be quite good on this subject . . . You know, I was born in a library.

BERGEN: You were actually born in a library? How is that possible?

NOBLE: Well, mother kept trying to tell Dad, but the librarian kept saying, "Shhhhhhhh!"

KIRKWOOD (*Laughs*): The librarian kept saying "Shh"! (*Take*) If your parents were smart they would've brought you back after two weeks.

NOBLE: They did, old boy . . . After all, I had to be renewed.

KIRKWOOD: Ray, there's a North American van leaving for the Grand Canyon. Why don't you get on it? Or better yet—get under it!

BERGEN: Please, that will do. Now that Professor Snerd has defined literature for us, we can go on. Professor Kirkwood, what would you say is your favorite book?

KIRKWOOD: Well, it used to be Louie over on 3rd Street, but the cops grabbed him.

NOBLE: Oh, too bad!

KIRKWOOD: Yeah, he was on his way to being "bookie of the month." (*Laughs*) Get it, bookie of the month! (*Take*) Ugh . . . that was a loser!

BERGEN: Professor Kirkwood your education is sadly lacking.

KIRKWOOD: You hurt me, boy. Why, I'll have you know I went to school . . . and I really enjoyed that day.

BERGEN: Do you mean to say you only went to school one day?

KIRKWOOD: You're supposed to go back?

BERGEN: Never mind. Let's get on. Now, Professor Snerd, who is your favorite author?

MORTIMER: Well, it's . . . er . . . gosh . . . I know it as well as I know my own name . . . It's . . . er . . . Nope—that's my own name . . . It's . . . er . . . No . . . He's dead . . . er . . . (*Sings*) "Oh when they begin the . . ."

BERGEN: Mortimer, all I asked you was—who is your favorite author?

MORTIMER: Oh, yeah—*Author* Godfrey!

BERGEN: That's ridiculous.

KIRKWOOD: Yeah. I hear he isn't around any more. He just fired himself!

BERGEN: That will do. Gentlemen, I'd like to get one sensible answer from this panel. Professor Noble, do you know Dickens' works?

NOBLE: No, but I'm glad he got the job.

PANEL: (*Ad libs agreement*: "Yes, he needs the work, he's a good fellow . . ." etc.)

BERGEN: I'm referring to Charles Dickens.

NOBLE: Oh, Charles Dickens—of course . . . How silly of me . . . His books have always occupied an important position in our house.

BERGEN: Is that so?

NOBLE: Yes, you see, we have a table with one short leg.

PANEL: (*Ad libs agreement*: "Clever," "Very good," etc.)

BERGEN: This is hard to believe. Haven't you read any of Dickens' famous classics? You know you might enjoy *Little Women*.

KIRKWOOD: Oh, I've enjoyed quite a few of them .

BERGEN: Kirkwood, we're still on the subject of Literature.

KIRKWOOD: I think I changed it for the better.

BERGEN: Now, you'll just have to stop your interruptions. I'm running out of patience.

KIRKWOOD: Nice timing. I'm running out of interruptions.

BERGEN: Oh, this is awful. I'm afraid you've all been neglecting the literary and cultural side of your life. Now, take me—my mind is always ripening.

KIRKWOOD: Naturally, it gets the full sun all day.

BERGEN: Kirkwood, I've had enough of your insults.

KIRKWOOD: Well, thank you—I always try to satisfy.

BERGEN: That will do—we must get on. Now, our modern writers have been compared unfavorably with the great fifteenth- and sixteenth-century authors such as Shakespeare, Chaucer and Bacon. Now, Mortimer, what do you think?

MORTIMER: I'll have some.

BERGEN: Some what?

MORTIMER: Bacon.

BERGEN: That's Francis Bacon.

MORTIMER: Francis Bacon? You mean it comes from a mule?

BERGEN: No, this Bacon is a man.

MORTIMER: Well, then count me out. I aint no cannibal!

BERGEN: Oh, I'm at my wit's end.

NOBLE: Careful you don't fall off, old boy. Just take it easy.

BERGEN: But this is awful, Ray. I'm supposed to be the moderator. What would you do if you were in my shoes?

NOBLE: I'd limp horribly, old boy. I wear size 11.

BERGEN: I shouldn't have asked. Gentlemen, this is a discussion on literature . . . Certainly you've read *some* books.

PANEL: (*Ad libs agreement*)

KIRKWOOD: I just read that book about a bad day at Santa Anita.

BERGEN: A book about a bad day at Santa Anita?

KIRKWOOD: Yeah, you know—*The Naked and the Dead* (*Laughs*) (*Take*) Oh, that was another loser.

NOBLE: Personally, I like those Edgar Rice Burroughs books about *Tarzan of the Apes*, even though they are unbelievable. After all, who would live with an ape?

KIRKWOOD: He hasn't met my wife. Ugh, what a beast!

BERGEN: Gentlemen, please. Mortimer, do you do much reading?

MORTIMER: Oh, yeah . . . Whenever I'm in my little library out in back, I always like to read the Sears-Roebuck catalog . . . 'Specially that spicy section on women's harness.

BERGEN: No. No. How about the best-sellers?

MORTIMER: How about them?

KIRKWOOD: I just read one of those best sellers . . . you know the one . . . *The Power of Getting Positively Stinking.*

BERGEN: That will do.

NOBLE: I say, did any of you chaps read that new English bestseller— *The Typewriter Murder Mystery*—or *Who Shifted Lady Chumley's Carriage?*

PANEL: (*Ad lib*: "No . . . How was it," etc. . . .)

MORTIMER: My favorite are those Mother Goose Stories like "Little Boy Blue Come Blow Your Nose" . . . or "You're a Better Man Than I Am, Rin-Tin-Tin."

KIRKWOOD: Well, we're back to my wife again!

BERGEN: Please, gentlemen . . .

KIRKWOOD: How about *Tom Swift and His Electric Nostril?* Anyone read that?

NOBLE: I say, chaps, the book I'm waiting for is the new Kinsey Report. This one's on *The Love Life of the Mashed Potato.*

BERGEN: *The Love Life of the Mashed Potato?*

NOBLE: Yes, old boy . . . You'd be surprised at what goes on under that gravy.

KIRKWOOD (*Laughs*): What goes on under that gravy! (*Take*) I gotta take a look some time.

BERGEN: That's enough, gentlemen . . . We're here to discuss the basic differences between modern and classical literature, and there are many of them. Mortimer, would you like to illustrate?

MORTIMER: No, I feel fine.

BERGEN: Here we go again! This is awful, panel. I'm just amazed at all this blind ignorance.

KIRKWOOD: Now, just a second, boy. I might've had a few, but I'm not blind.

BERGEN: We're not getting any place.

MORTIMER: I don't know about you fellows, but I'm writin' my own book.

PANEL: (*Ad libs*: "Atta boy, Mort." "Good work," etc.)

MORTIMER: Yup! They say any idiot can write a book—and if that's all it takes . . . er . . . I'm their boy.

BERGEN: What kind of book is it, Mortimer?

MORTIMER: It's about my cow Bessie . . . I call it—*With These Hands*.

NOBLE: I say, that one should win the *Pull* -itzer prize. Ho. Ho. Did you get it?

KIRKWOOD: All over us.

NOBLE: Really, Mortimer old boy, do you have a flair for writing?

MORTIMER: No, I've got a pencil. You can't write with a flare.

BERGEN: Of course not.

MORTIMER: Unless it's for light reading. Ho. Ho. I sorta outfoxed 'em there.

BERGEN: Mortimer, you're incorrigible.

MORTIMER: Gosh, I thought we were in C.B.S.

BERGEN: No, no. Now, gentlemen, I have something I must say.

KIRKWOOD: Well, as the farmer said to the hen—unburden yourself, boy.

BERGEN: I maintain that we're taking this subject too lightly. Now, you know what Socrates said about the importance of literature.

MORTIMER: Nope. I don't think I was listening.

BERGEN: He said it before you were born.

MORTIMER: Then I know I wasn't listening.

BERGEN: For your information, Socrates lived many years ago . . . in old Greece.

NOBLE: I say, he must have been a rancid old duffer.

BERGEN: Oh, this is terrible. I just cannot cope with the abysmal ignorance being shown here tonight . . . the monumental illiteracy . . . the crass superficiality . . . the utter incomprehension . . .

KIRKWOOD: AAAAA shaddup!

BERGEN: Now, this is absolutely . . .

SOUND: BUZZER

BERGEN: Thank goodness! That's the final buzzer. Before we leave I would like to say one final word to literature lovers everywhere. Remember—always keep the light of learning burning bright.

KIRKWOOD: That's a good idea. Let's all go out and get lit!

PANEL: (*Ad libs agreement.*)

BERGEN: Good night!

MUSIC: PLAYOFF

The Visitor
(*Lassie*)

by THELMA ROBINSON

Story by
WARREN WILSON *and*
CLAIRE KENNEDY

CATEGORY:

Television Children's Program

(ANY LENGTH)

THE VISITOR

by THELMA ROBINSON

The Visitor
was first presented by Robert Maxwell Associates,
under the direction of Maurice Geraghty,
in February of 1956,
with the following cast:

ELLEN MILLER · Jan Clayton
JEFF MILLER · Tommy Rettig
GRAMPS MILLER · George Cleveland
PORKY BROCKWAY · Donald Keeler
CLAY HORTON · Richard Garland
HARU YAMAGUCHI · Warren Nagata
MISS WITHERSPOON · Mary Alan Hokanson
BERT PULLEY · Steve Lowe
HOWIE BREWSTER · Douglas Smith
SIMON PULLEY · William Tannen
ART BREWSTER · Frank Richards
LASSIE

© Copyright, 1956
by Robert Maxwell Associates

FADE IN:

EXTERIOR MILLER BARNYARD—FULL PAN SHOT—DAY

> as JEFF comes riding in on his bike with LASSIE running beside him and PORKY, on his bike, close behind. Camera pans them all across the barnyard to the side door of the barn. JEFF rides inside the barn where he keeps his bike but PORKY pulls up outside.

MEDIUM CLOSE

> PORKY as he dismounts and rests his bike up against the barn. Camera pans him to barn door as JEFF and LASSIE come out. JEFF is carrying an official-looking application paper in his hand. It is folded in two.

PORKY: I'll betcha your Gramps is gonna say the same thing my Pop said—*no!*

JEFF: If Gramps won't sign I'll get Mom to do it.

PORKY: But your Mom's in Capitol City an' you said she won't be back till Monday an' Mr. Beasley said the application's gotta be in by tomorrow.

JEFF (*Biting his lips*): Yeah—that's right. Well, let's see what Gramps says.

TRAVELING SHOT

> JEFF, PORKY, LASSIE as they walk along the side of the barn to the front corner and turn it. We see GRAMPS trying to crank the pickup truck. The hood of the truck is open and he has obviously been working on it. His face is smudged and his hands are grease-stained. Giving vent to childish frustration, he viciously kicks at a front tire.

GRAMPS: No good pile uh junk, yuh!

TIGHT TWO SHOT

> JEFF and PORKY as they look at each other. Obviously, GRAMPS is not in the best of humor. PORKY urges JEFF forward. JEFF gulps and exits past camera with PORKY following.

MEDIUM CLOSE

> GRAMPS is now under the hood working with a pair of pliers. JEFF enters scene, forcing a smile.

JEFF: Hi, Gramps! (PORKY enters scene; either GRAMPS hasn't heard or he isn't responding. JEFF looks at PORKY who motions to the application in JEFF's hand and silently urges him to present it. JEFF unfolds the application.) I got somethin' for you to sign, Gramps.

GRAMPS: (*Without looking*): Got no time now!

TWO SHOT

> JEFF *and* PORKY *as* JEFF *looks at* PORKY *helplessly.* PORKY *gulps and takes a step toward* GRAMPS.

PORKY: Mr. Miller, it's very important.

GROUP SHOT

> GRAMPS *brings his head out from under the hood and moves around to the crank again.*

GRAMPS (*Over action*): Consarn gas-eatin' critter. (JEFF *and* PORKY *follow* GRAMPS.)

JEFF: Mr. Beasley at the 4-H Club said if we invite a farm boy from another country to come here for the summer ...

PORKY: Then maybe next summer *we* get to go to *his* country.

GRAMPS (*As he starts to crank again*): Fool crank's got a kick like a mule.

PORKY (*Innocently*): Doesn't the starter work? (*For the first time,* GRAMPS *looks at the boys.*)

GRAMPS: You think I'd be crankin' if it did? What do you kids want? (JEFF *leaps in, waving the application.*)

JEFF: It's the Farm Youth Exchange Program, Gramps. From the 4-H Club.

GRAMPS: Good thing—the 4-H.

JEFF (*Eagerly*): You're supposed to sign it. Y'got your pen clipped right on your overalls.

GRAMPS: Jes hang on to yer buttons there. What's it gonna cost?

JEFF: Nothin'.

PORKY: It's free!

GRAMPS: You sure?

PORKY and JEFF: Sure!

GRAMPS: Well, I reckon if it's somethin' fer 4-H ...

JEFF: Thanks, Gramps! (*He grabs* GRAMPS' *pen and spreads the application form on the truck's fender, eagerly pointing*) Here, Gramps, Sign here. (GRAMPS *laboriously forms his signature as the boys watch gleefully over his shoulder. The signing is completed.*) Gee, Gramps, you're swell!

PORKY (*Wistfully*): You sure are, Mr. Miller.

GRAMPS (*Touched but embarrassed*): Now scoot along, you two ... Let a man get to his work. (JEFF *and* PORKY *grin, then scamper off toward the house, followed by* LASSIE.)

CLOSE SHOT

GRAMPS *watches them with tenderness, then turns back to the crank.*

EXTERIOR KITCHEN DOOR—PORKY AND JEFF

PORKY: Gosh! It was real easy!
JEFF: Sure. My Gramps is okay!

Just then the sound of the pick-up motor is heard—strong and healthy. The boys stop, listen, then turn toward the sound. They look at each other and grin happily.

FADE OUT

FADE IN

EXTERIOR MILLER HOUSE—DAY

MISS WITHERSPOON, *a tall, sharp-faced woman—severely dressed—is tapping at the front door of the* MILLER *house. As she waits, she riffles efficiently through a sheaf of forms in her hand. After a moment it becomes obvious that no one is home.* MISS WITHERSPOON *glances around, then strides purposefully toward the barn.*

INTERIOR BARN—DAY

MISS WITHERSPOON *briskly inspects the barn and its contents, pausing now and then to make notes in a little book.*

MEDIUM SHOT

GRAMPS, *ambling along toward the barn. As he reaches the doorway, he stops still in surprise.*

MEDIUM SHOT

MISS WITHERSPOON *from* GRAMPS' *point of view. She is crouched down, notebook in hand, counting the chickens.*

MISS WITHERSPOON: One—two—three . . .

CLOSE SHOT

GRAMPS' *surprise replaced by indignation.*

GRAMPS: (*Loud*): Hey!

MEDIUM TWO SHOT

> MISS WITHERSPOON, *thrown off balance by the sudden crack of* GRAMPS' *voice, sends an empty tin can crashing to the floor. The racket causes the chickens to flutter frenziedly about the barn, squawking hysterically.*

EXTERIOR BARNYARD—FULL SHOT

> ELLEN *is coming around a corner of the barn carrying a basket of tomatoes. She starts toward the house when the noise of the clucking chickens causes her to turn and go toward the barn.*

INTERIOR BARN—TWO SHOT—GRAMPS AND MISS WITHERSPOON

GRAMPS: What ya doin' prowlin' 'round my barn?!

MISS WITHERSPOON (*As she recovers her balance*): Ha—you're Mr. Miller. Well, *I'm* Witherspoon from Eefee. There was no one home, so I thought I'd take a little tour on my own.

GRAMPS: Oh, you did!

MISS WITHERSPOON: I must say, Mr. Miller, I'm quite pleased with what I've seen so far.

GRAMPS: Oh, you are!

MISS WITHERSPOON: Yes. And what's more you have a good dry, clean barn here. (*With a satisfied nod*) Now I think I'd like to inspect the livestock and the house.

GRAMPS: Oh, you would—*would* you! Look here, Miss Eefee . . .

MISS WITHERSPOON: Miss *Witherspoon.* Eefee is the organization for whom I am Field Examiner.

GRAMPS: I don't give a tin horn *whose* field you examine—I jes' know you ain't goin' pokin' around here! (GRAMPS *in his fury takes a step toward* MISS WITHERSPOON, *with the intention, we feel, of hustling her bodily out of the barn. He is stopped by* ELLEN's *appearance.*)

ELLEN: Dad! What's happening?

GRAMPS: I caught this—woman—snoopin' around an' . . .

MISS WITHERSPOON: Now, now, Mr. Miller . . . not snooping. Please. Inspecting.

GRAMPS: I say it's snoopin'!

ELLEN: Wait a minute, Dad. (*To* MISS WITHERSPOON) I'm Ellen Miller.

MISS WITHERSPOON: I'm Agnes Witherspoon—Field Examiner for International Farm Youth Exchange.

ELLEN: Oh?

MISS WITHERSPOON: Yes, you see we like to inspect some things in person. It's merely a follow-up on Mr. Miller's application. The final step, so to speak. (ELLEN *looks to* GRAMPS *for an explanation while he glares incredulously at* MISS WITHERSPOON.)

GRAMPS: If this is some new-fangled trick for sellin' magazines or somethin' . . .

MISS WITHERSPOON: Mr. Miller, I have your application for a foreign boy to stay at your farm . . .

GRAMPS: I don't need no farm boy!

MISS WITHERSPOON: I said *foreign*, not farm!

GRAMPS: That's worse!

MEDIUM SHOT

> JEFF *and* LASSIE *peering around the barn door.*

MISS WITHERSPOON'S VOICE: Don't you want the boy?

GRAMPS' VOICE: I should say not! Never heard of such a thing.

> JEFF *reacts, showing concern. As* LASSIE *starts into the barn, he grabs and holds her back.*

TWO SHOT—GRAMPS AND MISS WITHERSPOON

MISS WITHERSPOON (*Holds paper in front of* GRAMPS—*sternly*): Do you deny this is your signature?

GRAMPS (*Peers at form*): I been tricked! The thing I signed was a 4-H paper fer neighbor kids to go back and forth to each other's farms . . .

MISS WITHERSPOON: You're very much mistaken, Mr. Miller. A boy is already on his way to you—a boy from Japan.

CLOSE SHOT

> GRAMPS *is horrified.*

GRAMPS: Japan! (*He sinks onto a bench.*)

EXTERIOR BARN

> JEFF *and* LASSIE *flattened against barn wall. After a fearful moment, they dart off.*

INTERIOR BARN—GROUP SHOT

> GRAMPS *is in a daze.* MISS WITHERSPOON *is vexed.* ELLEN *now holds the application paper and is studying it.*

ELLEN: This all looks very official and final, Miss Witherspoon.

MISS WITHERSPOON (*Distraught*): It is . . . and frankly, I . . . I don't
know what to do. The boy's already left Japan! What'll I do with
him? We thought you were responsible people.
ELLEN (*Goes to* MISS WITHERSPOON; *confidently*): I think you'll find
we are.

MEDIUM CLOSE SHOT—ELLEN AND
MISS WITHERSPOON

ELLEN (*Softly*): When can we expect the boy?
MISS WITHERSPOON: I'm not *quite* sure, but I'll let you know.
ELLEN (*Softly*): We'll be ready for him. (*She guides* MISS WITHER-
SPOON *out the barn door.*)

MEDIUM SHOT

GRAMPS, *rising out of his stupor. He stands up, glares around.*

GRAMPS: Jeff! (*He marches to the barn door. Bellowing*) Jeff Miller!
(*Muttering*) Where's that meddlin' boy? (*Bellowing*) Lassie!
Lassie!

TIGHT TWO SHOT

JEFF *and* LASSIE *hiding in the shrubbery. In spite of* JEFF'S
efforts to restrain her, the curious LASSIE *manages to break
away.*

MEDIUM CLOSE SHOT

GRAMPS, *as* LASSIE *comes into scene.*

GRAMPS (*Shouting angrily*): Where's Jeff? Go get him! (*LASSIE ignores
the command. She sits down stubbornly in front of* GRAMPS.) Y'hear
me! Go get Jeff! (*LASSIE merely flattens herself on her tummy, returning* GRAMPS' *glare.* GRAMPS *grunts, turns away in disgust and
stomps into the barn.*)

MEDIUM LONG SHOT—FEATURING ELLEN

She waves as MISS WITHERSPOON's *car drives off.*

MEDIUM CLOSE SHOT

JEFF *as* ELLEN *is about to pass the shrubbery, he hisses.*

JEFF: Mom!

MEDIUM CLOSE SHOT—ELLEN

She turns, sees JEFF.

ELLEN: So there you are, young man. Haven't you some explaining to do?

MEDIUM SHOT

JEFF *disentangles himself from the bush and comes out.*

JEFF: Gee, Mom, I thought Gramps understood about everything— and everything was all right!

ELLEN (*Searchingly*): Did you, really?

JEFF: I *thought* he did.

ELLEN: Well, sweetie, nearly all of the trouble in this world comes from people not understanding each other. I'm afraid you didn't do a very good job of explaining to Gramps. Why didn't you tell me about it?

JEFF: I forgot. I'm sorry, Mom.

ELLEN: Well, I guess we'd better go make plans (*Smiles ruefully*) for East meeting West at the Miller farm.

ANOTHER ANGLE

JEFF *and* ELLEN *start off rather solemnly toward the house.*

DISSOLVE TO

INTERIOR MILLER KITCHEN—NIGHT

With a look of concern, ELLEN *is hanging up the telephone receiver.* GRAMPS *watches from his chair, waiting for her to speak.* JEFF, *who has been thoughtfully clearing the supper table, stops and waits, too.*

ELLEN: News certainly travels fast around here. (*Goes to table; automatically starts to clear it*) What was that? The fourth or fifth call?

GRAMPS: T'won't be the last, nuther. Folks in these parts ain't gonna cotton to no kid from Japan.

JEFF: Who cares? He's not gonna be visitin' them. He's comin' to stay with us.

ELLEN (*To* JEFF): It's time for you to be in bed.

JEFF: Okay, Mom. (*As he starts to go, the telephone rings. Answering phone*) Hello ... Hi, Porky!

MEDIUM CLOSE SHOT—PORKY AT PHONE

PORKY: 'Lo, Jeff. 'Bout that halves-zees you gave me. Well, I'm givin' it back ... Ya see, I'm gonna be awful busy this summer—so I won't be seein' much of you ... (*Forlornly*) An' your visitor ... (*Pause*) Yeah. (*Pause*) 'Bye. (*Hangs up.*)

MEDIUM CLOSE SHOT

JEFF *hanging up receiver.*

JEFF (*To himself*): Gee . . . Even Porky . . . (As JEFF *goes,* ELLEN *and* GRAMPS *look after him, compassionate yet troubled.*)

FADE OUT

FADE IN:

EXTERIOR CALVERTON JUNCTION—DAY

ELLEN, GRAMPS, JEFF, CLAY HORTON *and* LASSIE *are waiting on the platform as a train pulls into the station.* ELLEN *glances around, chagrined by the conspicuous absence of other people.*

ELLEN (*To* CLAY): I hardly expected a welcoming committee, but I didn't think people would deliberately stay away.

CLAY: Oh, we have a welcoming committee of sorts. (*Nods off.*)

MEDIUM LONG SHOT—A BUILDING

as a small group of spectators duck out of sight.

FULL SHOT

While the military group is concentrating on the front end of the train, a solitary figure lugging a huge and very heavy Oriental traveling basket alights from the last car.

MEDIUM CLOSE SHOT

HARU YAMAGUCHI *neatly dressed in the shirt, baggy pants and broad-brimmed straw hat typical of the Japanese farm boy. He looks down the platform eagerly and beams and waves.*

HARU: Oh, so! This is me!

MEDIUM SHOT—MILLER GROUP—FROM HARU'S POINT OF VIEW

They turn and stop dead still, staring. Their faces reveal some of the uncertainty they feel at meeting this odd little stranger.

CLOSE SHOT

HARU *dragging his basket behind him. He has been taking tentative steps toward them, but now he stops, his smile disappearing. This is far from the hospitable welcome he had anticipated. As he looks forlornly from one to the other, his lip trembles for an instant before he is able sternly to control it.*

TIGHT TWO SHOT—JEFF AND LASSIE

LASSIE *whimpers and nudges* JEFF, *who still hesitates.* LASSIE, *drawn to the lonely little figure, dashes forward to greet* HARU.

TWO SHOT—HARU AND LASSIE

Eagerly, LASSIE *cavorts around him, barking excitedly and licking his hands, etc.*

GROUP SHOT

The awkward moment has now been broken by LASSIE'S *greeting.* JEFF *runs forward to* HARU. *The others follow more slowly, smiling.*

TWO SHOT—JEFF AND HARU

JEFF (*Haltingly*): Eesh-sho-nee kee-TAY koo-da-SA-ee! (*Please come with me.*) (*As* JEFF *waits expectantly,* HARU *looks embarrassed. More slowly*) Eesh-sho-nee kee-TAY koo-da-SA-ee! (*Please come with me.*)

HARU (*With some alarm*): You say there is hunger in the village?

JEFF (*Grinning sheepishly*): I was tryin' to say—"You're welcome. Please come with me." I read it in a Japanese dictionary.

HARU: Oh, yes. (*A little bow*) Please forgive this stupid one.

JEFF: Aw, I prob'ly said it all wrong.

HARU (*Anxiously*): Please do not blame yourself . . . Dust of many miles is in my ears. (*Others enter scene, camera angle widening.*)

JEFF: Well—anyway—here we all are. My Mom, my Gramps an' Clay Horton, the Constable.

There are ad lib greetings, such as: "Hello, Haru, good to see you." "Have a nice ride on the train, boy?" "Welcome to Calverton," *etc.* HARU *looks up at them, his confidence returning.*

JEFF: Well, let's get goin'. I bet you want to see the farm?

HARU: Yes! (*He eagerly picks up his basket and unceremoniously thrusts it into* ELLEN's *arms.* ELLEN, *taken by surprise, almost lets it fall.* CLAY, *at her side, swiftly relieves her of the weight.*)

MEDIUM CLOSE SHOT—HARU

HARU (*Surprised*): It is not the custom in this country . . . for the woman to carry such things?

CLAY (*Laughing*): It is definitely not the custom.

> *They all chuckle good-naturedly.* HARU, *after a moment, joins in the merriment. Camera features basket as we*

DISSOLVE TO

INTERIOR MILLER PARLOR—LATE DAY

> *The traveling basket is now open and* HARU *is ceremoniously distributing gifts. With his customary bow, he first presents a handsomely embroidered robe and cap to* GRAMPS.

HARU: Honorable One, this humble gift was selected for you by my father.

MEDIUM CLOSE SHOT

> LASSIE *smiling approval.*

GROUP SHOT

GRAMPS (*Examining robe gingerly*): This here's a mighty fancy bath-robe . . .

HARU: Excuse, please. In Japan no robe worn in bath. In Japan this robe is for occasions of happiness and good will. (HARU *excitedly takes another robe from his basket and gives it to* JEFF.) For you, Jeff-san. You like?

JEFF (*Uncertainly*): Sure . . . it's keen.

MEDIUM CLOSE SHOT

> GRAMPS *looking on disdainfully.*

GROUP SHOT

> HARU *hands* JEFF *a kimono and slippers.*

HARU: And you may give this to the woman, if she is worthy.

JEFF: Oh, *she* is! (*Turning to* ELLEN) Look, Mom, what's for you! (*He thrusts the kimono and slippers into* ELLEN's *arms.*)

ELLEN: It's beautiful. Thank you, Haru. (*Smiling ruefully*) I'll certainly try to be worthy . . .

MEDIUM SHOT

> LASSIE *watching happily.*

GROUP SHOT—FEATURING HARU

HARU (*To* JEFF, *beaming*): The woman in your house is indeed commendable.

JEFF (*Peering into basket*): What's all the rest of this stuff, Haru? (HARU *eagerly pulls out an assortment of packages.*)

HARU: Cherry blossom tea . . . ! Stewed fish eggs . . . (GRAMPS *shudders*) Pickled chrysanthemum petals! Dried eels! Jellied monkey livers . . .

JEFF: Monkey livers!

HARU: Rare delicacy! Also—bottled sparrow eggs . . . bamboo . . . and (*Hauls out string of tortured-looking dried "food"*) very fine fish heads! (*As he thrusts the fish at* ELLEN, *he notices the stunned expressions on the faces of his listeners*) I do not mean to seem ungrateful, but the food of your country is so strange . . . I feared I might not accustom myself to it . . .

ELLEN (*Holding up fish heads*): I hope I can accustom myself to preparing *these* . . .

HARU: Oh, very simple! Very simple! I show you!

ELLEN (*Flatly*): Thank you. That'll be fine . . .

JEFF: Haru, d'ya want to see your room now?

HARU: Oh, yes, Jeff-san! (HARU *snaps down the lid of his basket and picks it up. Smiling at* ELLEN) This time I carry! I catch on quick! You see! (*He starts to follow* JEFF, *but stops in the doorway.*)

CLOSE SHOT—HARU

A *frown crosses his face and he turns back to* GRAMPS.

HARU (*Tentatively*): There were no town visitors to greet me at train. Would not happen so in Japan . . .

CLOSE SHOT—GRAMPS

GRAMPS (*Uncomfortably*): Well—folks hereabouts keep pretty busy durin' the daytime . . .

GROUP SHOT—FEATURING HARU

HARU: Then they will come tonight. It is the tradition?

CLOSE SHOT—ELLEN

ELLEN: Well—no, I don't think so, Haru.

CLOSE SHOT—HARU

HARU (*Delighted and relieved*): This is good news! Now I am relieved!

GROUP SHOT

ELLEN: Why, what do you mean?

HARU: Oh, my father. Customs . . . traditions, nonsense! Such a speech he made me to learn! Now I can forget. All is well!

JEFF: Come on then, Haru! (JEFF *helps* HARU *with his basket and they both clatter out, followed by a happily cavorting* LASSIE.)

MEDIUM TWO SHOT

> ELLEN *and* GRAMPS *as they exchange somewhat shamefaced glances.*

FADE OUT

FADE IN:

EXTERIOR TRUCK GARDEN—FULL SHOT—JEFF, HARU— DAY

> *This is a small truck garden with a few rows of small, growing cabbage, tomato or pepper plants in the background.* JEFF *and* HARU *are just finishing the preparation of three new rows of planting for turnip seeds.* JEFF *looks up and sees* GRAMPS *and* LASSIE *approaching.*

JEFF: Hi, Gramps.

TWO SHOT—JEFF AND HARU

HARU: Hi, Mr. Miller-san.

> GRAMPS *and* LASSIE *enter scene.* GRAMPS *is carrying three one-pound bags of turnip seed (cloth bags).* LASSIE *moves over to* JEFF *to be petted.*

GRAMPS (*On entrance*): How you doin'? (*Looks up the rows*) Mmm —pretty good.

JEFF: This Haru's a slave driver. All work and no talk.

HARU: In the words of my father—busy tongue make idle hands.

GRAMPS: Your father's a smart man. Here's the turnip seed. We'll each take a row.

> JEFF *and* HARU *put their hoes aside and each takes a bag of seed.* JEFF *and* GRAMPS *fashion their bags into crude funnels by rolling down the excess and shaping them.* HARU *watches them and rolls his excess down, too, but doesn't shape his bag.*

JEFF (*Over action*): Boy, you sure know the right things to say and the right things to do, Haru.

HARU (*Over action*): Good habits must be learned early in life.

JEFF (*Looking up, teasing*): In the words of your father?

HARU (*Grinning*): This time—words of my mother.

> GRAMPS *grins, ruffles* HARU'*s hair and sets to work pouring seed into a furrow from the funneled bag with a rather lavish hand.* JEFF *follows suit.*

ANGLE TO FEATURE HARU

> *To him their method seems shockingly wasteful. He reacts with horror, and is about to protest, but then thinks better of it. He carefully pours a few seeds into his palm and starts to plant them one by one.*

FULL SHOT

> GRAMPS, JEFF *and* LASSIE *have progressed some ten feet further than* HARU. *Becoming aware of this,* GRAMPS *stops, then crosses to where* HARU *is working.*

MEDIUM CLOSE SHOT—HARU

> *To include* GRAMPS' *legs.* HARU *does not look up. His face is bunched into a little thundercloud of disapproval.*

MEDIUM TWO SHOT—HARU AND GRAMPS

GRAMPS: Here, boy. Let me show you. (*Demonstrates*) Catch on? (HARU *nods solemnly.* GRAMPS *gives him the bag of seed and watches while* HARU *goes back to work.*)

MEDIUM CLOSE SHOT—HARU

> *Doggedly he goes back to his own method.*

MEDIUM TWO SHOT—GRAMPS AND HARU

> GRAMPS *pushes his hat to the back of his head in irritation.*

GRAMPS: So that's it! (*During the following scene* HARU *continues his slow planting.*) I guess that speechifyin' look in his eyes means— turnips ain't planted so in Japan?

HARU: I did not speak.

GRAMPS: No. But you *thunk!*

HARU: In Japan seed very costly.

GRAMPS: In America *labor* very costly. You got me figured fer nothin' but a ramsquaddled ol' fool!

HARU (*Protesting*): Is not right.

GRAMPS: First there's the apple trees. Ya reckon they're too far apart, don't ya?

HARU (*Smiling*): Oh, yes.

GRAMPS: Same with the beans, taters, t'maters—everythin' else. Must waste—ain't that what ya say?

HARU (*Calmly*): I say—"In Japan is not so."

GRAMPS: I ain't in Japan! If we listen t'you we'd be bottlin' th' bath water—skeered a wastin' it!

HARU (*Earnestly*): Bath water very fine wood polish. Should *never* waste.

GRAMPS (*Stopped; mutters furiously*): Well, I'll be a ring-tailed 'possum! (*He glares at* HARU *fiercely, turns and stomps away.*)

ANOTHER ANGLE

> Featuring JEFF, LASSIE *and* HARU *watching* GRAMPS *go.* HARU *sighs.*

JEFF: Don't worry. Gramps'll calm down ...

HARU (*Philosophically*): Oh, sure. In Japan, *planting* different—but *people* the same. Gramps-san just like my uncle—Tomio Yamaguchi. (*As they go back to work ...*)

DISSOLVE TO

INTERIOR MILLER KITCHEN—TWILIGHT

> ELLEN *is cooking, setting the table, etc., when* GRAMPS *comes in from the hallway. She smiles at him warmly as he goes to the sink for a glass of water. On the window sill above the sink some of the jars of peas* ELLEN *has bottled are cooling.*

GRAMPS (*Disgustedly*): Peas with th' pods on! Don't need a hound dog t'smell out whose idea that was!

ELLEN: I don't know why I haven't done it before. They're delicious and *no* waste!

GRAMPS (*Roaring*): Waste!

ELLEN (*Startled*): Why, Dad!

GRAMPS: S'help me, if I hear th' word onct agin, Haru Yamaguchi-san goes packin'! (*A clatter and pounding is heard from outside.*) Now what? (ELLEN *runs out, followed by* GRAMPS.)

EXTERIOR MILLER YARD

> JEFF *is heaving large stones from a wheelbarrow and* HARU *is attacking the biggest with a sledge hammer.*

ELLEN: Whatever are you doing?

HARU (*Importantly*): Preparing a present—for you!

JEFF: We're making you a rock garden.

ELLEN: Really? Why, how lovely!

HARU: I am trained in this art. You will like.

ELLEN (*Thrilled*): I *know* I will!

GRAMPS: *Now* who's makin' a waste?

HARU (*Gentle reprimand*): Is no waste to make thing of beauty.

> ELLEN *glances affirmation of this to* GRAMPS *who "hmmphs."*

JEFF: Anyway, Haru says Mom can make kimono money on it if she wants.

ELLEN: Kimono money?

HARU: Old expression. Mean to have a few yen up sleeve.

ELLEN: I don't understand . . .

JEFF: Tomorrow—when we go to the dentist, Haru's gonna get wild strawberry plants and put them between the rocks.

HARU: You see, Mrs. Miller-san? Berries grow—you pick—sell berries. Make you little money—I hope so!

ELLEN: Thank you, Haru. (*Archly—to* GRAMPS) It's a very good idea. Maybe I can earn enough to buy an electric refrigerator.

> GRAMPS *glowers and enters the house.*

FADE OUT

FADE IN:

EXTERIOR WOODED AREA—MEDIUM SHOT

> HARU *is busily digging out wild strawberry plants with a trowel, putting them in a basket and happily singing a Japanese song.*

MEDIUM SHOT

> HOWIE BREWSTER *and* BERT PULLEY *tracking through brush. Although about the same age as* HARU, *they are a good deal taller and much heavier, and their faces are the faces of bullies. They carry slingshots—one twirling his around his finger as he walks. As the sound of* HARU'S *high-pitched singing is heard the boys stop and look at each other.*

BERT PULLEY: Wassat?

HOWIE BREWSTER: Dunno. Let's go see.

ANOTHER ANGLE

> As the boys reach a large rock behind which HARU is working.

MEDIUM LONG SHOT—FROM BOYS' POINT OF VIEW

HARU *busily digging up plants.*

MEDIUM SHOT—BERT PULLEY AND HOWIE BREWSTER

BERT (*Low*): It's the Jap kid! All by himself. Let's tackle him—see if he's yeller like his skin.

HOWIE: I gotta better idea. (*Holds up slingshot*) We bin lookin' for sumthin' to practice on. (BERT *nods.*)

MEDIUM CLOSE SHOT

HOWIE BREWSTER, *taking careful aim.*

MEDIUM SHOT

HARU *suddenly leaping and clutching his shoulder. He looks around in bewilderment.*

MEDIUM CLOSE SHOT—HOWIE BREWSTER AND BERT PULLEY

HOWIE: Got him!

BERT: Watch this. (BERT *takes aim.*)

MEDIUM CLOSE SHOT

HARU *hopping as a stone hits his open-sandaled foot. Again he looks around and this time spots the two bullies above him.*

MEDIUM SHOT

The boys from HARU's *point of view, sneering. They both take aim again.*

CLOSE SHOT

HARU, *a puzzled, hurt expression on his face.*

MEDIUM SHOT

HARU *hopping from one foot to the other as pebbles spurt up the dust around him.*

TWO SHOT—THE BOYS

HOWIE: Keep hoppin', slit-eyes!

BERT: Yeah—till ya get back to Japan-land.

MEDIUM CLOSE SHOT

HARU's *face goes cold with anger. Lips tightly clamped, he starts up toward the bullies, ducking stones as he goes. Just as he nears them, a stone catches him on the temple—throwing him off balance for a moment and drawing blood.*

FULL SHOT

HARU *reaches the boys and, using jiujitsu tactics, lunges at* BERT PULLEY. *Within seconds* HARU *has sent him sprawling on his back. Like greased lightning, he turns in time to intercept* HOWIE BREWSTER *who has approached from behind. Midst grunts and groans, they battle furiously.*

ANOTHER ANGLE

BERT PULLEY, *his face streaked with blood and dirt, starts for* HARU *again.* HARU, *who has managed to get a judo hold on* HOWIE BREWSTER, *flings him to one side and turns to meet the new attack. There is a scream of pain.*

MEDIUM CLOSE SHOT

HOWIE BREWSTER, *his face twisted in agony. Nursing his arm, he starts bawling in pain and fright.*

FULL SHOT

BERT PULLEY *breaks away from* HARU *and runs to* HOWIE.

HOWIE: My arm! My arm!

MEDIUM SHOT

HARU *standing, legs apart, panting—anticipating a new attack.*

FULL SHOT

BERT PULLEY *helps his friend to his feet.*

BERT *(Menacingly)*: You ain't heard the last a this! You just wait! *(With this the two bullies hobble off.)*

CLOSE SHOT

HARU *as he wipes blood from the side of his face.*

DISSOLVE TO

EXTERIOR MILLER YARD—DAY

GRAMPS, *driving his pick-up, turns into the yard.*

MEDIUM SHOT

> haru *working on the rock garden. There is a cut on his temple. Hearing the sound of the truck, he leaps up and runs to it.*

MEDIUM FULL SHOT

> gramps *is getting out of the truck. As he climbs out, an overwrought* haru *runs up.*

MEDIUM CLOSE SHOT

> gramps *startled as he sees the wound on* haru's *head.*

gramps: What'cha do to yourself?

haru: No do to self! Attack by two others!

gramps: Who? Why?

haru: Not sure. I think because skin yellow—eyes slant.

gramps (*Disgusted grunt*): Oh. (*The sound of a car taking a turn at high speed is heard.* gramps *and* haru *look in the direction.*) Here comes trouble. You git in the barn! (haru *hesitates*) Git! (gramps *shoves him toward barn.*)

LONG SHOT

> *The speeding car as it screeches onto the* miller *property.*

MEDIUM CLOSE SHOT

> simon pulley *and* art brewster *in car. These two overfed, grown bullies glare about, enraged. When they see* gramps, brewster *jerks the car to a stop and they leap out.*

brewster: All right, Miller. That Jap kid bust my Howie's arm! Where's he at?

gramps (*Incredulous*): Broke Howie's arm?

pulley: My Bert's got a deep gash crost his head. The kids'll be outta the fields fer weeks—an' you're gonna pay fer it!

CLOSE SHOT

> gramps *manages not to smile, but his eyes twinkle.*

gramps: You're talkin' crazy. Why, each a yer kid's twice as big as Haru!

GROUP SHOT

brewster: He fought dirty!

pulley: That sneaky judi-jitso!

GRAMPS: You better git along home. When you're simmered down, then we'll deal with this. (BREWSTER *advances on* GRAMPS *menacingly*.)

BREWSTER: I aim to git that Jap!

GRAMPS (*Exploding*): Git off'n my land, or I'll throw y'off . . .

BREWSTER (*Leering*): You an' who else? (HARU's *piping voice is heard.*)

HARU'S VOICE: Me! (*All three men whirl around toward* HARU.)

CLOSE SHOT

> HARU *has come out of the barn and is standing defiantly, a pitchfork in one hand and a horsewhip in the other.*

HARU (*Projecting*): Feel no fear, Gramps-san. I here!

MEDIUM GROUP SHOT—FEATURING GRAMPS

GRAMPS: We got no cause t'be afeart, Haru. (BREWSTER *and* PULLEY *are glowering at* HARU. BREWSTER *spits contemptuously, and starts toward the boy.*)

GRAMPS (*Enraged*): Git outta here, ya pewtrified polecats—er I'll use the horse whip on ya . . . an' the pitchfork, too!

> (PULLEY *grabs the angry* BREWSTER.)

PULLEY: Come on, Art, we got some rights too.

BREWSTER (*To* GRAMPS—*ominously*): This ain't the end by no means.

> As GRAMPS *and* HARU *glare, they jump in the car and go. Then* GRAMPS *goes to* HARU *and, gently taking the whip and pitchfork from him, goes into the barn.* HARU *follows.*

INTERIOR BARN

HARU: I sorry cause trouble to your house, Gramps-san.

GRAMPS (*Putting whip in its place*): Ain't no fault of yourn.

HARU: I sorry anyhow.

GRAMPS (*Putting pitchfork against wall*): Yer the one's been treated wrong.

HARU (*His eyes fill with sudden tears*): Shikata ga nai . . . (It can't be helped.)

TWO SHOT

> As GRAMPS *comes up to the boy.*

GRAMPS: What say?

HARU: What I say mean . . . (*Shrugs*) It can't be helped . . . (GRAMPS' *face suddenly lights with an idea.*)

GRAMPS: Say, Haru boy! Y'know what you an' me gonna do?

HARU: What, Gramps-san?

GRAMPS: We're gonna have a party! Ya really know how to cook a Japanese meal?

HARU: I know very good!

GRAMPS: Well, then, shake a leg! If we hustle, mebbe we can have it ready by th' time Ellen and Jeff get home.

HARU: I shake two legs! (*They laugh together as they exit from the barn.*)

GRAMPS: We'll eat on the floor, by heck! An' wear th' fancy bathrobes!

EXTERIOR BARN—CLOSE TWO SHOT

> HARU *stops and looks up at* GRAMPS *worshipfully.*

HARU: You very fine man, Gramps-san.

GRAMPS (*To cover his emotion*): Cut out yer palaverin', ya little monkey face. (*As he gives him a playful push and* HARU *laughs delightedly ...*)

DISSOLVE TO

INTERIOR MILLER KITCHEN—NIGHT

> GRAMPS, ELLEN, JEFF *and* HARU *are seated on pillows around a tablecloth which has been spread on the floor (or a very low table if this is feasible). Each has an empty rice bowl before him and there are numerous nearly consumed dishes of food scattered about.* LASSIE *has her own bowl.* GRAMPS, JEFF *and* HARU *wear their skullcaps and happi-coats—*GRAMPS *looking pompously comic.* ELLEN *is lovely, dressed in her kimono and wearing flowers in her hair.* HARU *has a neat band-aid on his forehead.*

ELLEN: Everything was delicious! (*To* GRAMPS *and* HARU) Aren't you two proud of yourselves!

HARU (*Pertly*): Very proud!

JEFF: This is a swell party! See, Lassie thinks so, too!

GRAMPS: Her bowl's clean as a whistle. (*Ruefully*) So's mine.

HARU: Now I teach you Japanese game. Okay?

> But at this moment a crash of glass is heard and a rock, with a note wrapped around it, lands among the dishes—breaking several. For an instant everyone is too startled to move. Then ELLEN snatches the note and reads aloud.

ELLEN: "Get that Nip kid out of town in twenty-four hours or suffer the consequences."

> *They stare at one another with mingled emotions and then, with an angry roar,* GRAMPS *heaves himself up and runs to the window. He yanks it up. From outside the sound of a retreating car can be heard.* GRAMPS *shouts after it:*

GRAMPS (*Shouting*): This is America, ya hear! What's more, next year we're gonna have another Japanese boy, an' a Chinese boy, an' mebbe even a Zulu boy, too! (*As* GRAMPS *shakes his fist after the car . . .*)

FADE OUT

FADE IN:

INTERIOR MILLER PARLOR—NEXT NIGHT

> *The window has been repaired. The* MILLERS, HARU, LASSIE *and* CLAY HORTON *wait in a tense silence which is broken by* HARU.

HARU: I go back to Japan, I think.

GRAMPS: Oh, no, you don't. You're stayin' put.

HARU: Better for everybody I go.

ELLEN: No, it wouldn't, Haru. We want you to stay.

JEFF: Besides we gotta finish Mom's rock garden.

ELLEN (*To* CLAY): What time is it, Clay?

CLAY (*Looking at watch*): Almost ten.

GRAMPS: See—they ain't comin'. Told ya it was all a bluff!

ELLEN (*To* HARU *and* JEFF): You boys go along to bed now.

HARU: You want me to sleep in Jeff-san's room?

ELLEN: You might as well since we put the cot up . . . Wouldn't it be fun?

JEFF: You bet! Come on, Haru! (JEFF *kisses* ELLEN *good night and* HARU *politely bows to the room as he,* JEFF *and* LASSIE *exit.*)

GRAMPS: Gonna turn in myself. Been a tryin' day. (GRAMPS *starts to exit.*)

CLAY: Well, I guess I'll get along, Ellen. (ELLEN *and* CLAY *follow* GRAMPS *toward the hall.*)

ELLEN: All right, Clay. And thanks a million for staying with us.

INTERIOR MILLER HALLWAY—MEDIUM SHOT—
SHOOTING TOWARD DOOR

CLAY: 'Night, Mr. Miller. (CLAY *opens the door.*)

GRAMPS: 'Night, Clay.

> ELLEN *and* CLAY *smile at each other somewhat wanly as* CLAY *exits.* GRAMPS *starts up the steps as* ELLEN *closes and bolts the door. She turns out the parlor light and walks down the hallway. Offstage we hear a car motor starting up.*

EXTERIOR MILLER DRIVEWAY—FULL SHOT—NIGHT

> *As* CLAY HORTON'S *car comes down the driveway and makes a left turn behind the rose hedge.*

EXTERIOR ROAD IN WOODED SECTION—MEDIUM SHOT

> *As* CLAY *pulls off the road and parks.*

CLOSE SHOT—CLAY HORTON BEHIND WHEEL

> *As he looks through the trees at the* MILLER *house.*

POINT OF VIEW SHOT—THE MILLER HOUSE

> *As seen through the trees. A light goes out on the second floor (*GRAMPS' *room). Then a light goes out in a downstairs window (the kitchen). There are still some lights visible, particularly in* JEFF'S *room.*

DISSOLVE TO

SAME POINT OF VIEW SHOT—THE MILLER HOUSE—
    LATER

> *Now all the lights are out. The house is dark.*

CLOSE SHOT—CLAY HORTON BEHIND WHEEL

> *He is twisted around now so he can look through the rear window of his car. His left arm is resting on the back of the seat. He takes a cigarette lighter out of his pocket, lights it and looks at his wrist watch.*

INSERT—CLAY'S WRIST WATCH

> *It says:* 11:30.

BACK TO SCENE

> CLAY *snaps the lighter shut, drops it into his pocket, turns to the wheel, puts the car lights on and steps on the starter.*

MEDIUM SHOT—CLAY'S CAR

As it pulls away. Camera holds on swirling dust for a moment, then we see two men—BREWSTER and PULLEY—come out of hiding in the wooded section and start across the road, looking offstage at CLAY's departing car. PULLEY is carrying a five-gallon can of what might be gasoline. They stop for a tight two so we can recognize their faces.

BREWSTER: It was Horton, all right. Good thing we laid low.

PULLEY: Yeah. (*Both men exit past camera toward the MILLER house.*)

EXTERIOR MILLER BARNYARD—MEDIUM SHOT

As the two men come around a corner of the barn cautiously. They look to see whether the way is clear.

INTERIOR JEFF'S BEDROOM—FULL SHOT—NIGHT

JEFF *and* HARU *are asleep, but not* LASSIE. *Her head is up and her ears pointed. She rises and moves to the window, looking out.*

EXTERIOR JEFF'S WINDOW—CLOSE SHOT

As LASSIE *looks out.*

THE TWO MEN—FROM LASSIE'S POINT OF VIEW

As they move slowly toward the barn door.

EXTERIOR JEFF'S WINDOW—MEDIUM CLOSE

As LASSIE *leaps out and takes a stance, growling softly.*

TWO SHOT—THE MEN

As they freeze in their tracks and turn toward LASSIE.

BREWSTER (*Low*): It's all right. She knows me. Here, Lassie. Here, girl.

FULL SHOT

As LASSIE *moves forward tentatively, not quite sure.*

PULLEY (*Low, jittery*): I seen what she did to Matt Willis.

BREWSTER (*Cajoling*): Here, Lassie. Come on, girl. (LASSIE, *recognizing* BREWSTER, *moves to him.* BREWSTER *pats her head.*) Nice girl. Good girl. (*Gently,* BREWSTER *leads* LASSIE *to the barn door. Quietly, he opens it and urges her inside with his knee. He closes the bottom half but the top half swings back against the barn, striking softly.*)

INTERIOR JEFF'S BEDROOM

> *As the sound of the barn door hitting the barn awakens* HARU. *He sits up and looks toward the window. Then he slips off his cot and goes to the window.*

EXTERIOR MILLER BARN—FROM HARU'S POINT OF VIEW

> *As* BREWSTER *and* PULLEY *disappear around the front corner of the barn.*

INTERIOR JEFF'S BEDROOM—FULL SHOT

> *As* HARU *goes to* JEFF'S *bed, starts to awaken him, changes his mind and returns to the window. He begins to climb out.*

EXTERIOR JEFF'S BEDROOM WINDOW

> *As* HARU *climbs out and exits past camera.*

EXTERIOR FRONT OF BARN—MEDIUM SHOT— BREWSTER AND PULLEY

> BREWSTER *is spreading straw along the barn wall and* PULLEY *is dousing it with gasoline.*

HARU'S VOICE: Why you do that? (BREWSTER *and* PULLEY *wheel and freeze.*)

HARU—FROM THEIR POINT OF VIEW

> *A brave but somewhat pitiful little character in his native night dress and bare feet.*

FULL SHOT

> *As* BREWSTER *drops the straw in his hands and lunges at* HARU. HARU *cries out but the cry is smothered and abortive as* BREWSTER'S *big hand covers his mouth.*

INTERIOR JEFF'S BEDROOM—MEDIUM CLOSE

> JEFF *as he sleeps soundly.*

THREE SHOT

> BREWSTER, PULLEY, HARU *as* HARU *struggles in* BREWSTER'S *arms.*

BREWSTER: Hurry up! Pour it on! (PULLEY *starts pouring the gasoline wildly.*)

INTERIOR BARN—MEDIUM SHOT

LASSIE, *realizing she has been tricked, barks frantically at the closed lower half of the door.*

INTERIOR JEFF'S BEDROOM—MEDIUM CLOSE

JEFF *awakens with a start, looks at* HARU's *empty cot.*

INTERIOR BARN—MEDIUM SHOT

LASSIE *has backed up and runs for the closed door.*

EXTERIOR BARN DOOR—CLOSE SHOT

As LASSIE *comes sailing over it.*

INTERIOR JEFF'S BEDROOM—FULL SHOT

As JEFF *leaps out of bed and runs to the window.*

EXTERIOR SIDE OF BARN—MEDIUM SHOT

As PULLEY *and* BREWSTER, *seeing* LASSIE *coming at them, let loose of* HARU *and run.* LASSIE *races into scene after them and hits* BREWSTER *and sends him sprawling.*

CLOSE SHOT

HARU, *as he watches. We hear mad growling offstage.*

EXTERIOR JEFF'S BEDROOM WINDOW—CLOSE SHOT

As he climbs out quickly and runs past camera.

EXTERIOR YARD—MEDIUM CLOSE

LASSIE *fighting with* BREWSTER.

MEDIUM CLOSE

HARU, *as* JEFF *runs into scene and throws his arms around* HARU.

JEFF (*Breathless*): You all right?
HARU: Yes, I fine.

INTERIOR MILLER UPPER HALLWAY—FULL SHOT

As ELLEN, *fastening the belt of her bathrobe races past camera to the stairs, just as* GRAMPS, *doing the same thing, comes out of his room.*

GRAMPS: What happened?
ELLEN'S VOICE: I don't know, but call Clay! (GRAMPS *races down the hall toward the stairs.*)

DISSOLVE

INTERIOR MILLER KITCHEN—CLOSE SHOT ON
BREWSTER'S ARM—NIGHT

> *There is a tourniquet above the elbow. It is fashioned of a
> short piece of clothes line with a stick in it.* CLAY HORTON's
> *hand is on the stick and* ELLEN's *hand is holding a damp,
> cold cloth against the gash in the arm. Camera dollies back
> to reveal* BREWSTER *in a chair at the table, his head hanging
> limply, his eyes closed. He is pale as a ghost. The tourniquet
> isn't stopping the flow of blood.* GRAMPS *is standing next to*
> ELLEN *holding a basin containing ice water.* ELLEN *takes the
> cloth off the wound, dips it into the ice water and presses it
> against the wound again.* JEFF, HARU *and* LASSIE *look on fear-
> fully.*

ELLEN: Can you tighten it any more, Clay?

CLAY: I'm afraid not. The arm's blue now.

GRAMPS: You picked a bad night to tackle with Lassie, Art. Doc Stew-
art operatin' in Creston an' Frank Weaver outta town. (BREWSTER
moans and his head rolls.)

ELLEN: He'll die if we don't stop the bleeding. (HARU's *face lights up.*)

HARU (*Quickly*): Excuse, please. (HARU *exits rapidly to the hallway as*
JEFF *looks offstage after him.*)

BREWSTER (*Mumbling it*): Don' lemme die. Please don' lemme die.

ELLEN: Jeff, get some more ice. (JEFF *exits to the ice-box.* HARU *enters
scene carrying a black lacquered box. The lid is off and he is looking
at something in it.*)

HARU: Mrs. Miller-san, please.

ELLEN: Yes, Haru. (JEFF *enters scene carrying a piece of ice.*)

JEFF: Here's the ice, Mom.

HARU: Wait, please. Before try ice, have something here in Japanese
kit aid Father give me when I leave Japan. (*He finds what he wants*)
Ah! Ancient remedy to stop river of blood. Powdered snake venom.
(HARU *produces, on his line, what resembles a miniature cardboard
salt shaker with Japanese lettering on it.*)

GRAMPS: Snake venom?

ELLEN: He's right. It's a blood coagulant. I remember from my first-
aid course. (HARU *gives it to* ELLEN. ELLEN *dusts it on the wound.
Everyone peers to see what the result is.* ELLEN *dusts more on.*)

GRAMPS: It's workin'!

ELLEN: Loosen the tourniquet, Clay. (CLAY *loosens the tourniquet slowly.* ELLEN *dusts more on.* GRAMPS *and* JEFF *are amazed.* HARU *takes it calmly. Finally the tourniquet is completely loose.* CLAY *takes it off* BREWSTER's *arm.*)

CLAY (*To* BREWSTER): You're going to be all right, Art. The Japanese boy saved your life. (BREWSTER *opens his eyes. He reaches out and touches* HARU.)

BREWSTER (*Weakly*): Thanks, sonny. (*Both* JEFF *and* GRAMPS *are proud as punch. They both put their arms around* HARU.)

GRAMPS: They don't come no better than you, Haru. Wouldn't be many did what you did after the way he treated you.

HARU: Kind act sometimes change strong enemy to strong friend.

JEFF (*Admiringly*): In the words of your father?

HARU (*Simply*): Yes.

FADE OUT

FADE IN:

EXTERIOR RAILROAD JUNCTION

> *The day of* HARU's *departure has arrived. This time a good many of the* MILLER *neighbors, including* PORKY, *have come to wave good-bye to* HARU. *They smile and wave as the* MILLER *car draws up near the station platform, where the train has already pulled in.*

ANOTHER ANGLE—TO FEATURE MILLER CAR

> *As* GRAMPS, ELLEN, JEFF, LASSIE, HARU *and* CLAY HORTON *get out, all laden with luggage and packages.*

FULL SHOT

> *There is an excited stir among the group of well-wishers as they see* HARU *and surge forward. Amongst them we see* ART BREWSTER, SIMON PULLEY *and their two sons.*

ANOTHER ANGLE

> HARU *standing by the car, smiling shyly at the crowd.* ELLEN *puts her hand fondly on his arm.*

ELLEN: You *will* write, won't you?

HARU (*Fervently*): With each new moon I will write. (*Turning to* JEFF) And you, Jeff-san, will send me promised letters?

JEFF: I sure will! (*The* MILLER *group struggles through the crowd with their packages.*)

CLAY: You all better wait here. I'll get this stuff on the train.

HARU (*Happily*): You present me too many gifts but my family has talent to appreciate.

ELLEN: You tell them we appreciate you.

HARU (*Softly*): Ahreegahto. (Thank you) (*Ah-reegah-to*)

ELLEN: You're welcome. (CLAY, *stacked with bundles, boards the train.*)

GRAMPS: Don't forget to send me those flower seeds from Japan, young fella.

HARU (*Emotionally*): I no forget, Gramps-san. I *never* forget you. (GRAMPS *pats his shoulder awkwardly. The train whistles as* CLAY *rejoins the group.*)

CLAY: Better get on board. (*They are going toward the Pullman when* ART BREWSTER *and* SIMON PULLEY, *followed by their sons, break through the crowd. Rather embarrassed, they thrust packages at* HARU.)

BREWSTER: Haru boy, I ain't much at makin' speeches, but I guess ya know how I feel.

PULLEY: That goes fer me double, Haru.

BREWSTER (*Taking small box from pocket*): T'aint much compared with the snake powder, but this here's fer ya pa.

HARU: I accept for him with gratitude. (*Train whistles—two short, urgent blasts.*)

CLAY: Sorry boy—time to go.

JEFF (*Moving closer to* HARU): Sayonara, Haru. (*Good-bye*)

HARU: Correction, Jeff-san. Bid me mata ai mashiyo. It means we will see each other again.

JEFF: Mata ai mashiyo. (*Ma-ta ai ma-shiyo*) (*As* CLAY *starts to boost* HARU *aboard.*)

HARU: One minute, Mr. Clay-san. (HARU *drops to his knees beside* LASSIE, *hugs and kisses her.* CLAY *swoops him up into his arms and into the train, which has begun to move. As train pulls out of the station,* ELLEN, GRAMPS, JEFF *and* CLAY *all call out* "Mata ai ma-shiyo," *and* LASSIE *barks her farewell as we*)

FADE OUT

The George Gobel Show

by HAL KANTER, HOWARD LEEDS,
HARRY WINKLER, EVERETT GREENBAUM

CATEGORY:

Television Comedy-Variety

(ONE HALF HOUR)

THE GEORGE GOBEL SHOW

by HAL KANTER, HOWARD LEEDS,
HARRY WINKLER, EVERETT GREENBAUM

The George Gobel Show
was presented on NBC-TV as a Gomalco Production
under the direction of Hal Kanter, Bud Yorkin and Rick Oxford
on November 12, 1955,
with the following cast:

GEORGE GOBEL · PEGGY KING · LEO DUROCHER
ALICE NUMBER FOUR · Jeff Donnell
ALICE NUMBER THREE · Jill Jorden
ALICE NUMBER TWO · Evelyn Russell
ALICE NUMBER ONE · Sue Englund

FADE UP—LEO DUROCHER

LEO: Good evening, ladies and gentlemen and friends of George Gobel. Due to circumstances beyond my control, I am Leo Durocher. I'm an executive with NBC—the National League Broad ... I mean, the National Broadcasting Company. I was traded even for a left-handed secretary with a good fast ball and a real good curve. One of my present duties is to see that things run smoothly on the George Gobel show. Tonight, they're not. Mr. Gobel is upset about something and has refused to go on. That's why I'm here—to straighten things out. So please stand by. Mr. Gobel will be with you in a moment. See you later. (*Waves, and we see he wears a baseball mitt. He reacts*) Oh. You never know. (*Shrugs.*)

MUSIC—"GOBELUES"—DISSOLVE TO TITLE CARD

The George Gobel Show . . . With George's guest, Leo Durocher ...

PEGGY KING

Pretty, perky Peggy King ...

TROTTER

John Scott Trotter and his marinated minstrels . . . and starring— George Gobel!

GOBEL FLIP

("Who Dresses Neatly")

YORKIN FLIP

("Who Dresses Conservatively")

KANTER FLIP

("Who Dresses Chickens")

WRITERS' FLIP

CUT TO: GEORGE'S SHADOW WALK. HE IS NOT THERE

ANNOUNCER (*Offstage*): And now, here is the star of our—oh, oh! Where's George? Hmmm. Looks like he's still in a fret. Let's take our cameras up to Mr. Durocher's office ...

FADE UP: ART CARD DEPICTING OFFICE DOOR MARKED "MR. LEO DUROCHER. PRIVATE."

ANNOUNCER'S VOICE: And now, as advertised previously, we take you behind the grim, gray walls of an executive's office.

DISSOLVE TO INTERIOR EXECUTIVE'S OFFICE

> LEO *paces beside his desk. Large swivel chair has back to camera.*

LEO: Georgie, boy, you've put us in a rough spot. Thousands of people are waiting to see you tonight. Thousands of people.

GEORGE (*Spins chair around*): Not only people. I get lots of fan mail from woodchucks and field mice, too.

LEO: George . . .

GEORGE: I'm very big with animals. I'm bigger with animals than I am with people.

LEO: George, you don't sound like the same sweet kid we all know and love.

GEORGE: Well, if I've changed, Mr. Durocher, it's *you* fellas who created this crew-cut Frankenfurter.

LEO: What do you mean, son?

GEORGE: Don't "son" me, Lippy! . . . And I'll tell you what I mean. I mean I'm tired of being treated like you guys are a bunch of shiny new white-wall tires and I'm a dirty curb!

LEO: Oh, now, Georgie-boy . . .

GEORGE: I've got feelings, too, you know. Underneath this "laugh, clown, laugh" face lies the sensitive soul of a youth who weeps unashamed on Arbor Day!

LEO (*Putting arm around him*): George, I'm sorry. Genuinely sorry. We had no idea you were so . . .

GEORGE (*Brushing him off*): You're just saying that. I know your game, Leo Durocher! I even know your batting average. You oughta be ashamed. (*Fist*) You see! (*Sobs*) To you, I'm only a tool to peddle soap and milk. I'm just a puppet with a wooden heart and a papier maché head. (*Buries his face in* LEO'*s chest and sobs.*)

LEO (*Patting him gently*): Now, now, George, you calm down and get this whole thing out of your system. You tell Uncle Leo exactly what's wrong and he'll help you.

GEORGE: He—he will?

LEO: Anything you want, you're going to get.

GEORGE: Anything?

LEO: We've already given you a choice time spot—the best cameramen, crew, studio, writers, directors, musicians—and if we've forgotten anything, you tell your Uncle Leo. (GEORGE *sniffles*) Now what is it?

GEORGE: I'm not included in the group-insurance plan!

LEO: No?

GEORGE: I want my seven-days' sick leave . . . and free check-ups from the company nurse . . . at the company hospital . . . the Rudy Vallee Memorial Clinic!

LEO: You have every right to expect that, George, and you'll get it. Now, go downstairs and start your show.

GEORGE: Not so fast there, buddy! I got one more squeak. A big one! My announcer!

LEO: Gilmore? What's wrong with him? He's one of the best.

GEORGE: Sure, he is. Only I just don't like the smart-alecky way he introduces me. Like on the very first show, he says, "And here's the star of our show, *whoever* he is . . ." That's not right. That's—that's undignified. It embarrasses me.

LEO: You know, George, you remind me of myself when I first broke into baseball. I was a shy, sensitive kid like you. Everything people said bothered me.

GEORGE: *You—shy? You,* the umpire eater?

LEO: George, I was so shy, in the locker room I turned my back when I oiled my glove! (*Turn away.*)

GEORGE: Gee. When did you change? And change you did.

LEO: One day I just decided to become a tough guy. That's what you should do. If you don't like Gilmore's introductions, walk up and tell him off. Get tough!

GEORGE: Okay! I'll tough up! (*Braces himself and growls. Then changes his mind*) Have you seen Art Gilmore? He's six foot three . . . sitting down. When he stands up, he's got knees where I've got armpits.

LEO: All right, George. I'll handle it for you. If you want a dignified introduction, you'll get one. Wait here.

GEORGE: Don't forget to touch first. (LEO *exits.* GEORGE *looks around, sees telephone. Picks it up and dials to himself—sings*) "I've got that dial feeling . . . got that dial feeling" . . . Hello? Dr. Gettleman, please. Doctor? George Gobel. Say, would you stop by my house and look at our little girl, Georgia? . . . Oh, there's nothing wrong with her. We're just proud of her. (*Hangs up.* PEGGY *enters*) Hi, Peggy.

PEGGY: George, what are you doing up here? Everybody's waiting— Uncle John . . . and the cast . . . and the studio audience.

GEORGE: We got a big audience tonight?

PEGGY: Oh, about three hundred people . . . and sixty woodchucks.

GEORGE: Well, I can't disappoint those woodchucks. C'mon ... (*They start to exit. Notice record player*)

PEGGY: Oh, look at this record; that's the number I'm gonna do tonight.

GEORGE: Let's hear how it goes, Pretty Perky.

PEGGY: But they're waiting for you, George.

GEORGE: Miss King, Herman and Lillian Gobel were married seven years before I was born. If I can make my own parents wait seven years, I can stall perfect strangers two or three more minutes! (*Puts record player on*) Serenade me, little gypsy . . . (*Into* PEGGY's *number.*)

SOUND: PHONE RINGS

PEGGY *answers it.*

PEGGY: Hello? Yes, Mr. Durocher? Oh, George is on his way down right now—You can tell Mr. Gilmore to start his introduction.

CUT TO GEORGE'S WALKDOWN SPOT

ANNOUNCER (*Offstage*): And now, ladies and gentlemen . . . (GEORGE *moves into shadows*) Here is the star of our show—whoever he is— George ...

GEORGE: Stop! Close the curtains! Cease the show! All off! Over! Out! Lights up! (*Lights up*) I'm sorry this happened, friends. But I'm not goin' on 'til I get that dignified introduction I was promised. (*Starts to go, turns back*) I'm not mad at *you.* You're okay in my book. And for being so patient while I get things fixed, we're going to show you a movie I took last summer while I was on a safari in the darkest depths of my corner grocery store. Take notes if you wish.

DUROCHER *looks up.*

LEO: All right, Gilmore—Mr. Gobel's introduction.

CUT TO: GEORGE'S WALKDOWN SPOT. HE STANDS IN SILHOUETTE

ANNOUNCER (*Offstage*): And now, ladies and gentlemen, I have the honor to present that noble humanitarian, pre-eminent philosopher and distinguished philanthropist, a man of humility and dignity who reflects the highest honor upon his family and community ... (*During this,* GEORGE *walks down, looks up at intervals*) . . . who has given unselfishly of himself to the world . . . One who will ever be remembered for his dynamic contributions to art, the theatre, literature, science, geopolitics, medicine and nuclear fission . . . a dedicated civilian soldier devoted to the good fight against evil, corruption and ignorance . . . A man whose name is synonymous with wisdom, vision, leadership and compassion—the star of our show— Mister George Washington Albert Schweitzer Leonardo Da Vinci Thomas Edison Luther Burbank Willie Mays Gobel!

GEORGE: That was a trifle long, but I think he captured me. Of course, there may be some of you who don't agree. Those who don't know the real me. People like—well, like my wife. Let me tell you about Alice. Boy, these women! How they change once they get you hooked. They just . . . You put a "Mrs." in front of a woman's name, that's like giving a cat his own fish market! It's not that I don't understand a woman's point of view, because I do. Understand, that is. A woman's point of view. I mean, after all, a wife has to be all things to her husband. Yes, indeed, as the Oriental philosopher, William Holden, has said: A wife is a many, many splendored thing. The best way to illustrate this is through the artifice of dramatization. A little artificial dramatization music, Uncle John.

MUSIC—A TROTTER ORIGINAL

Curtains part on GOBEL's *kitchen set.* GEORGE *walks in.*

GEORGE: Make like it's morning and this is our set designer's idea of the Gobel kitchen. We should live so good!

Sits at table. Picks up paper and buries himself behind it. Alice Number One enters in wrapper, her hair in curlers.

ALICE NUMBER ONE: Good morning, George. George come out from behind that newspaper.

GEORGE (*Looks around paper, reacts. Goes behind it again*): I believe I'll just stay here, Space Cadet. These "go to Europe" ads never looked better.

ALICE NUMBER ONE: You didn't used to talk that way.

GEORGE: You didn't used to look that way.

ALICE NUMBER ONE: We didn't used to have three children to wake and dress and feed and get off to school. You know what I am around here? I'm nothing but an overworked old hausfrau.

GEORGE: That beats being an underloved old maid, baby.

ALICE NUMBER ONE (GEORGE *goes behind paper.* ALICE *busies herself at stove*): You ready for your coffee? (*No answer*) Are you ready for coffee? (*No answer. So she pushes cup under paper, then pours coffee down crease in paper into cup.*)

GEORGE (*Slowly lowers paper*): You're just beggin' for a knuckle sandwich, baby!

ALICE NUMBER ONE: Now look, George Gobel—I'm tired of your attitude. You're not a husband . . . You're a—a bachelor with kitchen privileges!

GEORGE: Now, Alice—sweetie—if you're really, really upset, we can get a maid to help with the work. A real maid.

ALICE NUMBER ONE: And what'll we use for money, George? I don't suppose you've checked our finances lately, or . . .

GEORGE: Hold it. (*Comes down*) Do something with the lights, please. (*Background blacks out, leaving* GEORGE *in foreground*) See? The minute finance comes into the conversation, your wife is no longer your maid. Suddenly she's an entirely different person—a female bookkeeper. And they're the worst kind. Watch. (*Half turns*) No, Alice, I *haven't* checked our finances lately. What about them?

> *Lights go up in background, revealing* ALICE NUMBER TWO, *the bookkeeper.*

ALICE NUMBER TWO: We have a cash-on-hand surplus of three dollars and seven cents.

GEORGE (*To us*): See? (*Going up to her*) That's ridiculous, Alice. Where'd all our money go?

ALICE NUMBER TWO: That's what *I* want to know. When you gave me your last pay check, it was ten dollars short. What happened to that ten dollars, Shorty?

GEORGE: Let's see . . . er . . . I had a hole in my money belt and it slipped out?

ALICE NUMBER TWO: No, George . . .

GEORGE: I was rolled by a drunk? (*She shakes her head*) I . . . (*She shakes her head*) Okay. You caught me. You got me dead to rights. Alice, I took that ten dollars, chartered a plane and spent a gay, mad week in Mexico with a lady bullfighter!

ALICE NUMBER TWO: George Go——

GEORGE: Aaaaand if you say anything more, I won't give you the bull's ear!

ALICE NUMBER TWO: Oh, George, honestly! You're impossible!

GEORGE: Not at all. I'm very possible. In fact, I'm a true case history from Dr. Hudson's secret journal.

ALICE NUMBER TWO: Look at this budget, George. You've gone way overboard on unnecessary expenditures.

GEORGE: Just a minute now. I buy only what I need.

ALICE NUMBER TWO: I suppose you needed that new golf bag.

GEORGE: Yes, I did. It was getting pretty embarrassing carrying my clubs around in a laundry sack. Every time I got back to the car, I'd find a couple of dirty wet-wash bundles on the roof.

ALICE NUMBER TWO: All I know is we've got to cut down somewhere. Do you know what our biggest expense is?

GEORGE: Pipe cleaners for your mother.

ALICE NUMBER TWO: Oh, what's the use? No matter how hard I try to run an efficient home for you, you won't help at all! Always joking ... never serious ... spending money foolishly ... And I still want to know what you did with that ten dollars!

GEORGE: All right ... I'll tell you ... (*The hurt husband*) I'll tell you what I did with it ... I bought you a present, is what I did with it.

ALICE NUMBER TWO: A present? For me?

GEORGE: A bottle of perfume ... I've got it right here ... (*Takes it from pocket.*)

ALICE NUMBER TWO: Oh, George! What kind is it?

GEORGE: It's called "Utterly Depraved" ... It's domestic, but good.

ALICE NUMBER TWO (*Sniffs at bottle*): Umm! It's gorgeous! I'll go put some on!

GEORGE: Be careful ... It's very strong ... The girls who sell it wear lead jumpers.

ALICE NUMBER TWO: I'll be right back! Let me slip into something comfy.

GEORGE (*To camera*): See? If you spend money for something frivolous *they* like, it's okay ... Suddenly the carping bookkeeper becomes a real—well, see for yourself. (ALICE NUMBER THREE *enters in a provocative dress.* GEORGE *looks at her, then to camera*) Any questions?

ALICE NUMBER THREE: Darling—smell my perfume ... (GEORGE *sniffs his way to her ear*) Some more ... (*Tilts her other ear toward him*) Some more ... (*Tilts head forward.*)

GEORGE: I think you just ran out of ears.

ALICE NUMBER THREE: I mean here, George ... (*Indicates her neck*) I put a drop on my nape.

GEORGE: Well, now, I haven't sniffed a nape since 1936. (*Sniffs at her neck*) Ummm! These are sure better'n those pre-war napes.

ALICE NUMBER THREE: Come sit beside me . . . and tell me nice things . . . Tell me you still love me as much as when we were married. Sometimes I don't think you do, Poogie.

GEORGE: Of course I do, lovey. (*She cuddles up*) Easy, lovey . . . you're wrinkling Poogie's chest.

ALICE NUMBER THREE: That's what I mean, George.

GEORGE: That doesn't mean I don't love you, honey. I love you more than I ever did.

ALICE NUMBER THREE: Then why don't you show it?

GEORGE: Well, I do . . . in my own way. I mean, after you're married a long time, it's— well, it's kinda like an old smudge pot. It may not show a big flame in the orchard, but it's enough to keep the frost off the plums.

ALICE NUMBER THREE: Well, that does it! Nothing's sacred to you. Go on—you might as well go to work. I'm out of the mood now.

GEORGE: Mood? Mood? *What mood?*

ALICE NUMBER THREE: Oooh! (*She exits.* GEORGE *comes to camera.*)

GEORGE: See? Us husbands can't win. We're fighting against overwhelming odds. One man against a many-sided woman.

ALICE NUMBER ONE: And when you come home tonight, wipe your feet!

GEORGE: Okay, Bridget.

ALICE NUMBER TWO: And don't spend any money foolishly!

GEORGE: Yes, ma'am, Mrs. Bookkeeper.

ALICE NUMBER THREE: But *do* come home early, honey . . .

GEORGE: You can bet me, Ava. (*To us*) Anyway, that's what I mean . . . Wives are all things . . . maids and accountants and sweethearts. Put 'em all together and you've got my wife . . . (*Indicates curtains*) Mrs. Alice Gobel! (ALICE NUMBER FOUR *enters.*)

ALICE NUMBER FOUR: George . . . did you really mean it when you said that I'm all things to you . . . maid and bookkeeper and sweetheart?

GEORGE: Oh, you're even more, Alice. You're my pal . . . nursemaid to my children . . . an unregistered nurse and non-union plumber . . . my very own, personal Gina Lollobrigida. (*Sings*) "You're my everything!"

ALICE NUMBER FOUR: And you're *my* everything, funny honey-bunny. You're my . . .

GEORGE: Ah, ah! Don't tell me now, Alice. Come back next week and tell everybody.

ALICE NUMBER FOUR: Next week? Who's going to be here?

GEORGE: Well, let's see . . . (*Looks up*) Hey . . . who'll be here next Saturday?

ANNOUNCER: Don't ask me . . .

FADE UP—GEORGE AND ALICE NUMBER FOUR

GEORGE: Let's face a grim fact, friends . . . The girls who played the parts of all the Alices were just girls playing the parts of all the Alices. Alice Number One was Jill Jorden.

ALICE NUMBER ONE (*Enters*): Thank you and good night, George. (*To* ALICE NUMBER FOUR) Good night, Alice.

ALICE NUMBER FOUR: Good night, Jill.

GEORGE: Alice Number Two was Evelyn Russell.

ALICE NUMBER TWO: Thank you and good night, George. Good night, Alice.

ALICE NUMBER FOUR: Good night, Evelyn.

GEORGE: Alice Number Three was Sue Englund.

ALICE NUMBER THREE: 'Night, George, and thanks.

GEORGE: Must you go?

ALICE NUMBER FOUR: Good night, Sue!

GEORGE: Now, this Alice isn't the real Alice, either. She's the real Jeff Donnell.

ALICE NUMBER FOUR: See you next week, George. Good night. (*To camera*) 'Night, Real Alice.

GEORGE (*Sighs*): And they said King Solomon was a smart man! . . . Oh, well. Say, Mr. Durocher.

LEO (*Enters*): Yes, George?

GEORGE: Time to exercise Paragraph Three, Section Five of my contract.

LEO: Right. (*Hands him a ball glove, puts one on himself. They begin a game of catch.*)

GEORGE: So long, neighbors . . . (*They continue catching as we fade out.*)